Artificial Believers:

The Ascription of Belief

Afzal Ballim
Institut Dalle Molle ISSCO
University of Geneva
Geneva, Switzerland

Yorick Wilks
Computing Research Laboratory
New Mexico State University
Las Cruces, NM, USA

LEA LAWRENCE ERLBAUM ASSOCIATES, PUBLISHERS
1991   Hillsdale, New Jersey   Hove and London

Lawrence Erlbaum Associates, Inc., Publishers
365 Broadway
Hillsdale, New Jersey 07642

Library of Congress Cataloging-in-Publication Data

Ballim, Afzal.
    Artificial believers : the ascription of belief / Afzal Ballim, Yorick
Wilks.
        p.   cm.
    Includes bibliographical references and index.
    ISBN 0-8058-0453-6
    1. Belief and doubt--Computer simulation. 2. ViewGen. I. Wilks,
Yorick, 1939- . II. Title.
BF773.B34   1991
153.4--dc20   91-17539
                                                CIP

Printed in the United States of America
10 9 8 7 6 5 4 3 2 1

Table of Contents

Preface

A word of warning may be appropriate here, so that readers can decide where to begin the book, depending on their experience of, and interest in, the issues we discuss. The heart of the book is the presentation of an artificial intelligence (AI) program intended to simulate certain aspects of a human believer. We present it as painlessly as possible, but the account is technical in parts as it must be if it is to meet the normal standards of a monograph in artificial intelligence.

The technical core of this work is a prolog program *Viewgen*, one that maintains belief structures about the world and other believers, and is able to *ascribe* beliefs to others without direct evidence by using a form of default reasoning, a notion that we shall explain shortly. A further claim is that the structures, and associated reasoning, we propose also have consequences for identifying alternative descriptions of entities and for notions such as metaphor and speech acts. We argue that representational issues that have traditionally been considered as very different can be seen as closely related.

We believe the issues presented here are of considerable interest to an informed general reader and anyone with a background in any of the disciplines that make up what is nowadays called cognitive science: philosophy, linguistics, psychology, perhaps even neurophysiology, as well as AI itself, which constitutes the anchor subject of cognitive science, and the one that provides the key computational metaphor for mental processes.

So, a general reader should read the whole book. Anyone with a background in a component discipline of cognitive science may want to skip chapter 1 and those parts of chapter 2 that correspond to their specialities, since the account given might inadvertently offend them. An AI type who cares nothing for cognitive science (and there are some, in spite of the last paragraph) as well as the hardest liners, who want nothing but system details and are confused by prose, can begin at chapter 3.

A word of cynicism about cognitive science may be appropriate here, since the euphoria created by the birth of a new subject has not yet died down. The intellectual problems surrounding a subject that binds together practitioners from a range of disparate disciplines, each with its own history and methods of establishing truth, are enormous and unresolved. What establishes an acceptable truth in linguistics is just not the same as what does so in AI or psychology, and practitioners of one normally do not accept the evidence produced by the others, except in a cheery and wooly-minded way, so as not to give offense. It is rather like the way in which the jurisdictions of different countries, each with its own religious and moral traditions, often accept the validity of marriages contracted in others, only in a by-courtesy manner, so as not to cause offense or social disruption, although they remain "not real marriages."

This state of affairs has consequences for this book, one that draws from much of cognitive science, and attempts to show the consequences for a piece of work in AI. The background will inevitably seem partial and biased since it is written by us, who have no allegiance to the methods of verification in the other disciplines. If one were to take the claims of a strict philosophical operationalism seriously, then an apparently identical claim in any two such disciplines would actually mean something different, and they would be incommensurable and each could add no positive evidence for the other, simply because their meanings were determined by the methods of establishing truth in the two fields which are, by definition, different. That extreme view is surely too pessimistic but, at the moment, and until a uniform paradigm of research and evidence in cognitive science is developed, the reader is simply given a warning.

We have many acknowledgements to make: first, to three colleagues with whom we have collaborated at various times and whose ideas may be more present in the book than our citation of them recognizes: Janusz Bien, of the University of Warsaw, with whom Wilks collaborated on early versions of these ideas; also John Barnden and Eric Dietrich who were our colleagues at the Computing Research Laboratory, New Mexico State University.

We have benefited from being in various institutions that hosted this work: Wilks at the University of Essex, and both of us at the Computing Research Laboratory, and at the Institut pour les Etudes Semantiques et Cognitives at the University of Geneva. We owe a debt in the last case to the Fondazione Dalle Molle, which founded the Institute, and to Maghi King, its Director for her hospitality and support. The research has been supported at various times by the Science and Engineering Research Council (United Kingdom) and the Defense Advanced Research Projects Agency (United States) and we gratefully acknowledge this.

A wide range of colleagues have commented on and criticized the work at various times and places. It includes, in no order and with no attribution of responsibility whatever: Patrick Hanks, Nigel Shadbolt, Umberto Eco, Oliviero Stock, Andrea Basso, Aaron Sloman, Tony Maida, Dan Fass, Brian Slator, Richard Young, Patricia Wright, James Cowie, Mike Brady, Dan Dennett, Amos Tversky, Louise Guthrie, Gerald Gazdar, Roger Schvaneveldt, and Charles Martin. We must also acknowledge an enormous debt to Lisa Smith and Sylvia Candelaria de Ram for their critical and editorial assistance, and to Bea Guzman for much typing and correcting.

Plan of this Book

1. Introduction

We present an experimental approach to the question of what it is for an entity to believe, and to have beliefs about others' beliefs. Our intention is to pursue the second question as more primary than the first, and to do that by constructive, that is to say AI, techniques, rather than philosophical, logical or psychological ones. We need a practical, heuristic theory for the **ascription** of belief to others, whether they be human or artificial, because we cannot have direct evidence for the detail of what others believe. We shall place this task within computer dialogue systems in general and give a simple example of what the *ViewGen* program will do.

2. Preliminaries on the Nature of Belief

2.1 Philosophical Theories of Belief and Languages of Thought

The problem of relating "logics of belief" to the concrete reality of brain processes and behavior. Criticism of Fodor's views, that may be summarized as the language-of-thought-as-sentences-in-boxes view. Dennett's view of belief as a term in a language for describing and organizing our "theories" of other organisms,

5

chiefly people. The suitability of this view as a ground for artificial believers. The relation of belief to knowledge and to theories of meaning. Reasons for believing that a "computational theory of meaning" might best be tackled through an operational account of belief. A discussion of realist theories of meaning, including *Situation Semantics*, and why they are unsuitable as the basis for any theory of meaning, that treats belief as central, and aspires to computational or psychological realism. We then reexamine the notion of a language of thought as a vehicle for belief, and its relationship to actual and possible natural languages.

2.2 Problems of intensionality

This is a fundamental topic but one very difficult to treat in a plausible way within logic proper. Why is it essential to a computational account of belief?: Because believers do not agree about what entities there are in the world, as naive logics tend to assume. Moreover, they can and do disagree about whether or not one or more entities are located by a single description, and conversely for a set of descriptions — e.g., is Fred's aunt Jim's mother or not? We give a critical account of other proposals within the AI paradigm, particularly the so-called "fully intensional" SNePs approach.

2.3 Problems of relevance

Again, a belief calculus that is to be programmable must model not only what is relevant to an issue for the system itself but also what other agents will deem relevant (which may lead to quite different results from the system's "own" notion of relevance). We contrast our own assumptions with those of another linguistic approach to relevance that do not consider belief to be central, with a critical account of Sperber and Wilson.

2.4 Peripheral phenomena? Speech Acts and Metaphor

The role of these phenomena in the machine understanding of language; our argument for their centrality, even though they have been largely peripheral phenomena in AI; our reasons for thinking they can be brought into computational contact with, and explicated through, a belief theory; we discuss the speech act theory of Searle and show why it was initially inappropriate for computational modeling, particularly because of the confusion of criteria in its rules that ranged over both speakers and hearers. We argue that, on the contrary, a computational approach must be inherently solipsistic with all its criteria applying to the computations of a single dialogue participant: the computer model of the agent in this case, all other models of agents being models within that system. Things cannot be other than that, since there is no neutral, God's-eye (i.e., omniscient, all-knowing) view of dialogue interactions, such as is assumed by notions like "mutual belief" and "mutual knowledge." We also argue that in a strict sense, Davidson was right to see metaphor as *false belief*, but that this notion can be more positive and constructive than he intended.

2.5 Approaches to Belief in Natural Language Processing and Linguistics

Historical digression on why issues of belief were systematically ignored in linguistics and natural language processing (Schank, Hendrix, Grosz and others). Discussions of the cognitive accounts of belief in the work of Fauconnier, Dinsmore and Shadbolt.

We also discuss the computational speech act theory of Perrault et al. and point out similarities and differences with what we set out here: in particular that they assume (as a starting point because their interests are elsewhere) a complete partitioning of beliefs is psychologically and computationally impossible. An argument is made for a procedural, rather than the diagrammatic and set-theoretic, accounts that we find in the work of those authors. Our theory aims to model the construction and maintenance of such nested belief entities.

2.6 Approaches to Belief in AI

A discussion of the AI literature on belief: a separation of accounts based on modal (or first order) logic explicitly from more heuristic/procedural accounts. What is lacking in them all is any clear empirical notion of **belief ascription**, the key issue we propose to tackle. Discussion of the work of Shadbolt, Fauconnier, Moore, Konolige, Maida, Shapiro & Rapaport, Barnden, Levesque, Fagin, Halpern & Moses, and Martins & Shapiro.

3. Belief Ascription

3.1 Representational Structure

An account of the basic structure chosen to represent an environment or set of beliefs about a topic. Why this approach unifies beliefs about matters of fact and meaning: we cannot ignore or separate off believers whose misbeliefs are about meaning, as with one who believes "scone" means, say, "chair." The position on meaning that is assumed at this stage, and its relation to other aspects of meaning structure, assumed here but not incorporated in programs, particularly the associational aspects of meaning. Relation of these structures to hierarchical knowledge structures.

3.2 The Argument for Partitions or Environments as Basic

We contrast our approach, in which it is essential, computationally and theoretically, to isolate an environment (or belief set) in which to do computation, with others. Having found it, by the mechanisms yet to be described, we shall speak of "running utterance representations" within it, to produce inferences or output utterances. The advantages and disadvantages of partitioned systems, as against the "flat" ones of standard modal logic. Some background on partitioned systems in AI and discourse processing: Hendrix, Grosz, Reichman.

3.3 The Construction of Viewpoints

This is the basic operation of the system, in which environments are pushed-down into each other using a default rule of ascription to construct inner environments. These are deemed to represent **viewpoints**: the beliefs of A about B's beliefs. The recursivity of this process; constructing nested environments to any depth necessary, and the process representing ascription of belief to an inner believer even without direct evidence.

3.4 Limitations to Default Ascription

Why default rule fails in a range of cases: self-knowledge, expertise, fundamentalist believers etc. And why the default rule must be saved (if that proves possible). Saving the default rule with the aid of a theory of privileged evaluators, and lambda expressions for representing intensional expressions.

4. Experiments in Belief: *ViewGen*

Pulling together the various aspects of belief ascription described in section 3, to describe an algorithm for belief ascription. *ViewGen*: The implementation of this algorithm.

The capable evaluators in action, and the first explication of limited expertise and the ability, of a program, to grasp and reason with concepts it understands only vaguely or not at all. The crucial importance of the notion of vague and incomplete information in dealing with the real world. Examples of *ViewGen* in operation.

5. Global Issues: Reasoning with Viewpoints

5.1 Reasoning with Viewpoints

Some speculations on reasoning with viewpoints. Reasoning with viewpoints has two forms: viewpoint-internal reasoning; and viewpoint-external reasoning. Viewpoint-internal reasoning as, in a certain sense, equivalent to normal reasoning techniques using a closed-world assumption over the sentences in the viewpoint. However, viewpoint-internal reasoning is influenced by elements introduced for viewpoint-external reasoning. A discussion of these elements, and the outline of a language for viewpoint-external reasoning. Propagation as an example of viewpoint-external reasoning.

The work described here has all made the unrealistic, but wholly conventional, assumption that all beliefs have strength or probability 1. We explore the application of techniques such as Dempster-Shafer (statistical), and evidential reasoning and their application to reasoning with defaults, hierarchically organized material, and weakened beliefs. Current methods for representing strength of belief do so by attributing a numeric value to the belief, which we find unrealistic and hard to justify. Instead, we propose that beliefs are considered as being "weaker" or "stronger" with respect to each other. (A consequence is that many beliefs will not be directly comparable). We propose a calculus that abstracts away from numeric attribution of strengths of beliefs, retaining the desirable effects of numerical approaches, but without recourse to numbers.

5.2 Environments, Intensionality, Reference and Speech Acts

Why the environment and viewpoint mechanisms provide a new way of understanding classic problems of intensionality, de dicto/de re distinctions etc. and problems of reference identity between speakers. The essential asymmetricity in our use of the ascription process to produce a new intensional entity. Discussion of recent work by Cohen, Levesque, and others. The extension of this approach to speech acts in dialogue, viewed not as a reasoning problem (the conventional view of the authors we discuss) but as stored stereotypical forms, in a representation consistent with the representation of meaning we use throughout.

6. Further Extensions and Speculations

6.1 Metaphor Revisited

We have claimed that metaphorical, or continually extended, meaning is fundamental to our constructivist view of natural language. A natural way to envisage that within a belief model would be to model metaphor as the pushing down, within a believer, of one meaning structure or viewpoint within another (e.g., seeing one thing as another, or through another, as in seeing a car as a metaphorical horse). The idea here is to give a richer constructivist account of metaphor, as opposed to the usual property transfer approach. It should not be astonishing that a theory of belief could provide a basis for an account of metaphor since the latter phenomenon has been traditionally close to the idea of a point of view and, as we noted earlier, there can be no distinction in our view between beliefs about facts and about meanings. Is someone who thinks Thalassemia is a province of Greece, rather than a disease, wrong about facts or meanings? It does not matter, on our view. The idea is to see how far we can push the basic belief ascription machine to new tasks, in this case by taking intermediate meaning structures (e.g., "car") as phantom or pseudo-believers, and the product of the metaphor creation process as an asymmetric intensional object (e.g., car-as-horse).

6.2 Psychology and Effort Reviewed

Consequences of this theory for psychology include the percolation effect of beliefs ascribed within a system and their effects remaining after the ascription (compare to the classic sleeper effect). This phenomenon is a side-effect of computational processes and may correspond to ways in which unsupported beliefs propagate in human believers. Considerations of the computational effort in push-down ascriptions and how and when the inner environments should be preserved in memory, to avoid excess effort and resource use by the processor. Further complications of the believer's **self-model** and how this can be maintained, used and changed by the believer (cf. a public self, or self-image: how a believer thinks others see him). The believer's model of the inference processes of others and of the *ViewGen* model itself: what it is for a believer to have an active model of belief processes in others, and whether that affects computational matters.

One outcome of what we have proposed is that belief is not just an addition to a meaning theory as in conventional theories, where you must know what a proposition means before you can tell if it is true or believed. The present work suggests a more Quinean (or even Wittgensteinian) view: that belief wholes and their manipulation may support a quite different theory of meaning, one in which a theory of meaning is empty (as Tarskian, denotational, theories are for natural languages) if applied only to individual propositions apart from coherent "belief clusters" and if divorced from a theory of belief, plans, goals and action. In saying that we are falling back, as is sometimes done in AI, on a new version of "procedural theory of semantics or meaning," one in which what something means is a function of the ascription processes, and action/utterance outcomes, of which it forms a part. If we ask, what does "Prussia" mean to one who believes "Prussia invaded France in 1871?" We cannot answer that by any dictionary or denotational/referential processes, but only by an account of the interaction of metaphor, belief and meaning structure.

6.3 Practical and Social Matters

The practical consequences of an operational theory of belief in a computer for expert systems (including medical/legal systems), teaching systems, strategic systems, and advanced text understanding in particular is considering what it would be for a computer to be responsible in the way a human (or sometimes an animal) is.

6.4 Conclusion

References

Index

Chapter 1
Introduction

Chapter 1
Introduction

What could an *artificial believer* possibly be like? And would we want one, if it could be created? It is said that in Tibet streams turn wheels that, as they turn, pray on behalf of people and therefore, presumably, believe as well. More recently, Adams (1989) created the notion of an electric *MONK*, a device made to believe so as to relieve people of the burden of doing so. Yet these remote or fictional machines may not be taken seriously into consideration by a reader so early in the story. We shall begin therefore by asking how we know what belief itself is, and what constraints we must place on the notion.

People know what it is to believe because we all believe a vast number of things, even though it may not really make sense to talk of there being a number of our beliefs that we could count. Many of them will be true, some false, while some are not agreed to be true or false by experts, and some are neither true nor false in a different way because, even if we profess to believe them very hard, scientists might say that their truth or falsehood could not possibly be decided by the best and most precise methods available to human beings. But our knowing what it is to believe does not give us any real insight into what belief is, or what it would be like for a computer, or anything artificial, to believe as we do. After all, being able to see tells us nothing at all about the theory of vision or how to make a computer that can recognize shapes.

Anyone who reads magazines now knows that the goal of artificial intelligence (AI) is to make computers behave in human-like ways, though not necessarily in ways that are more than human, or super-human as some would put it. A mechanical shovel that can do the work of 100 men would not be considered AI, and a bank's computer that can tally a whole branch's accounts between 3:30 and

3:35 p.m. is almost certainly not AI: It is just very fast computer arithmetic. But definitions and borderlines do not matter here for our purposes. We shall take AI to be the writing and running of programs to do the things that are done in AI laboratories: that is over-simple and possibly vacuous but pretty clear, nonetheless. So, we would include getting computers to control robots, to reason, to see with TV cameras, to write music, to understand and translate English or Chinese, and to learn. That list is not complete, and those tasks are certainly not being done equally well by today's computers and AI theories. Given that we as humans believe things and it is no super-human task to do so, it will hardly be surprising that AI researchers want computers to believe things too, as part of some of their projects.

If we judge by the terms of ordinary speech, the job is perhaps already done, and may be simpler than we guessed. Someone believes he has $321.15 in his checking account, and goes to the automated teller outside his bank where it displays on its screen that he has exactly that sum. Many people would then say that the bank computer believes the same as he does. Some might go further and give all the credit to the machine by saying it **knows** he has $321.15 and that's what really counts, quite independently of what he believes because, if the computer and the customer disagree, it is always right and he will be in the wrong!

They could probably be made to see it differently given persuasive descriptions of situations where a customer had convinced the bank that the computer or its operators had made a mistake, and that his own figure was right and the computer's was wrong,with the result that it did not *know* anything, after all. That would probably happen if there were paper records of deposits and withdrawals and the bank could produce no conflicting ones. Hence, we need never admit that the computer *really* knows and we just believe things, because it will always be a matter of weighing available evidence, evidence external to the computer's stored data. Whatever it may mean for a computer to know or believe (the subject matter of this book) it can never rest on any special privilege attaching to computer stored information.

In this book we shall not be using "believe" to mean something weak and in some way short of real knowledge. We shall stick to the view that knowledge is no more than the special set of beliefs that scholars and administrators agree on, or teach in schools at the moment or, in nastier countries, enforce with an army and police. To adapt a well-known cliche about languages and dialects: knowledge for us is just belief with a bureaucracy behind it. Readers who care about this distinction will be relieved to know that we treat it more seriously later in the book.

But to return to where we were: many consider that computers already believe things and, if that is so, how can there be a problem about the existence of artificial believers? For those are, on that view, just computers with databases for doing tasks like checking account balances, which may also have a screen or voice module that produces statements in English declaring what is in their database. No one has any difficulty understanding the person who, for example, gets a second, duplicate, electricity bill after paying the first and who says: Oh, it believes I haven't paid. People now talk like this and are understood, so surely artificial believers are already a fact of commonsense everyday life!

1.1. How philosophers want this game played

Lined up against that way of talking, and against accepting the commonsense conclusion we have just presented, are two groups of people. First, there are philosophers for whom belief is a very complex notion to understand, one that cannot be separated from the idea of a mental state: in this case, a mental state of believing. When we go to the bank we can be said to be in a mental state of believing that there is $321.15 in the account. But the computer that then types $321.15 on the screen is in no mental state of any sort: it is just obeying an instruction to type out whatever number it finds in its registers. It is not in a mental state and therefore cannot believe anything whatsoever.

Philosophers who write like that would usually go on to say that no machine can be in any mental state of any kind, even in principle, and that remains a fundamental difference between computers and people (Searle 1980). They would maintain that position even if the machine went on to do much more surprising and interesting things than the automated teller, such as conducting an intelligent conversation on its screen about the account, one so clear and lucid that we became convinced a bank employee inside the building was typing to us as a joke.

That possibility is like the one Turing envisaged (1950) long before it was technically feasible. It is now a very close possibility, in that people can already be "fooled," if you like that phrase, that they are talking to a person when they are not. Turing's conclusion was that if one could not detect differences between the machine and a person over a reasonable period (and he wanted rather special constraints on the way the dialogue was set up, although they are of no concern here) then we might as well dispense with philosophical discussions of whether machines could think or believe or not and just concede that they did.

In one sense, as we noticed already, Turing's view has been accepted by the man in the street, at least as in regards to what is actually happening with computers and how we talk about them (see Turkle 1987), and certainly so if it is a matter of what is just around the time corner or in futurist TV stories. For most people there is no real distinction here between the fiction and the reality. And it is worth reminding ourselves that it is those ordinary people who control the English language and what we can and do say with it.

But Turing has not won his case with the philosophers. Indeed, why should he, since his test was intended to stop philosophical discussion of these issues, which he thought could go on forever, while they, naturally enough, have a very strong interest in keeping it going! But this is not a cynical book and we have no intention of reducing serious intellectual questions to employment, or trades union issues. As we shall see later, there is a wide range of philosophical opinion on what belief is, some of it not very far from Turing's own view. We shall survey and discuss these issues, thus paying our philosophical dues, as it were: But we must emphasize that this is **not** a philosophical book, since cheerfulness, in Dr. Johnson's phrase, will keep breaking in.

1.2. The minimum AI view of belief

To see why this is not a philosophical book, even though "belief" is a word that has served philosophy faithfully for centuries and will continue to do so, we must turn to the second group of intellectuals who are unhappy with the plain speaker's view that a bank's computer has beliefs about an account. This contains researchers in AI and natural language processing, amongst whom we count ourselves. Their view, in the simplest terms they could all agree on, (so we shall call it the minimum AI view of belief) whatever details they disagree about, is that the bank's computer cannot be said to believe anything, *not* because it is a machine, but because the whole setup is too simple to be called belief.

That position is quite different from the negative, philosophical one just discussed: It accepts that there could indeed be machine believers, artificial believers if you will, and that belief is central and essential to any attempt to produce intelligent conversational behavior from machines. It also assumes that belief cannot be equated with "whatever is in a machine's database," where by that phrase, we mean structures interpretable directly as low-level facts, like the contents of a bank account. The position of this book is close to those assumptions, but emphasizes in addition that belief requires the ability to understand *that other people* (or machines come to that) believe things different from what we ourselves believe. That is why no "database" view could possibly capture what it is for a person or machine to believe. We will risk the following claim: Belief for a machine or a person, to be a notion of any interest at all, requires at least the ability to understand that others have different beliefs from itself. Belief is, on that view, a matter of there being more than one believer, or at least belief in more than one believer, since the last man on the Earth still, in some sense, has beliefs.

Let us now set out why the AI approach to belief and other mental matters is different in principle from a philosophical investigation. As the reader will have noticed, philosophy will creep into these discussions whatever disclaimers we give, for we cannot completely eschew philosophical discussion of topics like belief: but the history of such topics is part of philosophy and nothing can be done about that. But there is something different about the AI approach to these age-old matters: It adds not only cheerfulness (or some might say, crude and ill-informed impertinence) but also hubris. AI researchers want to cut through philosophical discussion by engineering actual, performing, systems; and about that Turing was totally right. It is a new way with philosophical issues; one that Dreyfus once compared (1972) disparagingly to alchemy. He, too, was right, but not in quite the negative way he intended: Alchemy was a practical way of doing medieval philosophy and much more successful than its detractors would have us believe. For some historical reason that is not completely clear, it is the philosophers' account of alchemists that survives, rather than vice-versa. We must ensure that the same is not true of the history of AI.

1.3. A digression on methodology

Wittgenstein once said that philosophy leaves everything as it is, by which he meant only that it is not an empirical subject, or, as some would put it, is not a first-order subject with empirical consequences. The AI system to be described in this book also leaves philosophy as it is, by which we certainly do not mean that AI is not an empirical subject. We mean that our *computational* theory of belief is independent of philosophical theories of belief. It may seem more compatible with some than with others, and we shall note those similarities when we come to such theories in a while, but it is ultimately compatible with them all. One can adopt any theory whatever as to what belief *is*, and then adopt our computational view of belief ascription. And that, of course, is also what Wittgenstein meant: A philosophy of belief does not commit you to anything empirical, within AI, or psychology, or anywhere else, were you to set about constructing an artificial believer.

However, there is a form of modern philosophy, namely the application of logic specifically to AI activities and programs, which may appear less neutral with regard to our enterprise. There are researchers today who believe, unlike scientists in truly empirical disciplines, that certain types of formalization are not an activity subsequent to the expression and testing of empirical hypotheses (as has been widely believed appropriate for, say, physics) but should be involved from the outset in the very framing of hypotheses. This is a common view in AI, particularly in areas like belief, Moore (1977) being a standard reference to such a point of view.

Our view will be closer to that of traditional, more robust, sciences: Hypotheses and tests must precede a full formalization because there has to be something to formalize. A theory can only be axiomatized when it is a theory already. In all this we want to stick to what we view as the essentials, and not put the logicist cart before the theoretical/empirical horse. Our model is very much that of science or perhaps engineering, and not that of the second-order studies, like formalization. It is also true as a matter of observation that those logicist theories in this area have not yet produced any workable, functioning programs that can simulate believers even at the low-level we offer in this work. Colleagues of a logicist persuasion will characterize our rejection in a variety of ways, one of that might be an accusation of mere sleepwalking. We accept that at least in the sense Koestler (1959) intended when he claimed that, in the early phase of any science, sleepwalking is the desirable mode of progress: moving forward without knowing *exactly* what one is doing. That has certainly been the way in that AI has made progress until now, and we suspect that only in that way will artificial believers, like theories of gravity in the past, come into being.

Let us remain with this methodological issue for a moment: We are most certainly not advocating a view that can be parodied as Only Machine Performance Counts. A cocktail party version of that position is to consider an all talking, communicating, walking, singing, dancing machine entering a room. We all then concede that its designers have "solved the AI problem, alias the Turing test." The real problem arises when we find that the machine has no comprehensible program underlying its performance, but only a gigantic hack or kludge (alias "large impenetrable, structureless programs"), perhaps even a connectionist network (see later description). The standard version of this parable then appeals to us to accept that the achievement is therefore pointless: Performance has been achieved but with no science or insight, because the program that produced the behavior, being apparently without structure, may be as hard to understand as the human it simulates.

Colby was often accused in this way when his PARRY (1975) program turned out to be so successful in performance but so short on internal and logical structure: It was simply a fast pattern matcher, and its excellent human simulation in real-time was very depressing for those who thought logical structure, or extensive world-knowledge, essential. We believe, on the contrary, that the structures, rules and inference patterns we shall employ are the appropriate ones for this subject matter, and do capture something approaching plausible psychological realities.

This last is perhaps the most dangerous claim of all, one that has become popular and seductive in the age of cognitive science as we noted in the preface earlier. In one sense, we all know perfectly well that nothing less than an advanced neurophysiology could confirm or disconfirm AI theories as theories of the mind. We know equally well, unless we are extraordinary optimists, that such evidence is not now available and will not be in the foreseeable future: The gap between brain research and the formal analysis of concepts like belief is simply too wide. If one accepts that, then one must look elsewhere for the empirical verification of theories.

A more popular program within cognitive science, with the aim of establishing such verification, is the close connection that now exists between AI and psychology. In that alliance, or rather the AI-chauvinist version of it, the situation is simple: AI provides symbolic theories of the mind and runs programs, psychologists take those outputs and compare them with the results of experiments on human subjects. For some this is an appealing picture, not least because it reverses the relationship that linguists, for example, have sought to impose on AI: one where they were real theorists, and AI workers were the white-coated laboratory assistants who carried out the lesser task of confirming or disconfirming theories by mere computing. But that view (and, alas, cognitive science, whatever it may become, consists of little more than a montage of such views) is no more satisfactory with psychologists playing the laboratory assistant role, and we shall not avail ourselves of such possible tests here. To say that is not to deny that psychological realities should be incorporated in AI programs where possible, nor that some AI programs may be highly suggestive for possible human experiments. No, the reason is simply that the two subjects (like all such pairs, since subjects are largely defined by their standards of truth, proof, argument, and verification) are different, and there will always be alternative psychological explanations that may intervene between one such theory and the computational results, however close those may appear in a particular case.

All of this leaves us, as AI researchers, alone and falling back on only our own home-grown criteria, even though, as thoughtful researchers know only too well, these have not yet been fully defined. They do require at least some performance (as a necessary but not sufficient criterion) as well as requiring that structures be motivated and perspicuous and implemented in a range of ways. And also, we suggest, though this is not a popular view in AI these days, some notion of a *procedural theory*: one that provides plausible procedures that may, at best, preserve certain other principles of efficiency in the use of resources or information (or nonefficiency if we can find a way of motivating those, too).

This claim is particularly hard to justify, but all AI researchers know, in practice, how to tell a clear theory and implementation from a bad one, and that will have nothing to do with the logical structure used in a representation, or the formal semantics provided, but will have a great deal to do with judicious choice of notation, perspicuity, and the possibility of a reimplementation from published descriptions. It is with these traditions, then, that we wish to align ourselves. However, and this is most important, we take that point to be quite independent of the style of representation in the sense that our basic procedure is a default algorithm, even though this is, in fact, coded in a declarative prolog program *ViewGen*.

1.4. Limitations of the *ViewGen* system

No reader should imagine for a moment that we believe that the functioning of our program, together with its theory and description that we shall offer in this book, add up in any way at all to an *Artificial Believer*. We are not so presumptuous: What we do offer, and only that justifies the book's title, is a series of suggestions for ways forward, plus a program called *ViewGen* as a proof of possibility in the standard way we just described. That is the only way AI actually makes progress: very large-sounding titles, accompanied by very small, staggering, sleepwalking steps.

Let us admit that two other very important things are missing from what we offer: first, we do not tie *ViewGen*, our "belief engine," whose description occupies much of this book, to a natural language parser. By parser we mean any program whose function is to process actual sentences of English dialogue being conducted with the main *ViewGen* program, so as to yield the representation the program uses. Nor do we have the reverse procedures that would transfer *ViewGen's* beliefs back into English. Only with the aid of those transformation processes could *ViewGen* engage in real dialogues.

We are carrying out, with colleagues, the task of linking *ViewGen* directly to English sentences and its omission here is not accidental: indeed one of us has argued forcibly on other occasions (Wilks, 1976) that systems for the representation of knowledge and belief cannot, in the end, be "decoupled" from a parser. That is because the structures proposed are necessary for the parsing process itself if we believe, as most AI researchers do, that a natural language cannot be transformed to a meaning representation without the aid of such belief and knowledge structures. However, in order to convey the heart of our claims in a limited space we shall do just that, and the only token of good faith we can offer is that one of us has worked a great deal on parsers of English and continues to do so, and so such procedural steps are not omitted here simply from ignorance or unwillingness to tackle the issues that arise in their construction.

The second methodological omission in what follows is that we do not tie what we offer firmly to a theory of learning or knowledge acquisition. Once upon a time in AI, it was normal to present structural representations and then to add that it was too hard to explain right now how an organism could learn them, but that the issue would be dealt with later. Dreyfus (1972) in his classic and devastating critique of AI, argued that all this was the wrong way round: Humans were creatures that learned what they knew in a real world and so artificial entities of the same power would need to have just such a learning process. Learning, for him, was indispensable to AI, and not something that could be postponed.

Matters have changed since then: Machine Learning, within what we can still call the standard symbolic AI paradigm, has become an established sub-discipline (e.g., Langley, 1980), and more recently nonsymbolic, or connectionist, approaches (e.g., Smolensky, 1988) have made learning central to their approach. In this book we tread an uneasy path, albeit a conventional one on this issue and do not offer any serious account of how the beliefs we manipulate are derived or acquired, in part because we have deliberately cut ourselves off from a parser, as we just admitted, and natural language input would be the normal source of beliefs of the sort we shall deal with.

However, we shall say something about how beliefs can be acquired, and we must do so because our fundamental algorithm is a "default mechanism," one that assumes people ignore (and assume others ignore) the beliefs of others except where they are known to contradict their own. That statement is far too simple a description of what we propose, but put in that crudity it can be seen why we must address the issue of learning, or else a reader might well ask how, on our view of belief manipulations, anyone can ever learn anything at all! We deal with this issue in considerable detail below (sec. 3.4).

Again, if the beliefs that organisms have are to be treated in a serious and realistic way, then we have no excuse for limiting them to those beliefs that can be expressed symbolically or linguistically, or even to those that can become conscious. As two people walk towards each other in a busy street, each moves to the side and, except for rare comic clashes, manage to pass each other without anything needing to be said, which is to say with no symbolic or conscious messages passing between them. And yet one can reasonably say that this happens only because one of them believes that the other is going to pass to *his* left, while the other believes the same (but of the other person). Although there is no proof, it is simply common sense to say that, in those rare hesitations we observe, the individuals are recomputing their beliefs about the movements of the other, before making their own movements. We feel we can see in the faces that that is being done.

There is no reason whatever to think that such beliefs need be expressed at anything like a symbolic level: Dogs certainly seem to be in the same situation as we are at such times, and most of us feel no strong commitment to a *symbolic* folk-psychology for dogs, where by that phrase I mean something purporting to be a theory, but whose content is not more than what the average person thinks about mental states and functioning. Beliefs that could not have expression at any level of symbolic language will not come within our scope, even though it might well be possible to accommodate them into some plausible language of movement primitives. We shall restrict ourselves to beliefs that seem to have a natural symbolic content: to claims, general or specific, about the world and about plans based on them.

Hence we shall not address the issue of consciousness explicitly in this book (though see Wilks, 1984): It is of no importance for our claims and procedures whether or not the beliefs we describe here are consciously entertained or not. We are offering no explication of "conscious belief" in this system, and nothing we say depends on it. In (Wilks, ibid.) one of us has set out what it might be like to do that, but it is of no immediate importance to us here, except to note that it is an assumption of what we call "belief ascription" that vast numbers of beliefs are manipulated in complex cross-comparisons to achieve even a very small amount of response output in, say, an English dialogue. And since such responses are normally given very rapidly in everyday life, it is difficult to believe that the belief structures manipulated by those processes could ever become conscious, at least if that is taken to mean "entertained explicitly and serially." Even worse, we cannot imagine massive parallel computations going on consciously, since we are conscious, almost by definition, of one thing at a time.

Let us mention another self-imposed limitation: we shall discuss later, at least in regards to the work of others, the situation where people do not say what they believe, but lie. But in general we shall assume that utterances are not lies. There is an argument sometimes used to justify this assumption that claims descent from Kant: Namely that people must tell the truth most of the time or lying and indeed language itself would lose its meaning. We shall accept that argument for what it is worth, and build a system on the default assumption that utterances are true unless we have reason to believe otherwise.

We shall now end this methodological digression and return to the system we propose and the crucial notions we shall need to describe it.

1.5. Enriching the Belief Example

Suppose someone says "I'll leave you my watch in my will." This seems all very simple, but any formal account of the understanding of such an utterance, by a person or a machine, is very complex indeed.

A first observation is that anyone who says such a thing is not just making a prediction about their own future behavior, but is stating an intention and would be taken by a hearer, or a court to be entering into an obligation. This last remark is often made to sound more formal by calling such an utterance a **speech act** and, in particular, a speech act of obligation or promising. Speech acts have been an intensively studied field since Austin (1962) and Searle (1969), and we shall say something in a later chapter about the background they provide for our work, philosophically, linguistically and computationally. Much labor, including computational labor, has gone into "how you detect the speech act" said to underlie such an utterance. Our view will be that some of that labor was misdirected in that, although labelling the utterance PROMISE may be a useful thing to do, it is really circular and appeals only to those who like linguistic matters categorized and fixed. From our perspective, the important thing is what sort of changes of belief state we should expect in an automaton (our ideal "artificial believer") that can be said to understand that utterance when it reads it.

It is clear, and also essentially trivial, that the message conveyed by that promise to its principal hearer is simple, and yet cannot be wholly separated from a great number of beliefs we can hardly articulate or separate. Some are straightforward generalizations that apply to the speaker just because he (assuming it is a he) is a human being: e.g., *Speaker will die*, in this case. Others are trivial but wholly cultural: People normally decide ahead what will happen to their property when they die, and if they fail to do so, the courts decide for them. Much of that information will be contained in one dictionary definition of "will" which, in its turn, can conveniently be considered a set of beliefs, even though conventional dictionaries are not written that way.

Again, the speaker above assumes by default that the hearer knows the cultural facts about dying, and that without such beliefs on the hearer's part, what he had to say would not make sense, and the hearer would not be able to grasp the key issue that is his expression of an intention in another's favour, one to be followed up in writing.

We must notice something else, too: another belief we may not have already possessed, and which the utterance causes us to infer, namely that the speaker is likely to die before us (the hearer, person, or automaton) since otherwise the bequest makes no sense. This belief may be a total surprise to us, but we notice that it is not said explicitly: It is something we infer from what was said. It may not be a belief we already had about ourselves (though it could be) but is a belief we now attribute to the speaker. In the manner of speaking we shall adopt in this book, it is a belief that we now add to our view of the speaker's view of us. We shall write of everything exclusively from our own point of view or, rather, from the machine's point of view, if it is the automaton whose belief constructions we are considering. That is not blind selfishness, but merely recognizes the separateness of minds (including, we shall maintain, machine minds): Your beliefs are always your beliefs, and never ours, however close we become and no matter how much you reveal of yourself. This, elevated to a philosophical position, is usually called solipsism. We shall just treat it as computational common sense, while noting later how many AI writers and researchers forget it at times.

The last decision, to store that belief about the speaker dying first, in a computational zone we called our-view-of-the-speaker's-view of us, slipped by easily and yet we were very close to one of the key notions we shall need in all that follows: that not only must an understander, machine or human, have clusters of beliefs about entities and particularly about *other believers* in order to understand, but that the nature of those clusters is very important. That belief is held by us about the speaker, but it is also in turn about us as well since the promise implied "I, speaker, will die before the hearer of this." We are dealing here with the two different assumptions: First, that beliefs should be stored in clusters and, secondly, that this particular belief should be put in a particular cluster (or perhaps in several, but at least in the one for our beliefs about the speaker's beliefs about us). That there are clusters of beliefs at all is an important claim; (and we shall give a more theoretical justification of it in a late chapter) many researchers are quite happy with the alternative view that all our beliefs about everything are just stored as a vast, unsorted, pile that we rummage through no matter what the topic, or what we are seeking. It is as if we had a house with no rooms or drawers, but everything we owned was piled up in a garage: A pile we sorted right through each time, no matter whether we wanted a corkscrew or a clean pair of socks.

This heap-view-of-thought is one often associated with a position we have not defined fully yet but will generally refer to as *logicist*: It can be crudely portrayed as the view that some version, probably a very sophisticated version, of logic will serve for all our needs in building the artificial believer and reasoner. And on that view, beliefs are usually portrayed as an unstructured set of "propositions" or sentences believed. The details vary from theory to theory but the basics always remain the same (even in theories like *Situation Semantics*, Barwise and Perry, 1983, that explicitly disavow propositions, as we shall see later). It must be admitted that some movements within logic itself, particularly many-sorted logic, have been designed precisely to limit pointless sortings through the heap, but it will become clear in the background sections that follow that, by using "logicist" as a term to cover what we object to, we intend certain very specific developments, such as model-theoretic semantics, and the application, out of their natural area, of notions of soundness and completeness.

The reader will notice in the body of the book that, although we explicitly reject views we call logicist, we remain very inexplicit about how the "inferences" we refer to are to be done. We consider this reasonable: there are many, many ways of modelling the inferences that humans make without committing oneself to the acceptance of any theory or mechanism of the type we call "logicist."

It was Minsky with his so-called "frame" theory (1975) who first set out the argument, in AI at least, that knowledge and belief must be structured around topics: that you should put all you know about cars in one place, or what he would have called a "car frame.[1]" The notion that models of believers also constituted by such groupings of topic-sorted beliefs is an extension of frames. It was again Minsky in an earlier paper (1968) who set out the idea that human reasoners must have models of each other to reason. Our system of partitions, or as we shall call them **environments**, is in one sense just a conflation of those two ideas of Minsky's: That believers have models of each other and of other entities and that these models can be, as we shall put it, *nested* within each other so as to produce *spaces within which to do reasoning*. Others have made that conflation, and their work will be discussed in detail later. The important ideas to be introduced here are:

(a) that a model of a believer must contain substructures or environments consisting of "relevant" items for a topic (we shall return to that weasel notion "relevant"). Only thus can the "Heap" view of reasoning be avoided.

(b) that those environments can correspond to other believers as well as to inanimate entities (e.g., "cars," "gas prices," "architects," "Albuquerque").

(c) that the model of a believer (human or artificial) must be able to "nest" (or any equivalent metaphor) environments so as to model the way that the base believer can model the beliefs of other believers down to any level a situation requires. It is an additional assumption here that we ignore "puzzle" situations requiring psychologically impossible nesting levels (e.g., deep center-embeddings in sentences, such as "the dog the cat the rabbit liked bit died").

This last claim is a new one, fundamental for what follows, and we shall try to justify it in this section. Consider the inference we made (on hearing the "watch in the will" utterance cited earlier) that the speaker believed he would die before us. We shall describe that situation in terms of (c) cited earlier as follows: we or the system, the artificial believer we are constructing, have created an environment for our beliefs about the speaker (let us call him Uncle Frank) that now, after inference from what he said, (though not before) contains the belief that he will die before us. We keep referring to "us" and "we" because we are joint authors. If it grates on the reader it can be taken as a royal or dignified "we" for the purposes of contemplating

---

[1] Quillian's planes (1968) were a precursor of the general idea.

a singular death. And let us not worry here about the technicalities of the names or indices (a sort of logical pronoun) by which the formal expression of Uncle Frank's belief indicates who is who.

So, this new belief is in our environment for Uncle Frank, a space permanently dedicated to beliefs about him, which is no more than a grouping of beliefs we believe he has as well as anything else we want to store that is relevant to him, such as beliefs others have about him. We may want to store those somewhere else as well (such as in the environment for another person who believes those things about Uncle Frank) and there is no reason at all why beliefs cannot be kept in more than one place. Indeed, we shall argue later that that is a great benefit, and a further difference from reasoning your way through the Heap.

At this point it might be asked why this particular belief, since it is also about us (that he will die before us) is in the "Frank environment" and not put right away into a new deeper one we can call "Our environment for Frank's beliefs about us," which would be nested three deep instead of two. This is a difficult question and one to which we shall delay an answer, just noting that some would indeed take such a view (notably the school of Perrault and his colleagues (e.g., Perrault and Allen, 1980) which we shall discuss later in some detail) but that we believe for very general reasons of *efficiency, storage,* and *processing* that belief environments should be kept in as shallow a version as possible, and only deepened when needed. Those words, including "when needed," will get a lot of attention later on.

Let us see where we are: We have seen how a new belief can be added into our environment for Uncle Frank on the basis of what he said to us and inferences from it. Let us highlight the key fact that that belief may well differ from what we believe about ourselves and our state of life and health, and it may also rest a false inference in that he does not in fact believe it. Let us take those one at a time.

It may well differ from our own view of ourselves because we know we have a fatal disease that will kill us within six months, long before he goes though we believe Uncle Frank does not know this fact. Hence the environments we maintain for ourself and for Uncle Frank (including his belief about us) will differ in that regard. This is the crucial difference from the bank-teller computer and one reason why it cannot be said to have beliefs: an automaton with beliefs must at least be able to see that others have different beliefs and record that fact, and so it cannot be mere data-base with no nestings of belief, where everything is a putative "fact" at the same level. Our claim that machine belief requires nested belief to merit the term "belief" at all, and therefore at least two distinct believers, is very much in the tradition that, in so-called linguistic philosophy, argued against the possibility of a purely private language. Language, argued Wittgenstein (1958), requires a society, and we are assuming much the same about belief.

In the second situation, further discourse with Uncle Frank may show we are wrong about his beliefs concerning us: He really does know about our condition but is being too tactful to refer to it. Perhaps in later discourse he either comes straight out with it, or says something from which we can infer that he believes the truth. Our system's ascriptions of belief are, in the fashionable term, *defeasible*. Representing this situation, one we shall return to later, also requires a system of inference that recognizes contradiction and the need to revise beliefs. There are many mechanisms for doing this, we shall take one "off the shelf" as it were, since it is not central to our claims and theory, at least not unless it falls under what we intended earlier by the term "logicist" which, the reader will remember, by no means excluded all applications of logic.

If we choose, and many family relationships are of exactly that sort, we can make this story as complex as we wish, and that complexity will have to be reflected by the "depth of nesting" we deem appropriate for the analyzing system (which we are simulating in this introduction). For example, a preexisting belief of ours, held at the moment at which he made the offer of the watch, might well have been that he had always intended to leave it to his daughter Jane, which would then have been our belief about Uncle's intentions, based on some long-forgotten evidence. Thus, we would have inferred at the moment of the offer (now perhaps made with an emphasis on "you" in "I'm leaving **you** the watch in my will") that he had turned against Jane in some way. Or perhaps only that, Uncle Frank being a tricky one, intended us to believe that he no longer cared for Jane. All this was the stuff of Grice's (1969) analyses of meaning and intention long ago. The point we wish to make here is that those analyses are essentially matters of solipsistic belief in an analyzing automaton, best seen as levels of nesting of environments. The last possibility suggests a nesting of our view of Uncle Frank's view and of our view of Jane. We shall begin a more systematic account of such notions with the example cited later, but let us note two things in closing off this section of the discussion.

First, that to reduce to an algorithm exactly what is the appropriate "nesting level" for understanding is a very difficult matter. An extreme example would be the reported remark of Metternich on hearing of the death of a fellow statesman: "I wonder what he meant by that." We feel instinctively that that extreme is carrying matters too far, as it is to wonder *why* an algebra lecturer is telling us whatever he is in his exposition. Additional levels are sometimes just inappropriate. Real life, however, as Metternich knew as well as anyone, often does demand a number of such levels, but it may always remain a system-dependent choice: Some human understanders always go for more levels than others, as we all know from everyday life. Again, some situations make us prefer shallower levels than others, e.g., being in a hurry, still although taking an exam might have the reverse effect. This position may imply that we can *only* be modelling an individual, and not psychological generalizations as some colleagues would undoubtedly prefer. In that sense, AI is still alchemy.

Secondly, we expressed earlier our own conviction that the manipulation, construction, and maintenance of belief environments is not just a preliminary to the real business of dialogue understanding, often called "speech acts," but is the heart of the whole matter. We believe speech acts have been systematically over-rated in the philosophical literature, (although see chapter 5.2 later) and normally come down, in the end, either to being a vacuous classification of utterances (e.g., detecting Uncle Frank's remark as a promise, rather than a threat) or merely a con-centration on the way that humans can *bind* themselves with utterances treated like actions. This last is of great interest but also, we suggest, beyond the scope of the automatic understanding of discourse: It lies in some other realm and we return to it in the last chapter. In common sense terms Frank does not really bind himself at all with what he said: He may laugh it off later, and say it was a joke. More likely he may write a fresh codicil the following week leaving it all to Jane after all, in which case he was not bound in any way by his remark. We shall not be fascinated by that binding any further here, and suggest it is not part of computational reason-ing and understanding, whatever its other interest may be.

1.6. Nesting environments as a computational linguistics task

We can look at what we have discussed so far as a very traditional task in computational linguistics. We now set out a new example as the systematic com-parison of two sets of nested environments and then notice how that is precisely the paradigm of all computational linguistics demonstrations.

Consider the following dialogue between a user and a system even though it has a rather stagey, artificial quality, as one where we intend the system as an artificial believer. We go on to ask what structures it must be able to manipulate to understand what is said to it.

USER: Frank is coming tomorrow, I think.

SYSTEM: Perhaps I should leave.*(*)*

USER: Why?

SYSTEM: Coming from you that is a warning.

USER: Does Frank dislike you?

SYSTEM: I don't know*(**)*, but you think he does and that is what is important now.

Figure 1. 1. A Sample Dialogue.

The point of this dialogue is to cause the hearer/system to change its beliefs as a result of engaging in it. Those who remain attached to a "speech act" way of looking at things may want the system, as proof of having understood, to be able to label the user's first remark internally as a threat or warning, but we shall not do so, for the reasons mentioned earlier.

The method we shall adopt is to consider the points marked * and ** in the dialogue above, and construct environment nestings at those points, which will then be considered as the system's internal structures for the dialogue at those two points. Within those environments, when constructed, we shall consider the evaluation of the user's first utterance within those environments. "Evaluate" here is intended to have a standard computer science meaning, one we could put more adventurously as *running structural descriptions in given environments* (Bien 1976).

What utterance evaluation will mean in concrete terms is drawing plausible pragmatic inferences and, in that sense, our view of understanding is at one with the general consensus in AI in recent years: that "understanding language," slippery notion though it is, can be best be identified with the drawing of such pragmatic inferences in context. However, and as the reader will see, this notion of "running the representations of utterances in environments" will be a crucial one for us and gives our views a different twist from the conventional notion of understanding in AI.

In particular, at point * in Fig. 1.1 the system is evaluating the user's initial remark "Frank is coming tomorrow, I think" in the following nested environment:

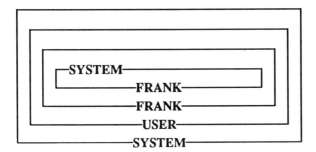

Figure 1. 2. What System believes the User believes Frank believes about the System.

This is the initial diagrammatic representation we shall use for the system's environment that contains its point of view of the user's beliefs, which in turn contains Frank's beliefs and so on. The whole represents the system's view of the user's view of Frank's view of the system. The innermost box called "System" has its label placed in a top left corner, rather than at the bottom, to show it is a *topic*: something that is believed about, rather than being a member of a chain of believers like the use of "System" on the outermost box. This is an important distinction, to be discussed fully later. Let us just accept it intuitively now, in the same way we do a box as a container for beliefs, as being either *about* a topic, if it has a top-left name, or *of* a believer, if it has a bottom-centered name on the box. Let us suppose too, that the belief "Frank dislikes System" resides in some formal representation in that inner environment, along with other beliefs, and that when the user's first sentence is "run" in that environment, the resulting inferences include the output at *.

Let us not worry either about why we chose just that order of just those constituents. The issue of the order of nesting is a tricky and complex one, but there may well be (as here) a default order that happens to correspond by default to the grammatical order of persons, i.e., I, you, he (= system, User, Frank). The point is to contrast what is in that nested environment with the one constructed by the system at point (**) in the conversation. There the system has evaluated just Frank's view of the system's self, that is to say he has run the user's same first sentence in the "shallower" environment:

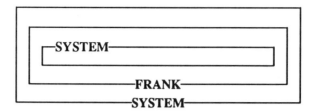

Figure 1. 3. What System believes Frank believes about the System.

where he discovers that he has no such information on what Frank thinks of him, and hence produces the different response he does at (**).

If we suppose some prior parsing of the input sentences has produced a semantic representation, one we shall not discuss at this stage, then the first question of principle is that of strategy for setting up environments. We shall distinguish the *presentation strategy* and the *insertional strategy*. The question for the presentation strategy is this: given any incoming information about an individual, how deep a level of nested environment should the system construct in order to incorporate it? A minimal strategy will be appropriate when, as we noted earlier, we listen to an algebra lecture but do not normally evaluate the input in terms of the presence of the speaker: One is not asking oneself "why is this mathematics lecturer telling me this?" and evaluating his motives and reasons for doing it. We shall call that a *minimal strategy:* one that has a very shallow environment with no level corresponding to the speaker.

What we shall call the *standard presentation strategy* for information is the one adopted in the nested environments cited earlier, where they are nested so as to include a level corresponding to the speaker (who is the user in this case) and then the individuals mentioned. At (*) the system evaluated the initial sentence while taking account of the speaker's motives, but at point (**) it does not take account of the speaker and the speaker/user does not occur in the nesting. This strategy allows a hearer either to disbelieve a speaker or to accept his apparent claims as he chooses (cf. Taylor and Whitehill 1981). Some readers will see immediately that we are leaping over huge intellectual difficulties here at high speed, hoping only that momentum will carry us forward. For example, we have not discussed at all how the system is to find appropriate stored environments, so as to nest them. If we require an environment containing all we know about Jane and can just go to the one labelled "Jane," then everything will be fine. But suppose beliefs about Jane appear in more than one place: suppose, for example, Jane is Frank's mother, then we have to know that so as to find them under another labelling.

Worse still, suppose we believe Jane is Frank's mother but the user, whose beliefs we (as the system) are "constructing," does not believe they are the same person. For him, then, facts about Frank's mother are not relevant to Jane and should not be in any environment representing her. The problem just mentioned is often known as that of "intensional description" or how we can represent and reason about situations where "the same person or thing" goes under many aliases, names and descriptions, not all of them known to everybody. We shall tackle this classic problem later.

In offering our own solution to it we shall seek to link it to practical problems of machine reasoning such as expertise (especially since expert systems these days have become for many outside the field the core of AI and how some of these environmentally-dependent descriptions can be "evaluated" by some experts, so as to get certain results, but not by others). To understand this idea in general terms, think of the way in which a doctor might evaluate the phrase "the cure for tuberculosis" so as to yield its "value," antibiotics, whereas many lay people could not get that, even though they could use a phrase like "the cure for tuberculosis," do have beliefs about the topic, and understand its meaning.

One important feature of this book will be our attempt to argue that a theory for manipulating belief environments correctly, and for showing how descriptions and utterances can be run in some but not others, will also be a process that gives the key to many traditional philosophical and computational problems concerning meaning itself.

Let us go back for a moment to the problem of strategies. To begin with there is the shallower kind of strategy, used by a reasoner to save resources and make things easy, whether from laziness or to keep resources for other problems in the understanding process. Then we can also imagine super-strategies (see examples cited later) that are deeper reflexive nestings, not only of the beliefs of the speaker and others, but also of the system itself. In such situations the system constructs ever deeper environments corresponding to what it believes somebody else believes about what it itself believes, etc.

Earlier we distinguished presentational strategies from what we called *insertion strategies*. When the system encounters an utterance like the first user's one (about Frank) in the dialogue of Fig. 1. the question arises as to where in the system this should be stored. This is just the case we touched on earlier when discussing which believer the "speaker dies before hearer" belief was *about*.

In the case of the user's sentence "Frank is coming tomorrow, I think," should the representation of that sentence be stored simply in the environment for the user, the person who said it, or in one for Frank, the person spoken about, or both? One possibility is a *"scatter-gun" strategy*, where the information is stored initially in all relevant places, i.e., in both the environment for the user and for Frank.

In 5.1 cited later, when describing *ViewGen*, we shall adopt a more conservative strategy, of putting a belief in the maximally relevant environment, a notion we shall explain later. For the form of the information to be stored, we shall simply assume some semantic representation (such as Wilks 1975/1986), but for illustration use simple predicate representations for sentences of a standard sort, even though we know them to be naive. Sometimes, when it causes no confusion, we shall simply put English sentences into boxes, as the simplest possible representations of the contents of beliefs.

In the next section we present this notation of nested boxes a little more concretely as a visual aid for the book and put the representation of some sample sentences into them. But before leaving this section, let us note why we have set up the last example as we did. We showed how an artifical or automatic believer would also be able to construct more than one environment nesting and compare the different inferences that can be drawn in them or, as we put it earlier, run the same discourse input in two different environments. That is not meant just as a fashionable gesture towards parallel processing, the ability to do more than one computation at once because, for our purposes here, it does not actually matter whether the two nestings are really computed at once or very nearly so, as they would be in any standard serial machine.

No, what is important to notice is that the use of environments series is not just to limit inference to manageable contexts (i.e., comprises special sets of "relevant" beliefs), but also so that a believer can compare the results of two such limited computations. This is crucial and, to put this suggestion in a historical perspective, let us notice that it is no more than an extension of almost every standard computational linguistics exercise.

Those, most readers will recall, began, historically and pedagogically, by noting that a single sentence (perhaps "time flies like an arrow") could have two syntactic structures, and if we were very lucky, context, decided which was appropriate. Again, at the level of word sense or other semantic ambiguity, one was shown a number of semantic interpretations and how semantic or pragmatic information made available to the system would limit them to only one interpretation. Winograd's thesis (1972) was essentially an exercise in doing that for the syntactic and semantic ambiguities of "Put the pyramid in the box on the block," and Wilks' system (1975/1986) performed the semantic task for sentences like "The soldiers fired at the women and I saw *several* fall," and settled the reference ambiguity of the pronoun "several" in doing so. Many other researchers did similar things and, in every case, the paradigm of computational linguistics was: Find multiple interpretations of a single input sentence at some chosen level (phonetic, morphological, syntactic, semantic) and resolve to one appropriate target.

In some sense, the treatment of the Frank dialogue cited earlier is also of this type. We have a single input utterance "Frank is coming tomorrow, I think," which is not ambiguous in this case, but which produces different inferences (that is to say different results or outcomes) when run separately in two nestings of environments. The system decides, by techniques yet to be described, which outcome is more appropriate. In that sense, the task we propose for our system is a standard computational linguistics one, but at a higher pragmatic level: The first utterance in the dialogue above is not ambiguous in any clear sense, just open to different interpretations in different environments, its output depending on the conversational context. And that last notion, so vague yet so omnipresent in this field, is given a precise explication by nested environments.

We should notice here that the role of belief processing in computational linguistics can be seen as much wider than pragmatics. Many of the classic examples of the field, even within what is normally called syntax, can be seen as belief based. Consider:

John told his mother about the murder in the park.

This belongs to an old and much-loved family of examples going back at least twenty-five years. It is conventionally dealt with as an issue in the syntax of prepositional phrase attachment (i.e,. whether 'in the park' depends directly on 'told' or 'murder'), although it is often conceded that the decision depends on semantic facts (for discussion of the issues see Wilks et al. 1985).

However, it is perfectly reasonable, we contend to see this as an issue of belief. If the system (alias *ViewGen*) processes the utterance in an environment that is the system's-view-of-speaker's-view-of-John then the attachment issue will be no more than the issue of whether or not that environment contains a belief (stored under a suitable topic) that there was or was not a murder in the park.

In practical fact, there will be more complex considerations, such as an inherited belief based on something like 'what everyone has read in the papers lately,' and that will actually simplify matters by being something like a generally known, publicly-accessible, fact.

The more serious complications (which should exist even under the 'linguistic' interpretation of the example, although they are normally ignored) are the *de re/de dicto* considerations of whose beliefs (speaker, John, the mother) are actually being assumed. Here our basic algorithm cuts through a great deal of the apparently sophisticated chatter such examples provoke. It is certainly possible to consider all the combinations of possibilities of the beliefs being *de re/de dicto* for each of the hearer, John, or the mother in turn (e.g., perhaps the speaker believes there really was a murder in the park but believes John believes it to have been only a traffic accident at a freeway junction).

We believe that a default rule should ascribe beliefs inward in the meeting until meeting explicitly contradicting material (or, in this case, confirming material, as to the crime's location) and that, in the absence of special information to the contrary, all such ascriptions are *de re* at every stage: that there is one presupposed murder and all participants have belief in it ascribed to them. We again, return to this issue in more detail later. Unless, as always, we encounter other beliefs that overturn that assumption.

This methodology, of dealing with linguistic examples in belief terms, extends more widely, as we shall see later in this book, where different beliefs about the senses others believe words to have lead to serious consequences. This is no more than treating lexicons as databases that vary from believer to believer, where the differences can sometimes be represented in a single believer, exactly as in our original bank-database example.

1.7. Pointers to background and the beginnings of notation

We have established so far that an AI system that takes part in discourse with other agents must be able to reason about the beliefs, and also such common-sense notions as the intentions, desires, and other *propositional attitudes of those agents*. We shall use this last, rather technical sounding, term to cover beliefs, intentions, etc., although without intending to imply a philosophical view in which a state of belief (say) is no more than a relationship between an agent and a "proposition."

This state of affairs is especially important in those common situations when the agents' beliefs differ from the system's own. Thus, the question of how to represent and reason about propositional attitudes is central to the study of discourse.

Clearly, this question is really about the beliefs that the system *ascribes* to the agents, on the evidence presented by the discourse itself and by context and prior information. The system's reasoning about beliefs therefore includes not only its reasoning *on the basis* of propositional attitudes that have already been ascribed but also the "ascriptional reasoning" involved in performing the ascriptions in the first place. This last phrase will become the name of our most central process in this book: We view the ascription problem as being a fundamental one, by which we mean the process (developed non-technically earlier) of how a believer (artificial or human) is to construct a symbolic entity that contains its best guess at the beliefs of another, but without any direct evidence. That is to say, how we ascribe beliefs (and huge sets of beliefs) to others within our own computations over representations.

Anyone tempted to say at this point that we need not ascribe, but can review the evidence we have for others' beliefs directly, should think again. We, all of us, talk every day with intelligent, normally educated, people on the assumption that they, like us, believe the Earth is round. We have no direct evidence for this and could not wait to establish it in the course of the conversation, any more than we could for the uncountable other beliefs we must infer in order to conduct a dialogue with one another. As we shall see later, these indirect ascriptions are very much matters of expertise: We assume doctors know, or believe correctly, a great deal about anatomy and pharmacology simply because they are doctors. Expert systems, taken in the widest sense, cannot possibly succeed unless they are not only expert, but are also able to engage in dialogue with those who are not. Naive expert systems, which is to say most or all of those that exist, are at bottom like our bank's automated teller: They have no concept that others have differing beliefs. Yet, as we argued strongly, dialogue is only possible on the basis that beliefs differ and are known to differ, including expert beliefs. A doctor cannot discuss with a patient unless he knows that the patient's beliefs about anatomy and treatment may be different from his own (correct) ones. For how else could a doctor interpret the patient who says "I have a pain in my stomach" unless he takes account of common misbeliefs about where the stomach is? Unless he can infer and construct a patient's, probably false, beliefs about anatomy, he cannot understand. Or, as we might put it, mere expertise is nothing without a representation of nonexpertise, and indeed of vagueness, which is an even more difficult representational problem.

This notion of ascription has been the focus of our past work on propositional attitudes leading up to this book (Ballim, 1986, 1987, 1988; Wilks and Ballim, 1987, 1988, 1989; Wilks and Bien, 1979, 1983). Ascriptional reasoning is profoundly dependent on the communicative context, general information that the system has about the world, and special information the system has about the agents at hand.

This book is about a theory of all that and a program that exemplifies it, called *ViewGen*. This program generates a type of environment known as a *viewpoint*. *A viewpoint is some person's beliefs about a topic*. Within *ViewGen*, all beliefs are ultimately beliefs held by the system (e.g., the system's beliefs about France, what the system believes John believes about cars, etc.) and so, trivially, lie within the system's viewpoint. The system's view of some topic (say, pneumonia) could be pictorially represented as:

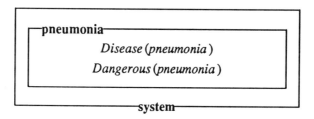

Figure 1. 4. Beliefs about Pneumonia.

As we noted earlier, the diagram contains two types of environments: first, there is the box labelled with "system" at the bottom, which is a "believer environment" or "viewpoint." Secondly, viewpoints contain "topic environments," such as the box labelled with "pneumonia" at the top of it. A topic environment contains a group of propositions about the "topic." So, for example, the above diagram conveys, now in a simple form of predicate calculus, that the system believes that pneumonia is dangerous and a disease. Topic boxes are motivated by concerns of limited reasoning. In short, it is envisaged that reasoning takes place "within" a topic environment, as if it were the environment of a procedure in a programming language.

Within *ViewGen*, environments are dynamically created and altered. *ViewGen's* "knowledge-base" can be seen as one large viewpoint containing a number of topic environments, each topic environment containing a group of "beliefs" that the system holds about the topic. Each proposition in a topic environment has at least one symbol identical to the name of the topic. Each such proposition is therefore *explicitly* about the topic. There are, however, implicit ways in which a proposition can be "about" (or "relevant to") a topic. The simplest cases are generated by inheritance in the usual way: For example, if John is a man, then any proposition in a "man" topic environment is implicitly or indirectly about John.

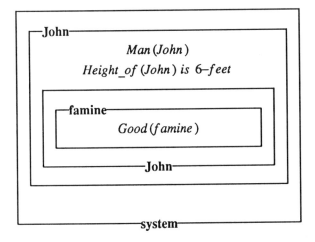

Figure 1.5. Beliefs about and of John.

If the "topic" of a topic environment is a person (someone capable of having beliefs themselves), then the topic environment may contain, in addition to the beliefs about the person, a viewpoint environment containing particular beliefs held by that person about various topics. Normally, this is only done for those beliefs of the person that conflict with the system's own beliefs about the topics. For example, suppose the system had beliefs about a person called John who believes that famine is good. This would be pictorially represented as in Figure 1.5.

The John viewpoint, shown as the box with "John" on the lower edge, is a *nested viewpoint*, as it is enclosed within the system viewpoint shown (through an intervening topic environment about John, shown as the box with "John" on its upper edge). For the sake of simplicity, in the diagram of a nested viewpoint we often leave out propositions that are not in the innermost topic box; e.g., in the

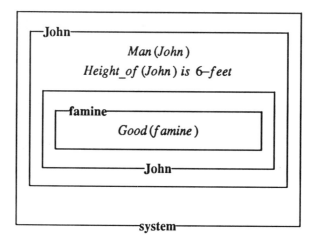

Figure 1. 6. Beliefs about and of John.

above we would leave out the beliefs that John is a man, and that he is six feet tall. Further simplifying this, we often leave out all but the innermost topic box, leaving it and the viewpoint boxes.

Hence, Figure 1.5 could be simplified as Figure 1.6.

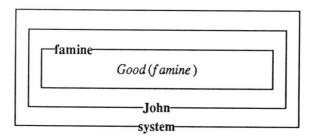

Figure 1. 7. Beliefs of John about famine.

The system stores its own beliefs, and the beliefs of other agents that differ from the system's own beliefs. Others' viewpoints are generated on demand, a position we find both computationally and psychologically more plausible than a "prestored nesting" view that other researchers hold, and that we shall discuss later. The process of generating a viewpoint can be regarded as an *amalgamation* mechanism that ascribes beliefs from one viewpoint to another (or, "pushing one environment down into another"); ascribing certain beliefs, transforming some, and blocking the ascription of others.

The simplest form of this algorithm, described in Wilks & Bien (1979, 1983), is that a viewpoint should be generated using a default rule for ascription of beliefs. The default ascriptional rule is to assume that another person's view is the same as one's own *except where there is explicit evidence to the contrary*. For example, suppose that at a certain stage the system believes that pneumonia is life-threatening and is indicated by current tests on a patient John, but that John believes that pneumonia is not life-threatening. Before the system comes to consider John's reasoning about pneumonia, the system's state is represented pictorially as in Figure 1.7.

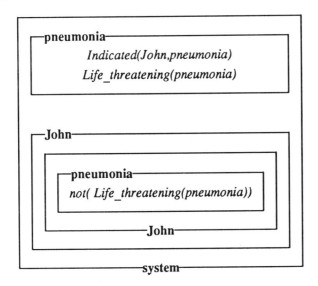

Figure 1. 8. John and pneumonia, the initial state.

The system can proceed to create a more complete environment for John's view of the disease by seeking to push the beliefs from the system's view of pneumonia (the upper most box in the diagram) into the topic environment for pneumonia within John's viewpoint. The belief that pneumonia is indicated is successfully pushed in, but the ascription of the belief that pneumonia is life-threatening is blocked by John's contradicting belief. The result is Figure 1.8.

This is simply a construction by the system, and in no way implies that John has beliefs that cannot be changed (to correct ones.) Thus far we have a pictorial notation, no more, and some idea of what a default algorithm for belief ascription

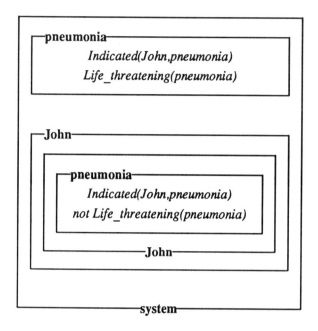

Figure 1. 9. John and Pneumonia, the resultant state.

might be like. As we shall see later, the notation must be made much more complex, there must be a program to implement it, and we must give a clear account of important classes of situation where the default algorithm does not work (we shall call these cases of "atypical belief"). But the basic idea of default reasoning about beliefs remains a powerful one: That we construct a belief ascription by assuming that others believe what we do about a topic *unless we have reason to believe otherwise.* Such an algorithm is not only simple, but also unavoidable (providing we can control atypical cases) because, as we noticed, we cannot have direct evidence for most of what other people believe.

Perhaps the most surprising fact about this approach to belief based on default is that it is original and obvious while yet not in the work of others, although it is beginning now to make an appearance (Perrault, 1990).

Chapter 2
Preliminaries on the Nature of Belief

Chapter 2.1
Philosophical theories of belief and languages of thought

It is a principle of this book that any procedural, symbolic theory of belief is logically independent of philosophical theories of belief: One could combine, in principle, any AI theory with any philosophical theory. Yet it may still be appropriate to review philosophical theories of belief in outline here or we shall have nothing more to refer to than common-sense as to what belief actually is.

2.1.1. Simple theories of belief

There are two basic, or primitive, theories of belief in the literature, which we may characterize roughly as:

(a) beliefs as simple properties of believers;

(b) beliefs as mere displayed behavior or propensity to behave.

One might say that the first is logically primitive and the second psychologically primitive. On the first view, *Mike (tall)* states a property of Mike and so does *Mike ("Cuba is an island")*, although many might prefer to see the first put as *Taller-than (Mike, 50%-of-people)*, in which case the second could appear more plausibly as *Believe (Mike, "Cuba is an island")*. The precise logical form of such expressions is not important here, although we shall return to the issue later: what is important is that a person having a belief is a property no different in type from that of their height is such and such, or that they were born on a given date.

This view (a) is, in one sense, not a philosophical theory at all: It is no more than a claim about how the relationship between beliefs and believers is to be *represented*. As such, its syntax could perfectly well accommodate the prevailing metaphor for belief in cognitive science: that a believer is like a box containing beliefs that could be written on separate slips of paper and pushed through a slot at the top. Detailed dispute about the primitive syntax of belief expressions can then concentrate on exactly what the entities in the second argument position are. Sentences seem poor candidates, since many beliefs do not have sentential objects, for one can have a belief regardless of the language, and hence the actual sentence that it is expressed in.

It is considerations like this last, of how you would test or explicate belief, that reduce the first primitive theory to the second. As stated earlier (and Braithwaite 1962 was an exponent of a more sophisticated version) it is little more than a reformulation of behaviorism: that mental terms, like belief, are to be understood in terms of associated behaviors, among which would be assent to statements (on the assumption that the subject is telling the truth). If we understand (b) in that way, then it suffers from the defect of all forms of behaviorism: It totally lacks structure and the ability to deal with similarities or differences between beliefs.

There is a probabilistic variant of (b) due to Ramsey (1931), one which has been the foundation of much formal work in the social sciences, and even AI (e.g., Pearl, 1985). For Ramsey, questions of belief were essentially matters of quantifiable behavior, and his standard example was *how much* one was prepared to bet on the truth of some proposition p, taken as a measure of one's belief in p.

The notion was original but, like all probabilistic theories of individual behavior, or propensity to behave, it always carried with it the difficulty of how one could gather the data the theory requires. In McCarthy's immortal words, "Where do all those numbers come from?" In a later section (5.1), we shall present a discrete calculus that offers some of the benefits of probabilistic theories of belief but without the continuous variables.

In the case of (a) as well, the interrelations of beliefs are in fact more complex than for properties in the normal sense: height, color, etc. do not have relationships of contradiction (although they may be contraries where several cannot be true at once) and hence there may be no benefit in assimilating the syntax of belief representation to that of conventional properties.

There has been an enormous amount of work on the nature of belief in this century and there can be no full survey of it here, nor is one necessary for our more modest goals. Virtually all of it attempts to do either (or occasionally both) of the tasks that (a) and (b) cover: providing a representation for belief or explaining what it is. And, as we noted, the notions are in practice not wholly separate. Moreover, those offering a representation for belief have usually gone on to give a *belief logic* as well, a task that can be simplified as showing why neither of "*X* believes *p*" and "*p*" entail each other , and why that fact matters. We shall return to logics of belief in some detail later, and for the purposes of this chapter will confine ourselves to more recent philosophical background on belief, which means: accounts alternative to (b) cited earlier.

2.1.2. Four contemporary philosophical theories of belief

In this section we shall consider briefly the following theories, all of which have had impact on the current state of cognitive science:

(c) Dennett's as-if theory
(d) Fodor's sentence-in-a-box theory
(e) Davidson's neo-Quinean theory
(f) Barwise & Perry's Situation Semantics

It is not usually profitable in AI to seek support for one's claims directly from philosophical theories: Their goals are usually too subtle and complex for them to be coopted as allies in AI struggles while their thrust is often against targets not explicitly revealed. However, our proposals are broadly consistent with Fodor's views, except perhaps where his claims are most distinctive, namely the grounding or semantics of internal representations. Quine's views about the coherence of the theories that make up an individual are very congenial to us, too. The general aims of situation semantics are, alas, all too congenial to almost everyone in cognitive science. The problem for us is that its distinctive proposals do not, in our view, give any firm or strong support or underpinning to AI representations or procedures.

2.1.2.1 Dennett

Dennett's theory of belief (1978, 1982) has proved popular with AI researchers: It seems to give them all they want and little they do not like. On his view terms like *believe* are part of an explanatory vocabulary humans use to model or describe their own and each other's activities in a way that is satisfactory overall.

Armed with such a theory, human beings are able to predict each other's behavior sufficiently well to live tolerably in society.

Such a view, justifying as it does common-sense talk about motives, beliefs, thoughts, etc., is often dismissively called a "folk psychology," and thought of as a reversion to behaviorism, since it seems to place little emphasis on "what really goes on inside people." It is also a descendant of nineteenth century theories like Vahinger's (1935), usually called As-If theories, according to which science as a whole deals with the universe as if a theory were true, whether or not it is in fact (whatever "in fact" may mean in such a context).

Like all views of belief, it has its points of breakdown, as when one asks someone (seriously) "Do you REALLY believe *p*?" Or, during the extraction of a false confession from a prisoner, say, or a statement of belief under interrogation by the Inquisition, the torturer may set exactly the admission he wants, but still yearns to know if the victim really believes whatever he has confessed to. In that situation, of course, behaviorism can have nothing helpful to say, but a sophisticated folk psychology can, with talk of "mental reservation" to admissions, etc.

The consequence of any view of this sort for AI is that an "artificial believer" is in a position no different from that of a human. We look at an entity's behavior and decide whether our overall theory of it (including "believe") works or not, in predicting its actions, communicating with it, controlling it, etc. It is this similarity that AI researchers like. This now is a much more sophisticated version of (b) cited earlier, in that nothing hangs on the equivalence of particular propositions and particular behaviors; it is the overall effect that counts, just as in the modern view of scientific theories, where one goes not for the crucial experiments, but for overall coherence or satisfaction.

Nor does Dennett deny the reality of mental states in the way that crude behaviorists would: it is just that he has a different way of looking at things. In terms of an "artificial believer," any consistent use of a belief primitive within the system's own internal representations would be allright, provided the general performance of the system is sufficiently good. Dennett's main claim is not that we do not have mental states (as classical behaviorists were thought to believe): it is just that the belief states of others have the theoretical status of, say, gravitational force between planets. In another striking passage he suggests that mental states may have no direct embodiment in hardware, just as when we say a hand-held calculator is doing multiplication, we do not mean there is some identifiable piece of hardware inside that is a multiplier, although there might be.

Whether one thinks that these analogies actually dismiss or downgrade mental states (as "being real") will depend on one's attitude to scientific realism, and whether or not gravitation is real, as well as a mere scientific construct.

Dennett certainly does not seem to mean that the belief-theory is a useful approximation, as opposed to a real, scientifically accessible fact. For it is part of his position that, as in regards to brains at least, such facts are not available. Here his position differs clearly from the scientific realism of Putnam (1960) as well as from Fodor's desire to make intentionality scientifically respectable in brain-science terms (the following). One critic has referred to "the nagging suspicion that Dennett is trying to sound as if he takes intentionality seriously (he wants to be able to say that ascriptions of beliefs are true) without paying the true costs" (Smith, 1988).

But Dennett's analogies with science only devalue the status of belief if one takes some scientific realist view that there is a *true theory* even if no current (or future) scientific theories actually express it. Some reflection may show that this view is actually antiscientific since the only theories there are as guides to the universe right now are the best ones we happen to have. On that "moving pointer" view (which some would say could not be realist), Dennett's analogy leaves belief in no worse position than any other phenomenon open to scientific investigation.

It could be interesting here to compare Dennett's view on belief with Katz's (1972) view that semantic primitives in linguistics have the status of entities like neutrinos, unobservable in principle but essential to the explanation of human behavior. Whether or not Katz was a realist on primitives, given that analogy, depends entirely on one's view of neutrinos, although, curiously, Katz was always taken to be a realist in drawing the analogy in the first place.

2.1.2.2 Fodor

Fodor's views (1975, 1980a, 1980b, 1987a) are a curious mixture of principle and common-sense. The common-sense is that he, like Dennett, seeks to defend a sophisticated-man-in-the-street view of belief while accepting (as Dennett does not) another metaphor for thought that the plain man often has: that beliefs are rather like sentences on slips of paper in a box in the head. The language in which the sentences are written he calls the Language of Thought (LOT): It is innate, not learned. We see here a tricky feature of folk psychology: It rests on many different metaphors and they may not all be consistent as a single theory. In fact, folk psychology has both behaviorist and mentalistic, alias internal-machinery-in-the head, aspects.

In a way quite different from Dennett, Fodor's view of things is also perfectly compatible with many AI theories of artificial believers and belief, although differences can arise about the question of a semantics for this lot in which the beliefs are expressed.

The origin of LOTs can be found as far back as Wilkins (1688), Leibniz (1951) and many others, and surfaces in such phrases as Fodor's "The recommended solution [to the problem of representing propositional attitudes or PAs] is ... to take the objects of PAs to be sentences of a *non*-natural language; in effect, formulae in an Internal Representational System," (Fodor, 1980b).

This "mental language" has been discussed under the term LOT not only by Fodor (cf. Harman, 1973; Field, 1978; Schiffer, 1978). On the LOT hypothesis, an agent has a belief if that agent possesses a statement in his mental language that expresses the meaning of the belief. Hence, if an agent believes that "Hamlet" was written by Francis Bacon, then that agent will have some expression in his internal language that represents Francis Bacon as being the author of the play "Hamlet.*U

Unfortunately, we have no direct access to what mental language humans use and are therefore left with several further questions to settle:

1)   Do all agents everywhere use the same LOT?

2)   If the languages of thought are different from agent to agent, then are they all covered by one idealized LOT?

3)   Can we proceed without assuming there must be uniformity over individual LOT's?

Positive answers to these questions serve to distinguish the *strong* or *realist uniformity hypothesis* (cf. Fodor, 1980b), the *weak uniformity hypothesis* (cf. Dennett, 1982), and what we shall call the attributive (or non-) *uniformity hypothesis* (adopted here), respectively.

An advantage of the strong uniformity hypothesis is that the LOT is determinate, i.e., there can be no problems in principle about the identity of the entities represented in the LOT. This may also be true for the weak uniformity hypothesis, via the idealized LOT. However, the attributive uniformity hypothesis suffers from the very indeterminacy inherent in natural language (see Quine, 1960), because the correspondence of LOTs (and the entities they contain or represent) can be established only by translating from LOT to natural language to LOT.

The indeterminacy problem is that without assuming representational uniformity we cannot know that the symbols used in any particular mental language mean the same thing in any other mental language. So the symbol "MAN" may represent a typical male member of the human race in one agent's mental language and may represent a jellyfish in another's.

Although the indeterminacy problem applies to the attributive uniformity hypothesis, the problem is trivial for a subjective system assuming the hypothesis. For such a system it is unimportant whether symbols in different LOTs really correspond. What is important is that the system believe there is a correspondence between its own LOT and another agent's LOT; that there is a "charitable" interpretation of the other agent's natural language to achieve this correspondence (cf. Davidson, 1967) and that the believed correspondence is confirmed by the satisfaction of the system's overall goals.

Regardless of whether LOTs exist and can be modelled, there is no way of showing, and no reason for assuming, that they have anything specifiable in common. As the problems that arise with the nonuniformity hypothesis are not insurmountable, there seems to be no appeal in adopting a uniformity hypothesis.

Another question is, to what extent should an internal language mirror the surface constructs of an external language? In other words, how many of the syntactic features of a natural language should be present in the internal representation? This question is extremely important because natural language is highly ambiguous and the choice of internal language decides where these ambiguities are resolved. For example, anaphora resolution (the resolution of pronouns to determine their referent) is a complex problem that might seem best resolved by the parsing mechanism that produces the internal representation from English, say. The alternative is to have pronominal terms within the internal language and to deal with anaphora when reasoning. That idea was put forward in Perry (1977, 1979, 1983); a related idea (that of representing quasi-indexicals) is proposed in Rapaport (1986) which we discuss in 2.2.5 later.

Fodor has always wanted to avoid the thickets of formal semantics (Montagovian, situation semantics etc., see 2.1.2.4 on these), while maintaining a position that is basically simple-minded realist about the semantics of the propositions in the LOT. He maintains that there is a straightforward denotational semantics of the sentences of the LOT, avoiding any kind of "meaning wholism" (of the kind associated with Quine) that would resist propositions being evaluated one-by-one against the real world (Fodor, 1987a). A curious feature of all this is that he conducts the discussion wholly in terms of the semantics of the LOT itself, and not of any natural language expressing its content. Hence, the problem that preoccupies many writers on belief, of how we can treat the semantics of the embedded proposition in "John believes it is raining," just does not arise for Fodor, because he has no problems about knowing *what it is* that people believe; he just knows and the LOT expresses that content. In that way he is utterly and completely in the tradition of Chomsky, of knowing the contents of heads.

Many AI researchers of more logicist persuasions do want to rest the semantics of any possible internal representation language in a computer on some version of formal semantics, and they certainly share with Fodor the assumption that the semantics of the representation language is the heart of the issue. Fodor wants a more abstract folk psychology than Dennett, one for educated folk who talk of "mental states," rather than plain men in the street who talk of belief and desire, and he also wants that theory to be semantically grounded in a formally conventional, but non-technical, way.

In later parts of this book, we shall argue that both Fodor and the formal semanticists share a common error: They ignore the extent to which their expressions, including sentences in LOT, retain crucial features of natural languages. In the case of LOT this is almost self-evident, but for logic-based representation languages the case will need to be made.

We shall assume a quite different kind of grounding, in humans and computers, by means of some form of **procedural semantics** (Wilks, 1982 and many other references in that paper), which Fodor and logicists both reject, and which holds that a grounding can be given in terms of actual computational procedures, rather than by another language or set of entities, whether wet or hard entities in the brain or computer, respectively. To put the matter at its crudest, to utter meaningful language does not always require that there be some **thing** we are talking about. This is a serious issue we shall return to on a number of occasions later.

Fodor's apparent alienation from AI approaches is not easy to explain, given his basic materialism (about the brain-mind relation) and the obvious compatibility between LOT and the representation-semantics assumed by much naive AI. The answer is probably aesthetic. Much of the structural underpinning of Fodor's theories: the modularity of mental theories, the nature of the LOT, the claims that tree structures are essential to mental representations, etc., all come directly from Chomsky's work (1964), and it may be that Fodor has inherited along with them Chomsky's total distaste for things computational.

2.1.2.3 Davidson

Davidson has developed a view of belief that could be described broadly as Quinean (1960), at least in so far as it takes seriously the problem of the necessary separateness of human believers: that they are, in a certain sense, scientists making sense of a solipsistic universe.

Davidson's (1967) major difference with Quine lies in the former's observation that all beliefs rest on other beliefs, which never "bottom out" to empirical observations in the way Quine (1960) and generations of empircists had hoped. A set of interconnected beliefs face the world as a whole, in some sense. In the case of language acquisition, and against Quine's theory of radical, or indeterminate, translation, most beliefs we infer as being those of our interlocutor (whether colleague, native or Martian) will turn out to be true, because of what Davidson calls 'principles of charity' (ibid.), namely that we share forms of life and belief and, were that not so, and were we not able to attribute those to others in a more-or-less "charitable" manner, we could not communicate at all.

Or, to put the matter another way, to treat our fellow citizens in conversation as if they were members of an alien tribe (a favorite image of Quine's) is to succumb to something like mental disorder. It is this insight that our default rule (see 3.4) for typical beliefs seeks to capture, just as our technique for what we shall call *atypical belief* will cover the cases that separate us as individuals.

Quine's own (ibid.) view of belief is also consistent with the general approach adopted in this book: namely that intensional logic (see 2.2), as normally understood, is not the way to capture belief, largely because it is inherently piecemeal, or what we earlier termed a Heap-view-of-knowledge, while what is crucial is the way human beliefs, as systems, are integrated, and defended. We shall have little to say here about the defense and adjustment of belief in the face of new and inconvenient information. What does reflect a Quinean preoccupation is that, for us too, a theory of meaning should follow from (rather than being prior to) a system for the integration, relation and adjustment of a system of beliefs. Formal semantics, as we shall argue later, is fundamentally a Heap view, whereas scientific enquiry, like human belief structures in general, requires organic wholes.

2.1.2.4 Situation Semantics (SS)

Quine's theory is, in Barwise and Perry's (1983) phrase, **innocent**: in it, as in their own theory of situation semantics, no special treatment is required for belief. Beliefs are (again in Barwise and Perry's phrase) "efficiently classified" by minds and topics. It is just that observation that our environment view seeks to capture in a computational environment. Barwise and Perry also make a strong assumption of extrinsic information, explicit and objective, and hence no theory of "information for subjects" (Fodor's phrase in 1987a) and hence no theory of belief at all on our view.

Situation semantics (SS) is a theory that has been influenced to a great degree by AI, as its authors make clear (ibid.). It is also (though completely unacknowledged by its authors) very much a relic of a Wittgensteinian Picture Theory of Truth: It is an attempt to have a semantics of real world situations and their representations, of structures, that is, rather than objects. Although the system of this book is procedural in essence, and therefore to a considerable degree representationally neutral, those are certainly the representational choices we would make. Our major difference with Barwise and Perry (BP) lies in the fact that they are preoccupied by representation to such a degree that no clear or distinctive view of belief can emerge from their work, even though they claim exactly the contrary (ibid.).

However, Devlin's (1991) version of SS devotes a great more space to discussion of belief, in contrast to knowledge particularly, and we shall therefore discuss his account in more detail. One thing Devlin does not do is provide what all AI programmers ultimately look for from logicians; a proper axiomatization of their theory. That is because Devlin, like Barwise and Perry, gives no proper axiomatic or deductive account of key notions like belief. So, if he does not offer what logicist accounts of these phenomena normally take as central, what else might AI researchers get in the way of philosophical, notational or anecdotal, support?

Our main criticism will be that Devlin gives no comprehensible account of knowledge (as opposed to belief) and that, without it, nothing can be a realist theory in any interesting sense. From that we shall infer, perhaps unfairly, that he is not so much a soft realist as a closet representationalist, a position that offers little to AI researchers over and above what they already have.

Devlin's account of mental states (p.113ff.) takes a position on the NO side of the classic question "Does the same brain or computer state imply the same mental state?" This is one of the classic dilemmas in the Fodor/Putnam arguments at the heart of cognitive science. But his reason is unlike the ones normally given along with that same answer: Devlin argues that the computer would not have the interconnections of belief, the contextuality with other beliefs that humans would, and to have a mental state is to entertain a belief connected to other beliefs.

The point fails to tell on what appears to be its immediate target since he gives no reason whatever to believe that, if a computer were sophisticated enough to reproduce a brain structure precisely, it would not also be sophisticated enough to display or express the interconnectedness of variables, etc., that underpin the relationships between human beliefs. But that target is unimportant to Devlin's point, since what he actually wants to display is part of what he means by the "relational nature of belief", as opposed to a standard realist account of belief where it involves a relation between a mental state and the world, or something like it. It will be Devlin's case that knowledge is relational, but belief is not: It is a mental state and nonrelational. Yet, as we saw in discussing mental states, for him beliefs are inherently relational with respect to other beliefs, and that constitutes part of what it is to be a mental state and shows (for Devlin at least) why computers cannot have them.

None of this supports any form of realism, of course: it is a contingent fact that those who say no to the question also tend to be realists in the modern tradition descending from Kripke. But, as we shall see, Devlin is not a serious realist in any sense.

2.1.2.4.1 Mental states

The key concept of "notion" is, for Devlin, both a descriptive language for intentionality and a way of correcting what SS has often been accused of, namely an ontological promiscuity of entities.

However, Devlin's claims about notions and the brain are not unique, e.g.:

"...we regard intentionality as a basic property of the brain, a property realized in the brain, but one that occupies a higher level than the molecular or neuron-synapse" (p.125)

or again:

"We do, however, conceive of notions as being realized as certain
configurations in the structure of the brain, configurations that are
(sometimes) associated with certain objects in the world..." (p.127)

Similar claims that their favorite theoretical entities are undoubtedly coded in
brains have been made by as mixed a bunch as Chomsky, Searle (quoted in full and
explicitly on p.122 and certainly not to his credit) and Schank, yet that does nothing at all to make the claim less vacuous and unsupported by any shred of evidence. It is just an idle bet against the future of science.

The last quoted passage makes pretty clear that "notions" are to be Devlin's
own Cartesian thalamus: a magic organ that ties the mental to the brain and to the
outer world. Our case will be that, whatever this trick is, and it is not a particularly
new one, it cannot be the basis for any clear-eyed realism, which we take to be a
theory, like Kripke's, where what things refer to and what knowledge is about does
not depend on any particular identities of bits of mind and bits of brain, and certainly not on what minds happen to "cognitively individuate":

"The uniformities (*e.g., situations, individuals, locations, types* — AB
& YW) will certainly include those entities that are cognitively individuated by the agent, but need not be restricted exclusively to those"
(p.118).

The last clause, could, of course, let a great deal through, and the tone here is
not basically realist at all, but cognitivist and representationalist. The problem for
the commentator here, as with so much of the SS literature, is whether there is anything distinctive at all, anything to distinguish what we are offered from the great
mass of unreflective knowledge representation in AI.

2.1.2.4.1 Belief and Knowledge

It is surely a necessary condition for any theory to be realist that it give some
account of knowledge of, as opposed to belief for. According to much current
orthodoxy with which SS wishes to align itself, knowledge requires access to the
real world in a way the latter does not. If it turns out that Devlin's version of SS
can offer no account of knowledge that will be another respect in which SS has
failed at exactly the point at that it claimed to offer most: a well-founded (in the
sense formal semanticists attach to such terms) theory, and something superior to
the efforts of AI researchers with their rather ill-formed metaphysics of "representa-
tionalism." That Devlin cannot offer such a theory is something he freely admits at

the end of his discussion:

"Given the notion of causation, whether or not a belief constitutes knowledge is simply a matter of fact concerning the origin or causal support for A's belief that p. There is no demand that A have evidence for, or be aware of, that origin or support. Indeed from her point of view she simply believes that p... From the agent's point of view, there is nothing to distinguish a belief ...from knowledge." (p.149)

This is slightly breathtaking in that, although it is all true, it is exactly the sort of argumentation that any realist must dismiss as irrelevant psychological solipsism. Devlin tries to escape in the following paragraph by setting out conditions for "knowing that you know," but they are vacuous once there is no distinction for the agent between knowledge and belief because of inaccessible causal relations. Russell's argument of the stopped clock, used by Devlin elsewhere in the book without acknowledgement, shows that accessibility cannot do the trick for establishing knowledge either. This is because seeing, at 12:04, the clock stopped at 12:04 does not give you knowledge that it is 12:04, even though it is). Once the casual distinction between knowledge and belief has gone, there cannot be one between "believing that you know" and "knowing that you know." Nothing can then be done to recover the distinction that has been lost.

Devlin's starting point was actually quite different, that knowledge is relational but belief is not (a view one might expect him to want to establish in order to buttress SS):

"Thus *knows* is not an intentional mental state in the sense of belief or desire. It is a relation. The mental state involved in knows is that of belief. What makes a belief state give rise to a knowing, is the way that state was either caused by, or else causally sustained by, information." (p. 147)

This is plainly at odds with Devlin's attempt to retain the knowledge-belief distinction in terms of "believing that you know," etc. It simply concedes a version of the knowledge-belief distinction in which it is in principle inaccessible to the agent concerned. And that restriction would be no problem at all for a realist: however Devlin realizes that under this inaccessibility condition, what he has established will do little for him cognitively, which is why he resists it. His knowledge-belief distinction can only be one for other agents, and not for an agent itself, and so cannot be connected directly to the issue of mental states at all. What he has established is in fact not far from what many AI-representationalists hold, and hold in a way that neither wants nor needs any support from SS. But the point here is that, necessary or not, Devlin's SS cannot possibly *offer* it.

The real problem for Devlin is further back in his formalism. The difference between knowledge and belief is not apparent there either, but is simply added in later by a claim about causation.

A proposition, the object or content of a belief, is said (Devlin 1991, p.126) to be an object of the form:

$$s \models \sigma;$$

this object shows that a situation *s* supports or confirms an infon (or conjunction of infons) σ. Situation *s* may be the world *w*, in which case the belief is true and σ is fact. This is, of course, odd in that a belief, and its associated proposition, seems on this view of things to involve access to a situation in the world necessarily, even though, in fact, people believe things (e.g., "God is good") without having any particular situation in mind that might support them. Devlin's account is hard to square with the common sense views that one believes propositions and that they are of the form σ, rather than the more complex form mentioned earlier and that support is not within the content of a belief.

Saying that is not merely expressing a preference for a certain conventional kind of belief-object. Devlin himself gets muddled at times and refers to objects in the σ position as the belief object, an understandable error. Again, if objects replacing *s* really are situations in the world (suppose we can imagine how real concrete situations, as opposed to their descriptions, might, just might, enter into a symbolic formalism) then how can belief be nonrelational (with respect to the world) as Devlin promised? If, on the other hand, and more plausibly, belief for him is nonrelational with respect to the world, then *s* objects are merely descriptions of propositions that give support to σ, and he is describing a formalism with no essential difference from any AI formalism in, say, truth maintenance form, (e.g., Doyle, 1979) where propositions have support sets of the same type. If that is a correct account, it fits his earlier claim that propositions are not independent of other beliefs, but again is a wholly representationalist view.

In so far as his earlier chapter 2 throws light on the interpretation of the symbolic form, it seems that when *s* is replaced by abstract situations (i.e., not *w* itself) then the relationship above between *s* and σ is one of set membership only, in which case infons cannot be entities distinct from situations at all, as set membership can only hold between entities of the same type, by definition. Yet that chapter also seems to suggest that when *s* is the set of world situations *w*, then the relationship the form expresses cannot be set membership since the world is not an infon or set of infons. But, in that case, we seem to have an odd formalism where the meaning of the relational connective varies with what satisfies one of the variables it connects, and that is incompatible with one's normal understanding of a relation.

His crucial claim about the interdependence of propositions he rests on a bizarre example close to classic ones in the philosophy of mind lierature. On p.129 he claims that an automaton that had the same lowest level structure as a mind/brain believing a proposition (i.e., at the bit/synapse level) would nevertheless not be in the same intentional state of belief as the human because:

> "in the absence of the rest of the network of interrelated beliefs (and other intentional states) this particular mental state is just that, an isolated state."

This misuse of a classic example type is pointless, in that it establishes nothing other than that Devlin believes propositions to be inherently related to other propositions, an unexceptionable belief. If an automaton could pass the initial conditions for this *Gedankenexperiment*, (i.e., for one proposition), it could also pass a stronger test in which it had a copy of a whole brain state, including the representation of all the other propositions related to the one in question!

But to return to our theme: all Devlin has shown is that beliefs are related to other beliefs, which almost anyone could accept, and that, in the terms his demonstration was made, the s or w occurring in the propositional form is not the world at all, but some representation of a support set of other beliefs. It cannot actually be the world, or any part of it, or his claim that beliefs are nonrelational falls, and belief cannot then be distinguished from knowledge even syntactically.

To see how far we have come from where Devlin wanted to be, we only have to recall his claim (p.126) that:

> "our approach will be to classify beliefs by their external significance; that is to say, by what they are about."

In the light of his formalisms and his arguments, there is no way at all that he can be said to have done that.

2.1.2.4.3 Notions and folk psychology

We have argued that there is no clear sense in which beliefs in Devlin's scheme of things are about the world, at least not in any stronger sense than any representational formalism is about the world. There is no place for the world in his formalism for belief, and knowledge is not in a different formal position from belief, except through the magic of notions which, as we saw, connect both to brain states and to world objects.

"What now of my assertion that beliefs about objects in the world are always in terms of *notions* of those objects, rather than the objects themselves? On the face of it, this seems to fly in the face of the professed agent-relativity of individuals .... As emphasized by the quote from Searle on p.78, an individual only exists as such because the agent concerned individuates it as such" (p.131).

On the face of it, which is to say in terms of the Kripke *Londres/London* example by which *notions* were introduced, this seems to be consistent with the "agent-relativity" of individuals, rather than its negation! Notions are, in effect, the different intensions that individuals have, and hence, almost by definition, agent-dependent.

Devlin is, from our point of view, in an impossible (even though familiar) dilemma over ontology, one that comes from his desire, like that of SS adherents in general, to please too many people at once. On the one hand notions are agent-relative (since they are brain-coded) and even folk-relative because of the "common identification of individuals across an entire species, or community, of agents" (ibid.). That is very much an "up to a point" phenomenon: God, the Jews, the American-Irish, the Mid-West, Central America, the Moral Majority, Free Speech, Democracy, blasphemy etc., are all disputable and hard-to-pin-down as to their boundaries or membership. And even if they could be made common across the species, it would be no more than folk-psychology, and not at all the stuff of realism.

And yet, Devlin can blandly pin his structures to the world with no problems as when he tells us that two notions of the city of London (it self, denoted by l) appear in differently structured beliefs (so far, so conventional) and that those two beliefs have the same content *pi*:

w: = << pretty, 1, 1>>

"where pi is the proposition   w:= <<pretty, 1, 1>>."

But this residual shred of realism is (a) almost impossible to square with the folk-psychology of notions, for how can it be that denotata just happen to be out there to correspond to notions that we have the greatest difficulty in establishing across communities, and which are, in any case, said to be individuated only by a brain or groups of brains? And (b) the realism or offer has nothing to do whatever with situations or SS, but is the simplest minded denotationism, not at all advanced beyond Frege. What revolution in semantics can spring from any of this? Surely formal realist metaphysics is not just a matter of notion-democracy?

We could end with a more general question about logic-based systems: how could it possibly be that the systems of the logical schoolmen could turn out to have been right all along about the structures processed by brains produced by evolution? Is that possibility any stranger than any piece of speculative science turning out to be right by the scientific standards of its time? Or, is it any stranger than the belief that mental structure is closely related to natural language, another phenomenon of much more recent provenance (a question to which we now turn in 2.1.3)? This line of argument is a familiar one, but has taken a more radical form than anything in this book with Winograd and Flores' (1986) critique, based on phenomenology, of all symbolic or rational modelling of human mental processes. One should remember, too, that phenomonenology is, in an odd way, an inheritor of a more scientific tradition than is AI, cognitive science, and traditional Western scholarship.

Phenomenology, with its biological emphasis on humans being part of the real physical world and continuously and inseparably connected to it, is part of the same trend as Heidegger's (1962) championing the pre-Socratic philosophers against Plato on the ground that the latter set Western thought on the wrong track with his emphasis on logic, reason, and the separability of humans from the world.

Phenomenology is thus not just barbarous antiscience as many now believe without reading any. It is anticulture and scholarship that is what the whole of logic, AI, lexicography, and the encyclopedia tradition represents. Cybernetics was in the scientific tradition (orientated to networks, number and quantities) and connectionism is a reversion to that. One might consider (and we shall end the chapter later with such a claim) that engineering may be the only honorable escape from the humanities for AI.

2.1.3. AI representations as candidates for Languages of Thought

For the purposes of what follows, we will assume what has been the standard minimum AI hypothesis for many years (the recent connectionist revival notwithstanding), that mental activities like language understanding, planning, reasoning, etc., can be modelled interestingly and satisfactorily by means of a symbolic language. We will further assume that such languages may be considered candidates for LOTs. AI researchers did not have the notion of a LOT revealed to them by Fodor, only the catchy name; it had always been one of their working assumptions, even though they were not prepared to defend it philosophically. Indeed, this assumption was AI's initial entry ticket into cognitive science.

Maida has asserted (1986, 1988), that one must accept a "uniformity hypothesis" about languages of thought, in general, and about the representation of belief in different agents, in particular, in order to proceed with cognitive science and to construct AI programs capable of reasoning about beliefs, which is to say that agents all have the same LOT. We think that this hypothesis is unwarranted. Instead, we argue for a different hypothesis: an *attributive uniformity hypothesis*. This hypothesis has none of the unverifiable ontological commitments of Maida's, yet it provides cognitive scientists and artificial intelligence researchers with everything they need. It will follow from this that Maida's assumption is "idle": it does no work in cognitive science.

2.1.3.1. The realist uniformity hypothesis

Maida's uniformity claim is that all humans have the same LOT in their heads, and that this uniform language is what we use to form or express beliefs (see also, Fodor, 1975; Konolige, 1983). We called this claim the strong or *realist uniformity hypothesis* (RUH). A weaker version (the weak uniformity hypothesis that we noted earlier) is that all languages of thought are covered by some idealized mental language, rather in the way Chomsky claimed that all natural languages express universal structural constraints, and that makes them, for him, a natural family.

RUH appeals not only to late-Chomskyans but also to the logically oriented. It would indeed be nice if there were some universal language, like LOT, which could be contrasted with the variety and messiness of natural languages, which appear to be the only symbolic constructs we have access to when modelling the mind. If LOT existed it would give us a stationary target, as it were: a unitary basis underlying the diverse behaviors we observe.

Many, like Maida, have investigated phenomena associated with belief by assuming the existence of LOT (e.g., Moore 1977; Levesque, 1984; Konolige, 1983, 1985). It is telling that those researchers concentrate on establishing the universality of methods for reasoning within already established belief spaces, rather than on the more important problems (for us, at least) of constructing belief spaces and concomitant methods for belief space interaction for the interaction of those belief spaces. For example, Maida has attempted to prove that all agents reason with *modus ponens* (Maida, 1986). It is much more likely, on the contrary, that no such proof could conceivably be given, were sets of inferences by individuals taken as data. The use of modus ponens by others can only be (at best) a default assumption about fellow reasoners.

2.1.3.2. The attributive uniformity hypothesis

Let us now set out the contrasting position. The *attributive uniformity hypothesis* (AUH) is that questions concerning the existence of a uniform language of thought are *irrelevant* to cognitive science and AI. All that is important is that we be able to attribute beliefs uniformly when couched in some representation scheme. AUH is *not* the assumption that there are different languages of thought, rather, it is the view that there is no way of showing, and no reasoning for assuming, the existence in humans of a universal LOT. However, the irrelevance of universality is only part of the hypothesis, it also claims that it is unimportant whether or not the internal representation system of humans is a *language*, in the Chomskyan sense, i.e., having certain generative properties. One could never establish that humans' internal representation systems constitute Chomskyan, generative, languages because, quite simply, it is not possible to show that the hypothesized languages generate all and only the thoughts humans can believe. In summary, although AUH is compatible with the view that humans have internal representation systems in their heads, it asserts that it is irrelevant whether there is a universal system and whether it is a language or not.

It is part of our position that AUH is compatible with cognitive science *as a science*. Cognitive science is the discipline that seeks to explain cognitive capacities in humans and other (intelligent) information processing systems. Such explanations (whether connectionist or not) *attribute* an internal representation scheme that represents the environment of the system. As AUH-ers, we are merely pointing out that (a) there is no reason to assume that the scheme actually exists in heads and (b) even if humans actually have internal schemes there is no reason to assume there is a universal one that is also a generative language, like English or Italian. The only assumptions needed are that (a) human cognition can be explained (this is just the cognitive science assumption), and B) beliefs are useful in framing such explanations. AUH is scientific because it is falsifiable (cf. Churchland, 1979). Indeed, AUH has more of a claim to a scientific basis than RUH, which amounts to what some have called Chomsky's long term bet on genetics, in that it is just a way of pushing confirmation and falsifiability indefinitely into the future.

AUH does not *entail* that all of cognitive science (especially not AI) is a science. AI systems that model, say, belief systems (or any higher cognitive function) can be viewed as modelling individuals, in this case hypothetical and fictitious individuals. If one accepts this view, and if one accepts Fodor's (and others') view of what constitutes a science, then one is not doing science in an AI of individuals but engineering, what Dreyfus preferred to call alchemy. More recently, Weyhrauch termed it the "construction of the computer individual" (Weyhrauch, 1980). We think that to see things this way can be a liberating freedom, not a criticism: it might make AI workers more intellectually honest. They would then talk less about about their programs being theories or experiments, which are normally deviant uses of these terms.

2.1.3.3. The role of natural languages

An important contrast between the two approaches to uniformity distinguished earlier is their attitudes towards natural languages. It is a crucial consequence of any uniformity view that the LOT cannot be a natural language. This follows because LOT is genetically determined to be the same in all humans, even though they speak quite different natural languages. It is, as always, a logical possibility that all human heads run in a single language that also happens, by chance, to be a natural language, say Italian. But we shall not consider this a serious empirical possibility.

Now, there is no reason why AUH should imply any particular view on the question of whether any of the range of internal representation schemes in heads (if there are any) can be a natural language or not. If LOT (or any internal scheme) is not a natural language, then there arises the classic problem of the translation to and from it and the natural language used by the head's owner, as well as the yet more serious problem of how concepts can be added to a language of thought that is in some way fixed (most notoriously, this is a problem for Fodor's genetically-fixed LOT). The translation/acquisition problem exists for all parties in this dispute (i.e., for RUH-ers and AUH-ers) but only for RUH-ers is this problem a conceptual, rather than an empirical one.

Among the well-known problems associated with the view that the internal scheme is a natural language is the issue of indexicals, to which we shall turn in the next section. There is, however, an aspect of AUH to which natural languages are essential. It is not the internal issue at all, but rather the role of language in keeping the behaviors, beliefs, goals, etc. of different organisms in harmony to some acceptable degree. This degree is impossible to specify, but we all know it from everyday life: However different our beliefs, attitudes, goals, etc. may be, we can remain in some general social harmony by means of the exchange of language signals, even though we have no access whatever to what lies in the other head, behind those signals. Moreover, a natural language, processed by any of us as individual humans or machines is, in general, the only symbolic evidence we have on which to base our construction of the beliefs and attitudes of those other agents.

So far, so obvious. But on the RUH, natural language is somehow dispensable in principle; it has an accidental quality. On that view, heads are known to run the same LOT, and there could, in principle, be quite different ways of communicating between LOT-using-heads than through the crude and misleading translations into LOM (language of the mouth). The attitude of this book, and of Wittgensteinians everywhere, of course, is that this suggestion is fantastic nonsense, a nonsense to which the RUH leads and that constitutes a further argument against it. We have no access to LOTs, no evidence whatever that they are uniform, and hence natural languages are essential, not dispensable, and indeed the only clues we could have (this side of the neurophysiological millennium) as to what any LOT might be like. The candidates we have at the moment in logics, programs, etc. are all blatant outgrowths and specializations of natural languages.

In summary, Maida is just wrong about the necessity for RUH: AI models of beliefs can proceed on AUH. If researchers persist with RUH they will find it difficult to produce actual programs, unless they concede that those programs can only model an individual. Those done on AUH which produce constructions of actual belief sets (not proofs about other individuals, independently of their belief sets) are clearly attempts to model individuals (e.g., Wilks & Bien, 1979, 1983; Ballim 1987).

Secondly, we have touched on, in a way not normally done, a well-known issue in AI/cognitive science: engineering versus science. If we are right, the best scientific assumption is that human cognition can be explained and modelled by attributing only those internal representation schemes sufficient to support beliefs. This assumption is also the best engineering assumption because we can still view AI as being about individuals, namely, the artificial individuals we create by programming. We shall consider those artificial individuals as holding the RUH by virtue of having uniform default hypotheses about the individuals they in turn model. A simple way of stating this rather convoluted thought is that AI workers, as engineers, can do science only by creating artificial miniscientists, which is to say, indirectly. Those alchemists who wanted to construct the homunculus were, of course, in exactly the same position as perhaps was God and those mothers now known euphemistically as "domestic engineers." There is no way of construing AI as "doing science" in any direct manner.

Chapter 2.2
Problems of intensionality

2.2.1. Intensional objects and their identification

Intensional logic rests on observations like the following:

$$P \text{ --|---> } a \text{ believes } P$$

$$a \text{ believes } P \text{ --|---> } P$$

which is to say that, for any proposition P, it does not follow (does not entail) that any a believes it and, conversely, the fact that some a believes a proposition P, does not entail that P is true.

On these two truisms rests the whole of intensional logic, which of course must not be confused with intentions (see 2.1.2.2). Another conventional way of looking at the same matter is to talk in terms of substitutability failure: suppose P contains the name of an individual p, and Q is another proposition differing from P only in that it has another name or description q for the very same individual as is named by p. Let us write those as P(p) and Q(q) respectively. Then, within the standard view of first order logic:

$$P(p) \text{ <----> } Q(q)$$

However

$$a \text{ believes } P(p) \quad \text{ <---|---> } a \text{ believes } Q(q)$$

That only makes, in a formal manner, the point that we cannot infer (at least not in any strong logical form) that, because someone believes something under one name or description, then they also believe the same thing under another name or description, even though, since the objects are the same, what is true under one must be true under the other. If I believe I am meeting Mary's best friend at the station at 6:00 tonight, I may not also know I am meeting Ruth at the station at 6:00 tonight, even though I know Ruth perfectly well, and it is actually true that I am meeting Ruth at the station tonight. And that will be perfectly plausible if no one happened to tell me that Ruth is also Mary's best friend maybe by oversight, maybe as a joke or a surprise, who knows?

These peculiarities of belief contexts, known for millenia in one form or another, are the stuff of intensional logic, but the solutions normally offered (some were touched on in 2.1) are based on a misconception. The nonentailments listed earlier are true, but probably are not worth remedying by anything that remains a logic. The work of Kripke and those who followed him attempted to show that there could be, under certain constraints, a logic of intension worthy of the name, a deductive calculus of a different type. We suggest that that may be false, in the sense that the nonentailments above cannot be usefully remedied at all: they are mere matters of fact about limitations on deduction.

Kripke's basic idea (to parody a complex and difficult theory) was that there could be a (possibly infinite) range of logically possible worlds, within each of which deduction could be done, as it could across worlds with the Leibnizian notion of "true in all possible worlds." Each world contained individuals under a single description, however implausible (e.g., Socrates in one world would be a female three-legged dog). To every (consistent) set of beliefs there corresponded some set of such worlds consistent with it.

The core of this idea was to be found in Carnap (1956), but Kripke gave a formal semantics for the notion of possible world, and introduced the notion of "rigid designator" to ensure that individuals could be related across worlds even if they shared no properties sufficiently significant to recognizing them as the same individual. The need for such a mechanism was unacceptable to some (e.g., Quine 1960), as was the sheer promiscuity of the creation of individuals that this scheme allowed. Quine could never, as he put it accept the "possible man in that doorway."

And yet, in other ways, Kripke's vision was very restrictive since like Carnap, Kripke required the same basic individuals in all possible worlds independently, that is, of their baroque descriptions. The whole system had a highly nonconstructive flavor, in the sense of not being based on clear operations that could be made computational, and the same criticism has been made of the work of Montague (1974, cf. Potts 1975, Wilks 1976). Hintikka (1973), among others, has attempted to remedy this with a more constructive notion of "possible world."

Let us return to the phenomena at this point, and note that inferences that trespass across the nonentailment barrier are actually made by all of us all the time. We believe (truly) that Ulan Bator is the capital of Outer Mongolia and suddenly, in order to make a joke in a letter, we have to ask ourselves whether the recipient will believe that, too. For this particular P in the formula above, can we infer that a, the recipient, believes P? It is simply an empirical matter of judgment about another's education and geographical competence. Maybe we are not sure but decide to risk the joke anyway. There is nothing of logic, deduction or entailment here, even though such inferences are and must be made, quite without official license. They are not normally conscious, nor are they about individual propositions, as opposed to being about great swathes of organized expert knowledge. Joe, for example, used to teach geography before he became a dean, so surely we can risk that inference in his case? But no, maybe not, because, surprisingly, on becoming an administrator, he repressed all memory of his old subject, or perhaps, even when teaching the stuff, he always confused Ulan Bator with Lhasa. These are simply not logical matters, and it is useless to seek any kind of logical principle that will rescue us from the profound but vacuous nonentailments.

Inference in such cases is real, everyday, an empirical matter, and the core subject matter of this book. We hold that it is done normally, but not randomly, by the operation of certain default rules, operating beliefs already classified into environments or belief spaces. We shall return later to the justification of that particular point but now want to turn to the general form in which we shall discuss intensionality examples, and then contrast our approach with another AI system, one not using partitioned spaces, but which also claims to deal with intensionality.

2.2.2. Dealing with intensional objects in this book

It is natural in a system of partitioned environment notation to treat environments as intensional objects: to treat the Jim-object, pushed down into the Frank-object, as not just yielding an environment by computation that is Frank's-view-of-Jim, but also as a intensional object we might call Jim-for-Frank.

The names and descriptions attached to environments correspond to the names and descriptions in play in constituent propositions, but we should resist any tendency to think of the environments as being a meaning or referent of the expressions they are named for. The environment names, as far as their meanings go, are simply derivative: dependent, in the best Fregean tradition, on whatever meanings the environment names are assigned on the basis of their participation in the (contained) propositions.

Let us now consider two simple cases of intensional objects and see how the basic default algorithm deals with them:

CASE 1 (Two-for-me-one-for-you): The system believes that Frank and Jim's-father are two people, but that Mary, whose point of view is being computed, believes them to be the same person.

CASE 2 (One-for-me-two-for-you): Mary believes Frank and Jim's-father to be separate people, whereas the system believes them to be the same individual.

Scenarios such as these are common, and arise over such mundane matters as believing or not believing that John's-house is the same as the house-on-the-corner-of-X-and-Y-streets.

2.2.3. Two-for-me-one-for-you

Processing of the first case will begin with the system having three topic environments for Frank, Jim's-father and Mary. Two questions that arise are: What intensional object(s) (i.e., environments) should Mary's viewpoint contain? and what should be the beliefs about those intensional objects? Let us say that the system has beliefs about Frank and Jim's father as shown in Figure 2.1. The first question can be restated as "given certain intensional objects in one viewpoint (the system's, in this case), what are the corresponding intensional objects in the system's version of another viewpoint (Mary's)?" Extending the normal default rule for belief ascription to cope with intensional object ascription, we would say, naturally enough, that intensional objects in one environment directly correspond to identically named (or described) intensional objects in another environment, *unless there is counter evidence to believing this*. This notion of correspondence of intensional objects between environments can be expressed as beliefs, but these beliefs must be of a type different from those we have previously discussed. In section 3.3

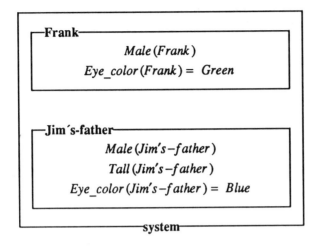

Figure 2.1 System beliefs about Frank and Jim's-father.

we shall describe fully the way in which that (single) environment is constructed, and how its construction will be an inherently asymmetric process, allowing the system to construct (for Mary) Frank-as-Jim's-father or Jim's-father-as-Frank. Which one we finally obtain will depend on the order of the ascription from the two components shown earlier.

2.2.3.1. One-for-me-two-for-you

In the second case, where the system believes in one individual but Mary two, then the natural computation of Mary's view of either Frank or Jim's-father is simply to copy the system's single representation, changing "Frank" to "Jim's-father" as necessary. This is shown in the following figure.

These are not merely aliases, but are best thought of as dual ascriptions, performed by making two identical copies. Further information about Mary's beliefs would then presumably cause the contents of the two environments to differ, since she presumably has at least some differing beliefs about what are (for her) distinct individuals.

However, she does have, as we might put it, one crucial belief differing from the system's: namely, that these are not the same person, even though that is not a belief she can have explicitly for obvious reasons. One cannot be said to have the belief that two entities are identical if one had never contemplated them as separate.

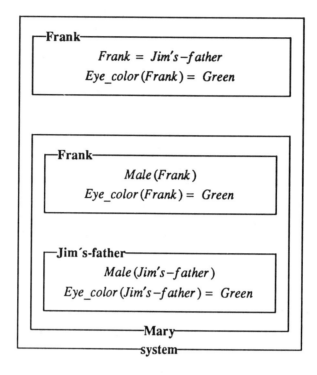

Figure 2.2 Treatment of CASE 2 in the Frank/Jim's-father example.

The only belief she could be said to (implicitly) have is that there are two descriptions available ("Frank" and "Jim's father") for the same person.

Neither CASE 1 nor CASE 2 turn out to be particularly problematic, and the situation is no different if the entities about whose identity there is dispute are non-believers rather than believers. That would be like classic but natural casees such as a difference between dialogue participants as to whether Tegucigalpa and Capital-of-Honduras are, or are not, the same city or whether Rome or Avignon should be identified with City-of-the-Popes.

Let us now turn to another way of describing intensional problems and then, finally, to a particular formalism (SNePs) based on intensionality, which does not adopt a partitioned approach like the one we advocate. In that way we hope to make clear by contrast the virtues of partitioning, and then treat the partitioned objects or environments as intensional entities.

2.2.4. Belief reportage and the *de dicto/de re* distinction

There exists another tradition in logic for discussing intensionality matters, one that we find less helpful than the method of viewpoints, and which is normally called the *de dicto/de re* distinction. A standard introduction to it goes as follows (following Rapaport, 1986):

Ralph sees a person whom he believes to be the janitor stealing classified documents. Unknown to Ralph, the janitor has won the lottery.

A standard account of that is to say that Ralph believes *de dicto* that the janitor is a spy, where *de dicto (=of the utterance)* can be glossed roughly as "what Ralph explicitly would assent to on the basis of what he believes." Whereas Ralph believes *de re* that the winner of the lottery is a spy, where *de re (=of the thing itself)* is to be glossed as "What Ralph believes of the thing, whatever the thing turns out to be," and this last phrase is normally taken as the way to pin down *de re* interpretations and is the key to the whole game.

All the nonsubstitutability in opaque contexts such as belief can now be brought to bear and we have, on a standard account (where DD is *de dicto* and DR is *de re*):

BelDD(Ralph, janitor is spy)

janitor = lottery_winner

BelDR(Ralph, lottery_winner is spy)

This is (classically) a valid conclusion if we are allowed to swap DR for DD when making the substitution. However, the following is not a proper reference:

BelDD(Ralph, janitor is spy)

janitor = lottery_winner

BelDD(Ralph, lottery_winner is spy)

because Ralph does not know the lottery winner and the janitor to be one and the same person. All this is just a rewriting of earlier examples and discussion using different terminology.

To us, the distinction here is precisely one of viewpoints, and better described in that way: The first inference (to a *de re* conclusion) cannot be drawn in any space that "is" Ralph's. We all consider our own beliefs to be *de re* and, consistently with the diagnosis of *de re* identifications as "whatever anything turns out to be," Ralph can properly and sincerely say "That man, the janitor, is a spy whoever he is" and "That man, the janitor, is a spy under whatever description he goes." But none of that leads to the inference under discussion simply because Ralph lacks the relevant belief in equivalence. It also means that there is no content to the standard claim that Ralph actually believes anything *de re* at all about the lottery winner. One can imagine a person who conceded that his own beliefs were only *de dicto* and not *de re*, but that would be a very odd situation indeed: perhaps a certain kind of Christian modernist who recited one of the creeds regularly and said he believed it *de dicto* but without any particular *de re* attachment to entities.

Another way of putting all this is that *de re* vs. *de dicto* is a viewpoint rather than a substitution problem and is better seen as such. We only deem a belief *de dicto* when it is being talked about as a belief of someone else, and we assume all our own beliefs are *de re*, as are those who agree with us about identification issues! The *de re* belief cited earlier, then, is not a belief of Ralph at all, but a belief of the system, being misreported as a belief of Ralph.

Rapaport (1986) claims that an AI system must have separate ways of representing the *de dicto* and *de re* beliefs if it is to be capable of reasoning correctly about behavior. We hold that this is simply another case where a belief report does not correspond directly to the belief it purports to (for an argument for representing certain *de re* beliefs differently from *de dicto* belief, see Bach & Harnish, 1979; Bach, 1982; Dretske, 1981).

Another type of belief sentence sometimes distinguished is called *de se*, and is a belief involving a pronominal reference to the believer. An example is sentence (S2.2):

(S2.2) Alison believes that she is poor.

A *de se* belief is sometimes said to have *de dicto* and *de re* readings (ibid.). The *de dicto* reading is that Alison believes that she (Alison) is poor. The *de re* reading is that Alison believes that she (whoever she may be) is poor, even in the case where Alison is an amnesiac and does not know that she is named Alison (see SEC cited later for further discussion of this issue). One thing should be clear from these peculiar examples: Although a representational system should be capable of representing all these readings, the real problems lie in interpreting the sentences.

2.2.5. Rapaport's version of the SNePs system

We now proceed to some description and criticism of a particular system of meaning representation, one that is also presented as a belief representation: the SNePs system. Rapaport and Shapiro (Rapaport, 1986; Shapiro & Rapaport, 1986) are concerned with intensional representation schemes, rather than extensional ones, and with the representation of *de dicto, de re, de se* and nested beliefs, as well as the problem of what they term "quasi-indexical" belief reports.

SNePs is fundamentally a network representation with the special property of being, as its authors put it, "wholly intensional," in that none of the nodes of the network are claimed to stand directly for entities or classes of entities in the world. Given the highly "symbolist" orientation of the present book, and its assumption that brains, like computers, have direct access only to symbols and that any semantics must accept that obvious fact, we naturally find the assumptions behind SNePs attractive. In this section we shall examine Rapaport's version of SNePs, in which a major claim (Rapaport, 1986) is that quasi-indexical belief reports pose a special problem because the quasi-indicators cannot be replaced by coreferential terms without losing the intended meaning of the sentence, i.e., quasi-indexicals are special intensional entities in their own right and should be included in any representation scheme. Quasi-indexicals, as we shall see, are at the heart of the intensionality problem.

An indexical is an expression (like "I," "this," "that") that depends on who utters it for its (complete) meaning. Quasi-indexicals (QI) are indexicals that occur within intensional contexts (such as a "believes" context). Sometimes an additional condition is added: that the indexical in the intensional context must represent the use of an indicator (pronoun) by another person (Rapaport, 1986).

Here we want to examine Rapaport's claims about quasi-indexicals (QI), and ask if the phenomenon is as he describes it (NO); ask if his observations commit him to representing the phenomena in his particular formal language for belief (NO); then ask if he has achieved such a representation (YES); and ask finally whether it is doing him any good (NO). The answers we shall arrive at are those in the parentheses.

In what follows it will be important to distinguish between linguistic questions about English and its analysis on the one hand, and questions about the representation of belief in some quasi-formal language on the other. Earlier, we accepted the general consensus in cognitive science that these cannot be the same thing, even though it is logically possible (and compatible with genetic inheritance) that all human beings could in fact have some natural language, say Italian, as their uniform LOT. Part of our complaint against Rapaport is that he consistently confuses the two levels of discussion by bringing into belief representations issues that make sense only in the world of sentences, such as pronouns and truth conditions.

Nothing Rapaport says denies that beliefs can be expressed internally in a natural language. Anyone who believes a LOT is a natural language will have problems with pronouns: at least they will if their LOT is a natural language with pronouns. There could, of course, be natural languages without pronouns in principle, and it would certainly seem an unnecessary structural complexity in a language of belief and thought to have pronouns in it. Yet, curiously enough, and whether or not he does believe a LOT is a natural language (presumably he would deny it: SNePs does not look much like one), Rapaport's position on QIs does seem to involve just that complexity.

2.2.5.1. The truth of English sentences

A major claim of Rapaport is that QIs cannot be replaced by extensionally equivalent terms in propositions. He further claims that this is important for representing beliefs. In other words, representational schemes should represent QIs, and separately from the things they indicate. Rapaport gives the example of a person, John, who has been appointed editor of *Cognitive Science* without his knowledge. Rapaport gives the sentences (1 and 2) to indicate John's beliefs about the situation:

(1) John believes that the editor of *Cognitive Science* is rich.

(2) John believes that he himself is not rich. (Rapaport, 1986, p.379)

Suppose that (3) is inferred from the information that John is editor of *Cognitive Science*, and that John believes that the editor of *Cognitive Science* is rich. Rapaport says that the system should not infer (3) because it is inconsistent with (2), where the 'he*' in (3) cannot be replaced by 'John' because it would be wrong to do so (John does not believe that he himself is rich). The symbol '<he*' is Rapaport's notation for a QI. Unfortunately Rapaport never provides any rules governing the use of this symbol.

(3) John believes that he* is rich. (Rapaport, 1986, p.379)

Rapaport uses this example as an argument for having QIs in a formal belief representation, as distinct from extensionally equivalent terms. However, this does not at all follow from the example.

First, Rapaport has glossed over the information that John does not believe himself to be editor of *Cognitive Science*. A system holding both (1), (2) and that John does not believe himself to be editor of *Cognitive Science* would not draw (3) as an inference. So this is not a problem for a system reasoning with the beliefs with which Rapaport provides it.

Secondly, there is no problem in replacing 'he*' by 'John' in (3) as long as (3) is not taken to be something that John would say, i.e., John would not say that John is rich but (3) is a quite acceptable sentence if uttered by someone who knows that John is editor of *Cognitive Science* to another person who also knows this fact.

The problems that Rapaport cites (of drawing wrong inferences by substituting coreferent terms, and of being unable to replace QIs in general by their referents) are not representation problems; rather they are problems of ENGLISH usage. Rapaport contends that systems reasoning about beliefs in the above manner must represent QIs correctly to prevent the inference of (3). However, as we see it, the problem is not how you represent a belief, but rather how you interpret and generate belief sentences.

Rapaport's strong argument for QIs in the representation is that the 'he himself' in (2), which is also a QI, cannot be replaced by 'John' if John is an amnesiac about his own name. This argument is compelling because, if John is amnesiac about his own name, then we might agree that he cannot have beliefs about 'John,' yet he can still have beliefs about himself. So, even though John believes that he is himself poor, he does not (necessarily) believe that 'John' is poor. It is because (3) covers this type of situation that Rapaport advocates having QIs in formal belief representations. However, this is not an argument for representing QIs, it is an argument for de-coupling the name of an entity (or rather the concept of the name of an entity) from the concept of the entity itself. Consider (4) as a representation of (2) within some system's beliefs:

(4) SYSTEM believes   GENSYM001 believes GENSYM001 is poor
    SYSTEM believes   GENSYM001 is named 'John'

There is no ambiguity about this representation, nor are there any QIs within the scope of what John believes. The system represents John by the arbitrarily generated symbol 'GENSYM001' and has a name that it can attach to this symbol. If John is a known amnesiac about his name then the system will not ascribe the belief that John is named 'John' to John himself. This solution is found in Moore & Hendrix (1979; their 'SYS' symbol) and in Wilks & Bien (1979, 1983; their '*' symbol).

There is a general issue of great importance beneath this apparently small point: this book, like LOT theorists and Rapaport, accepts the fact that a representation system for beliefs and their cognitive contents must have certain features of natural languages. The issue here is what particular features that should include, e.g., pronouns or their equivalents.

2.2.5.2. Belief diagrams

The question now arises as to whether the SNePs notation for belief computations that Rapaport presents actually contains QIs or not. Rapaport explains his diagram (Rapaport, 1986, figure 13, p.406; reproduced here as Figure 2.3) for the sentence "John believes he* is rich" by saying that "The role that he* plays in the English sentence is represented by node m5; its quasi-indexical nature is represented by means of node m7" (p. 405). The diagram is already a shorthand and, in the fuller version, the node m10 is tied to nodes m3, m9, and m4. Very roughly, the complex m10, m9, m3 and m4 represents a belief by an agent connected to John that there is richness, whereas the complex m7, m3, m4, m6 represents a belief by an agent connected to John about an entity that is an ego. These subcomplexes are not directly connected, but are so only through common terminals.

There is an expository problem here in separating general issues concerning the interpretation of the diagram from issues that bear on our central concern: the relation of natural to formal/belief languages and how that is treated in Rapaport's system. The former problem can be thrown into immediate relief by asking first why the diagram does not represent "John believes of something referring to itself that it is rich?" That question brings out, maybe unfairly, the lack of apparent connection between the John who believes and the individual represented in the belief. The raising of this question is a price Rapaport is prepared to pay for his insistence on the difference between John as believer and his representation of himself within

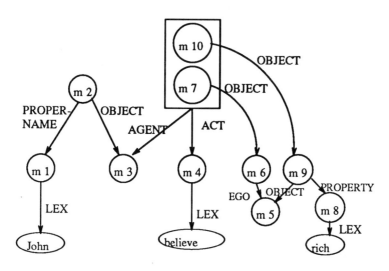

Figure 2.3 Rapaport's SNePs network for "John believes that he* is rich."

the belief; a correct distinction but one that can be more naturally achieved (see 3.1), without the mysteries imposed by the QI.

It is true that there is a routing back from m6, m5, m9, m10, m3 that goes from the object of belief back to John, but what is there in that routing that suggests, let alone guarantees, that they are the same person? Moreover, if this network is embedded in a general network of other beliefs (as SNePs envisages, rather than being a set of disjoint sentence representations), with other arcs leaving terminals, then how can such a tracing be done reliably? The routing requires identifications, at best, across something like the following: "Of all the things that are rich and are the object of a selfreferential belief, one can be traced by the concept of an act of belief to a believer who is also in relation to a proper name John!"

It seems that SNePs networks cannot really be partitioned, in the classic sense of Hendrix (1979) and in the way we assume in this book. If the OBJECT arc in Figure 1 is taken as an approximation to a belief-partition delimiter (or left-hand "scope bracket") then we seem to have no determinate way of inserting the closing bracket or end of the partition. One could put this by saying that, in SNePs, information attached to a node is always attached to that node, which means, among other things, that the name of a concept can be detached from the concept itself in some contexts but not others (cf. Barnden, 1986).

A more alarming possibility that lurks here is that there can be beliefs with "unattached pronouns": that I can just believe "He did it" without attaching "he," or maybe even "it!" This comes out clearly in the "routing problem" round the SNePs network noted earlier: a routing that leaves the inner "JOHN" node unscoped and floating. It is our contention that, although one can contemplate a sentence like "He did it" out of all context, and presumably construct an appropriate representation, it simply makes no sense to talk of that as a candidate for a belief.

The problem arises from confusing things one can say about English sentences (e.g., pronoun resolution, their truth conditions, etc.) with things one can say only about beliefs. Our case is that Rapaport, and the more generally the SNePs style of representation, confuse these repeatedly.

Our contention is that Rapaport's assumptions lead to a representation both implausible and overcomplex, but another question now arises. In the diagram given there is now no possibility that the node m5 (the concept of John within John's belief, i.e., he* in the original sentence according to Rapaport) is ambiguous; it is tied by an EGO arc back to John. That is to say, the diagram appears (in English parsing terms) to refer the identity of he*, however bizarrely, to John. So where exactly is the QI property in the figure, which would seem to demand some degree of indefiniteness about that referent of he* to John?

On the other hand, our diagnosis of the routing problem suggests that, after all, m5 may not be resolved to John, even though Rapaport evidently thinks it is. In that case, he does have genuine QI-ness in his system; but who could possibly want an untraceable, unresolvable network? The QI-ness we can detect is not anything Rapaport or any other computer scientist should want.

A minor historical complication here is Perry's argument (referred to by Rapaport but not quoted or discussed) that considers indexicals to have some essential role in logical languages; but we need not consider that in any detail because Perry concludes that a nonindexical internal representation is neither necessary nor sufficient to account for the use of "I" (Perry, 1979, 1983). The consequence of Perry's view does not support Rapaport, since the former is concerned essentially with "I" and not pronouns in belief contexts in general. Nothing in Rapaport's discussions refers essentially to the pronoun "I."

2.2.5.3. Self-models without indexicals

In his paper, Rapaport also seeks to show that Wilks & Bien (1979, 1983), like everyone else he discusses, fail to appreciate the importance of QIs. The form of his criticism is to show that the "belief construction heuristic" given there (essentially the one of this book) produces unacceptable results when applied to selfembedded beliefs, in particular the System's view of John's view of himself, achieved by the mechanism we describe by procedurally embedding the System's model of John in itself. The paper Rapaport criticizes warns the reader explicitly that the default mechanism for belief embedding cannot in general be applied to selfembedding (Rapaport ibid. p. 115). So, Rapaport is right but we were already aware of the problem, and indeed it has been subsequently solved with a notion of belief blocking that is now part of the *ViewGen* program (see later in this book). More importantly for our present purposes, problems with the default algorithm and the constraints on its application have nothing to do with the QI issues raised by Rapaport. These are, we repeat, purely a function of the odd assumptions behind SNePs diagrams, and do not arise in other systems of belief representation, but only in English sentences.

Chapter 2.3
Problems of relevance

An ascriptional reasoning system must address the issue of relevance because, in ascribing a belief or other attitude to an agent, a system must seek to ensure that the belief is relevant to the discourse interpretation needs of the moment. This can involve considerable complexity, even in apparently straightforward cases. For example, when considering whether or not to ascribe a belief **seriously-ill(father-of(fred))** into a topic environment about John, we will take into account whether or not the topic environment **fred's-father** is within an environment that contains an identity such as **john=fred's-father** or not. The first belief will be relevant to the topic only if such an identity belief appears in an intervening belief space. This example also involves intensionality problems of the kind discussed in the last section, but the relevance problems are now additional and independent. Adequate and efficient determination of relevance is especially important in our view, since we are concerned with on-the-fly ascription during discourse interactions. Relevance is a part of the inference-control problem that crops up for *all* reasoning systems.

It has been claimed that the interpretation of utterances by humans can be explained on the basis of the maximization of relevance (Sperber & Wilson, 1986). Although we have serious doubts about the adequacy of Sperber and Wilson's approach and about their characterization of the notion of relevance itself, the basic idea that relevance-maximization is a useful heuristic in utterance interpretation may be correct. We shall discuss their system critically in the last part of this chapter.

Relevance is a complex, variegated notion that has received intense study in its own right, for instance in formal logic (e.g., Anderson & Belnap, 1975), discourse theory (Grosz, 1977; Sperber & Wilson, 1986; Wilks, 1986, Blakemore,

1987), AI problem solving (Subramanian & Genesereth, 1987), and elsewhere. Our general strategy at present is to seek simple, powerful heuristics that will provide a useful basis for the environment generation processes that are our current focus.

In the following, we consider the fate of a proposition P entering the system through the interpretation of natural language input. We assume this proposition is to be taken as a belief of some agent A (perhaps of the system itself). We consider the question of whether the proposition should be inserted into a topic-environment E, for some topic T, within A's viewpoint, because of being construed as relevant to T. We assume that initially P is placed at top level within A's viewpoint — i.e., not inside any particular topic environment. Notice that if P is placed inside E it may later become a candidate for pushing into some other environment, and so on.

The over-arching strategic question about the role of relevance in our system is about *when* relevance determination is done; to what extent should the determination be "zealous" or "lazy" (a distinction of John Barnden's in Ballim, Wilks and Barnden, 1991)? A totally zealous approach would consider inserting P in E as soon as P arrives. A totally lazy approach would leave all relevance to be determined on demand; that is, during the course of reasoning about A's view of T, certain beliefs in A's viewpoint (but outside E) would be determined to have become relevant, and therefore to have become candidates for pushing into E.

It is worth reminding oneself here that zeal only makes sense up to the level of resources available to be committed. Rieger's (1975) inference program is probably the best known case of zeal-without-regard-for-resource in the literature; it worked on what one might call "the principle of greatest effort" or the-more-the-merrier, and remains a warning to everyone. To make the program function at all, Rieger had to cut off inferences after an arbitrary seven steps.

Our approach will be zealous at least to the extent of having a basic rule that zealously deems as relevant those propositions that explicitly mention the topic. Thus if T is John then the proposition **seriously-ill(wife-of(John))** is relevant. This explicit-mention rule has been the basis of our initial approach to relevance. The presently reported extensions will only account for a limited portion of the full relevance capability that a complete environment-generating system should have. Even with that limitation, a significant problem to be addressed is that of deciding what other manageable and useful types of zeal should be added. Suppose T is John, E contains a proposition stating that John is Peter's father, and P says that Peter's father is seriously ill. Then, surely, P is relevant to John and is a candidate for being pushed into E zealously just as much as the proposition stating directly that *John* is seriously ill would be.

Another possible addition of zeal involves inheritance down taxonomic links. Suppose again that John is the topic. Let E state that John is a medical patient, and let P say that patients are afraid of the disease thalassemia. Should P be deemed relevant zealously? We suggest that (usually) it should not be, because of the possibly large number of general propositions about patients (and superordinate categories). On the other hand, if the topic were a joint one involving patients in general as well as John,[2] then P would stand to be deemed relevant anyway, simply by the basic explicit-mention rule. In this specific example we also confront the issue of P's potentially being marked as medical expertise, so that it would only be deemed relevant if the agent A in whose viewpoint E lies was believed to be expert on medical matters. Such attention to agent-relative extent of expertise is a feature of the current *ViewGen* program.

A special case of the taxonomic issue is when, instead of a proposition like the above P (saying patients are afraid of thalassemia) we consider a proposition P that is itself taken to be taxonomic, such as one saying that patients are clients. It may be that such taxonomic information, indirectly related to the given topic (John), should be zealously deemed as relevant. The question of how zealously the relevance processing traverses taxonomic chains is a matter we are still investigating.

Inheritance down taxonomies is traditionally concerned with *(quasi) universal* statements about categories of objects, e.g., *all* (or *most*) patients are afraid of disease. However, *existential* statements about categories could also come into play in the relevance issue. Consider a proposition P saying that *some patient or other* in a particular hospital ward is afraid of cancer, and suppose John is held to be in that ward. Then P is, in principle, relevant to John (though it need not zealously be deemed to be), because it lends a nontrivial amount of support to the hypothesis that John is afraid of cancer.

---

[2] There is no reason in principle why topic-names should be single, simple terms like "John," even though we have not gone far beyond those in *ViewGen*.

2.3.1. Sperber and Wilson's approach to relevance

We have just outlined the general principles of our approach to relevance in our system, and we shall now turn for contrast, as in earlier chapters, to some completely different work, in this case Sperber and Wilson's (1982, 1986) work on the centrality of relevance. Like our own, this claims allegiance to a general "information processing paradigm," and also descends from the insights of Grice (1969) that understanding is a matter of inference from what is said and what is assumed.

Sperber and Wilson's starting point is to show how one might repair the major lacunae in the work of Grice. Exactly what information is to be assumed in the inference processes associated with dialogue, and how is it accessed and manipulated? Sperber and Wilson (SW) have made strong claims concerning those, and we shall argue that their claims are misleading or false. Our further claim, naturally enough, and this book is its expression, is that our approach, for all its shortcomings and lack of development, addresses the problems more directly. One aspect of the comparison we shall offer will be that SW's system remains, at bottom, a process-free linguistic approach, best seen as maintaining certain Chomskyan principles in a plainly pragmatic area, whereas what we offer is a process-orientated account, firmly within the AI-Psychology tradition.

In making that point, no suggestion is intended that the existence of actual programs, such as *ViewGen*, is of any theoretical significance in itself. Indeed, it would be wrong to do so because there is much work, in psychology for example, firmly within the information-processing paradigm that does not have associated programs, as well as work within AI itself where no programs are written, although important points about representation are nevertheless made. In separating SW, then, from other work in the way we shall do, it is not the existence or absence of programs that is at issue when one refers to the information-processing paradigm.

We shall make the contrast we want by continuing to develop examples like those of earlier chapters, where we need some way of distinguishing formally between what one participant in a dialogue believes and what another does, and those two may be quite different, even though the two people communicate perfectly well. The need for that can be seen very easily. Suppose a doctor is talking to a patient and says:

Where in your stomach is that pain, Mr. Smith?

indicating, as he says it, an area of the lower belly. The doctor accepts, by his statement, a lay representation of where the stomach is, i.e., way below its actual location. In order to communicate satisfactorily with Mr. Smith, he assumes the false belief he believes Mr. Smith to have, based on what the patient said on presenting his symptoms. The doctor does not himself believe or assert that belief.

Attempts have been made to describe such phenomena within an informal logic of presupposition, but the above is not an example of presupposition by any definition of the term. In any case, the delimitation of that notion is beside the point if what is essential to the example is capturing some notion of "belief space," if one can say WHOSE beliefs they are.

The need for such a representational facility has long been recognized in philosophy (e.g. Donnellan 1966), psychology (e.g. Johnson-Laird 1983), linguistics (Shadbolt 1983) and AI, particularly in the pioneering work of Perrault and Allen (1980). There has not been such recognition in all AI work on inference and understanding of the last ten years, and our case will be that, whatever the plausibility and sophistication of its claims, there is not that recognition in SW, and it is a fatal drawback.

We shall refer to that representational requirement as "recursive cognitive solipsism" (to use an old philosophical term that Fodor, 1980b has deployed for other purposes): the requirement that a model of discourse understanding is solipsistic in the sense of modelling only some particular entity's understanding. Hence, the simultaneous modelling of the beliefs of others must be the systems, or principal entity's, beliefs about those beliefs. Moreover, it must be possible to model the "belief of" operator recursively, so it can be applied as deeply as is needed for a particular example. It is just such matters we set out formally in Section 3.

2.3.2. Sperber & Wilson's account of "understanding"

In recent years Sperber & Wilson (1982, 1986) have set out a more general account of reasoning than that of "mutual knowledge" (see 2.4.2). They call it a "theory of relevance," and its starting point is Grice's four maxims of communication (Grice, 1975). They argue that these four can be reduced to one, that of Relation or "Be relevant," and their theory is intended to give content to that rather bare injunction.

The aim of SW's analysis can be stated as one of making explicit the appropriate inferences so as to show, within a single logical space:

- what is said by a speaker,

- what additional implicit items of information must be brought to bear by a hearer,

- what inferences follow from the above, including those Grice would have called "implicatures."

A key term for SW is "contextual implications" (nontrivial inferences that can be drawn from context and utterance combined), for:

> "having contextual implications in a given context is a necessary and sufficient condition for relevance" (ibid., p.73)

where deriving the contextual implications is, in effect, the establishment of the relevance of an utterance. A key requirement will be a procedure for establishing what the context is (in the sense of a set of propositions as input to an inference procedure) for a given utterance.

Things get much more interesting when claims move to a quantitative stage and specify the inferences appropriate for understanding in terms of the processing resources available or offer quantitative selection of the MOST appropriate inference or inferences. This has been done within AI/Psychology under the term "resource limited processing" (e.g., Norman & Bobrow, 1975) and as a special case within the field of natural language processing as "least effort" or "preference" theories (e.g., Bien, 1983; Wilks, 1975).

SW's version starts with their Principle of Relevance (ibid., p.75), which is "the single principle governing every aspect of comprehension":

> "The speaker tries to express the proposition which is the most relevant one possible to the hearer."

This is a counsel of perfection, of course, and may, like all such principles, not be adhered to by the speaker. Here we shall understand it in reverse, as it were, in keeping with the hearer-oriented aspect of SW, as a principle that the hearer is well advised to believe the speaker is observing. But the reader should note in passing that this is not a trivial gloss, since this principle refers only to the speaker's intentions. It is one of the continuing themes of our critique that such perspective switching by SW leads to muddle throughout.

The content of the principle is on p.75 and we shall call it THE CLAIM:

Of two utterances that take the same amount of processing, it is the one with the most contextual implications that will be the more relevant; and, of two utterances which have the same number of contextual implications, it is the one which takes the least amount of processing that will be the more relevant. (Sperber & Wilson, 1982, p.75)

Some care is needed now in interpreting this in terms of processing by a hearer (and SW seem to intend this: "...the hearer has to supply...." p.73, since "relevant" in the claim and the principle may not refer to the same items. This is a problem for SW, one that we will not attempt to solve comprehensively for them here. The real origin of the problem is the ultimate incompatibility of a Gricean speaker's-intention approach with one based on hearer's-information-processing, let alone with an abstract nondirectional model based on notions of Chomskyan competence, although SW preserve elements of all these.

2.3.2.1. The thalassemia example

Let us set out their principal illustrative example for their case: the thalassemia example (pp.74-5), with their own numbering of examples:

(19) Susan, who has thalassemia, is getting married to Bill.

(20) Susan is getting married to Bill, who has thalassemia.

(21) Susan, who has thalassemia, is getting married to Bill, and 1967 was a very good year for Bordeaux wine.

(22a) People who are getting married should consult a doctor about the possible hereditary risks to their children.

(22b) Two people both of whom have thalassemia should be warned against having children.

(22c) Susan has thalassemia.

In this context both (19) and (20) carry the contextual implication that Susan and Bill should consult a doctor, but (20) also carries the implication that Susan and Bill should be warned against having children. The sentences in (19) and (20) are almost identical in linguistic and lexical structure. Suppose that processing involves identifying the propositions expressed by the utterance, OCcomputing its nontrivial implications, and matching each of these against the propositions in the context to see if further nontrivial implications can be derived. Then (19) and (20) should take roughly equal amounts of processing. In this context since (20) yields more contextual implications than (19), with the same amount of processing, it should be more relevant than (19) and this seems intuitively correct. By contrast, (19) and (21) have the single contextual implication that Susan and Bill should consult a doctor. (21) is linguistically more complex than (19). On the above assumptions about processing, (21) will thus require more processing and be predicted as less relevant in context; again, this prediction seems to be intuitively correct.

Let us put four immediate considerations against this:

a) What serious quantitative information processing comparison can be going on in which a hearer can be considered as comparing the relevance of two *different utterances* (outside explicit psychological laboratory tests, that is), as distinct from a realistic situation where a hearer compares two alternative interpretations of a single utterance so as to select the more relevant? A hearer is normally offered an utterance, not several, from which to choose.

(b) It is true, as SW note, that (20) produces the (undoubtedly nontrivial) implication that the couple should consult a doctor, but surely that must have required a great deal of processing to obtain: the location and application of an AND rule, and the location and application of some form of modus ponens to (20)+(22b) AND (22c)? Or do SW somehow imagine that the actual inference itself, normally set out as explicit steps, does not require processing effort? If they believe that they should not use the metaphor at all, but leave it in the hands of others.

If the processing required by inferencing is taken into account, as they seem to intend, then the assumption of equal processing effort required by (19) and (20) is plainly ludicrous, since the accessing of a rule of conjunction and its application has a clearly quantifiable cost. In general, the safe assumption, other matters being equal (which, of course, they are not), is that more implications will require more processing effort, exactly the opposite of what their claim suggests.

(c) What basis can there possibly be for assuming, as SW still do at this point in their account, that (19), (20) and (21) all access the same context, and that access will require the same effort in all three cases (for, if it does not, then the comparisons drawn so far fall to pieces)?

Since (22c) is already present explicitly as part of (19), the context invoked by (19) cannot include (22c) as it does here (or, if it does, then other parts of utterances can occur explicitly in contexts, which will have other disastrous consequences for SW's claim). Hence the assumption that (19) and (20) "require the same processing effort" will be quite false if that effort includes context-location (and in the next section they concede that it does). If the effort is not the same then we have another case where the claim fails to apply, since neither equality is satisfied, although that, too, can give no comfort to SW.

Again, must (21) with its mention of Bordeaux draw into the context propositions about wine? These can be kept out only by making the indefensible assumption that this simply IS the context, achieved cost-free, and declining to discuss the matter further. If the mention of Bordeaux did draw in that wider context, at correspondingly greater effort than those drawn in by (19) and (20), then again the whole comparative farrago would fall to bits, since the assumption that (21) will yield the same number of contextual implications as (19) may well turn out false. A little ingenuity here could certainly produce a context for, and reply to, (21).

Gazdar and Good (1982) have pointed out that if a hearer has additional or idiosyncratic information about, or interest in a topic mentioned, then this may well give rise to a great number of nontrivial implications. Had the speaker said, in place of (21), "Susan, who has thalassemia, is getting married to Bill, who is a wine expert," then a wine expert hearer could have correctly inferred a great deal about Bill. SW, lacking any clear notion of what a hearer or speaker believe, separately or about each other, have no defense to this and make none in their reply to Gazdar and Good (Smith ed., 1982). In a properly founded theory, of course, it would be a requirement that the inferencing was constrained to a sub-space of assumptions that was the hearer's view of what the speaker believed the hearer believed. That would meet Gazdar and Good's point, for a hearer behaving appropriately would then not draw such "expertise" inferences if he believed the speaker did not know he was in possession of such information. Only in that way can context-finding deal with apparently irrelevant input (and real errors by speakers and hearers can, of course, occur concerning such information).

(d) Finally, the conclusions drawn by SW depend crucially on the context's containing the particular premises cited and not others, equally likely to be postulated by a hearer. (22b') is as plausible to a layperson as (22b), and (22d') may be widely believed by normal selfish individuals (and in their paper SW produce a context with a similar selfish belief about the function of charities):

(22b') Thalassemia is a form of bone cancer.

(22d') It is unwise to marry a woman with cancer, as she would need too much attention.

From the whole context (22a 22b', 22c and 22d'), (19) now has the implications that they should consult a doctor and that it is unwise of him to marry her. Sentence (20) also has the same two implications from that context, whereas with SW's context, (20) carried one more implication. It is obvious that the number depends crucially on the context located, and nothing general or significant follows as SW believe, from the particular examples they chose.

2.3.2.2. Locating the context

At this point in the exposition, SW introduce a principle that draws the whole theory closer to reality, but has the effect of negating much of what has gone before. They now face up to the consequences of the fact that locating contexts is a matter of processing effort:

" We want to argue ... that the search for the interpretation on which an utterance will be most relevant involves search for the context which will make this interpretation possible. In other words, determination of the context is not a prerequisite to the comprehension process, but a part of it." (ibid., p.76)

But are we faced at this point by the withdrawal of a minor simplifying assumption, one that can now be withdrawn without ill-effect; or is it rather that the recognition that context finding costs processing effort (one accepted by all those in the AI Psychology tradition who have discussed the issue) makes nonsense of the claim and everything based on it? The following definitions would at least remove the obvious absurdities in SW's position:

New principles for hearers (and for speakers, who assume hearers are using them):

(1) MAXIMIZE the number of contextual implications drawn for some total given processing effort (up to some arbitrary maximum per unit time, say, one to be empirically determined) for interpretation of input, location of context, and drawing of implications;

(2) MINIMIZE amount of processing for context-finding so as to leave more available for drawing contextual implications under (1).

These proposals, too, may well not stand up to any detailed examination, but they are at least procedurally plausible and not self-evidently self-contradictory (although they are not independent). Whereas, on SW's account, the hearer is under an injunction simultaneously to maximize and minimize the same sort of thing, in that the hearer is to minimize effort overall, while at the same time maximizing the number of contextual implications whose production must require effort! Our hunch, for what it is worth, is that SW should go simply for a least-processing-effort theory (as we have ourselves) for it is not clear what help having more contextual implications is.

In their reply to Gazdar and Good, SW (1982) deny that they assume "processing speed is constant" (ibid., p.106) and so, they argue, processing per unit time considerations are not relevant. They also claim that context-finding processing is noninferential, as distinct from the inferential processing that draws implications, and so no considerations drawn from summing processing capacities are appropriate in discussion of their system. This is, we believe, the merest obfuscation, and nothing SW write gives any support to the view that there are separate processing capacities that cannot be added. It is certainly possible that the brain does have separate capacities for the two processes, ones that cannot be added, but claiming that would require some shred of physiological evidence, above and beyond the undoubted convenience to SW. Moreover, such a concession would be quite at variance with the discovery that "determination of context is not a prerequisite to the comprehension process but a part of it" (ibid., p.76).

Given (1) and (2) cited earlier, some version of SW's claim could now be reinstated, and they might well feel that these new principles are just what they intended and have expressed (cf., " ...we would suggest that the amount of processing tends to remain roughly constant throughout a stretch of discourse" (p.77), if that is taken to mean processing per unit time!), but they certainly have not, and indeed are unable to do so, because the claim was stated on the basis of the false assumptions about cost-freeness, a matter of complete irrelevance to logical complexity and inferential effort. It would be hard to find in the recent linguistic literature a clearer example of the bad effects of the hangover of beliefs in the autonomy and primacy of syntax.

2.3.3. Cognitive Solipsism

We drew attention earlier to the fact that SW have no clear or consistent appreciation of the fact that real inference must go on somewhere and, in a model of human communication, that it must be in a hearer model or a speaker model (where each may, and must, contain models of the other). This lack surfaces in their work at intervals, as when they discuss the "common ground," which is their version of "mutual knowledge": the set of facts, serving as potential contexts, that both conversational participants know. But on SW's account, there is no method or theory to explain the difference between:

(a) premises/beliefs believed by the hearer to be held by the speaker when speaking;

(b) general knowledge known by the hearer and believed to be imputed to him by the speaker;

(c) enthymemic beliefs, not retrieved by the hearer from anywhere, but constructed by him, as part of a context, and imputed by him to the speaker on the basis only of what is said (i.e., not believed previously by the hearer, nor previously believed by him to be held by the speaker).

Enthymemic constructions are beliefs attributed to a speaker so as to cause implications to follow from what is already in the inference space, i.e., the current utterance. We produced, out of the blue, more or less plausible premises (22b') and (22d'), but as to how this process can be modelled algorithmically, no one has much to say. It is the great problem in SW's theory and for all those working in this area. No theory that fails to reflect these distinctions in some well-motivated way can be taken seriously in this area.

Investigations that do make them are the very stuff of much work in AI, both logical-theoretical (e.g., Moore, 1977) and programmed-applied (e.g., Perrault and Allen, 1980). In the important latter series of papers the notions of belief, speech acts, plans, reference, inference and models of the other were ingeniously explored, and the above distinctions were fundamental. A crucial advantage of work like the latter is that it can show the continuity of relevance and inference with human plans and goals, and what someone is talking FOR. There is no way this can be done with SW's work, and that must be a serious shortcoming in a general theory of pragmatics.

The greatest lacuna in the list is (c) and it is, at the moment, no more than an aspiration for all research workers, but SW do not see this because they have no procedural grasp of what can and cannot be done, so for them the very difficult is all one with the well-understood.

Let us summarize our objection to SW's theory: Their errors all stem from their conviction that there is an objectively right context set of propositions, one that can be assumed independently of how it is located, and independently of what individuals may in fact believe. Let us now summarize an alternative account of these matters, one in which those features are built in from the very beginning.

2.3.4. Another view of the medical example

Let us now set out as briefly as possible our view of one of SW's principal examples, making use of the *ViewGen* techniques, although not yet in the formal detail we shall apply later, and retaining the spirit, although not at all the letter, of SW's thalassemia example. The purpose here is to show that, contrary to SW's position, an analysis that can take account of differing points of view or belief sets is utterly crucial in dealing with examples of this kind, and that its total absence in SW's theoretical apparatus undermines everything they have to say.

Let us enrich the scenario a little as follows. The personae will be a doctor, who is hopefully an expert, and of whom we will suppose the system to be a model. There will be a fiancee, who knows the broad facts about the disease, and a fiance who does not, beyond that it is a disease. The doctor believes them both to carry the disease, and is aware of their different degrees of informedness. Let us also suppose they meet the doctor separately on this matter, and that the following dialogue takes place with the male partner:

| He: | My fiancee believes I have thalassemia. |
| Doctor: | You do and so does she. |

At this point, the doctor knows that nothing important (e.g., about children) follows *for the patient* and he must now break the bad news in detail. Whereas, had he been talking to the other partner:

Doctor:	You have thalassemia.
She:	Does he have it too?
Doctor:	Yes.

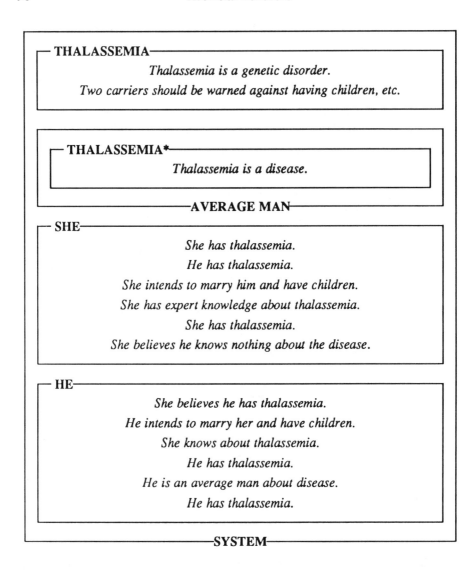

Figure 2.4. The doctor/system's view of two patients.

At which point, the doctor knows that much more follows for this patient and can behave appropriately. It cannot be argued that these distinctions are unimportant, at least by anyone who subscribes to the fundamental Gricean insights about human communication. But, as we have seen in the first part of this section, SW cannot possibly distinguish these situations with their limited theoretical mechanisms.

It will be pretty clear how the environments we have described (contexts in SW's sense) can be constructed to correspond to the doctor/system's views of his two patients. Using the notation developed in the introduction cited earlier we can suppose the following environments (Figure 2.4).

We can further suppose that "He" and "She" as variables cause no problems in this limited world and that the states of the environments shown earlier are after the dialogues have taken place. We can then consider what follows in certain environments (that the doctor/system constructs by push-down of environments at the appropriate moment), using ordinary inference rules (Figure 2.5).

The last environment contains "He has thalassemia" but no additional consequences follow. Notice that this nesting uses THALASSEMIA*, the average man's view of the disease, because although she does know details of the disease, he (the fiance) does not know what it is she does know. This point will become important later when dealing with intensional objects that are only evaluable by certain (informed) agents.

Even after further exchanges:

He: Does she know she has it too?
Doctor: Yes.

Nothing beyond the conclusion that they both have it follows because he cannot compute the key fact about the disease that she knows. Our submission is that the above method is rather more realistic that SW's proposals, and it is worth noting that it has nothing at all to do with the number of propositions that follow within any context/environment. Only some method like ours can explain how the doctor treats the patients differently in a way that no impersonal "heuristic of relevance" could possibly do alone. To put the matter at its crudest: relevance must be to *someone*.

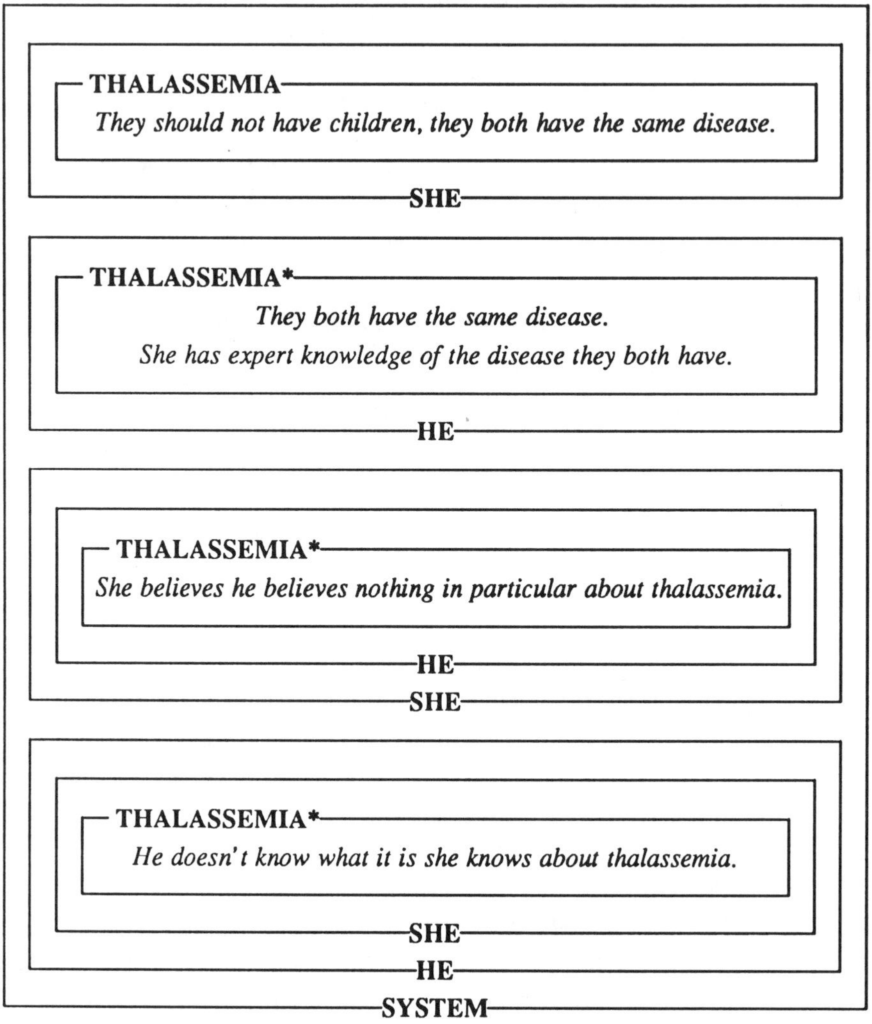

Figure 2.5. The doctor/system's view of the patient's views.

Chapter 2.4
Peripheral phenomena? Speech acts and metaphor

Let us now turn to these two phenomena which we, like many writers, assume to be central and not (as conservative schools of thought still hold) peripheral to human reasoning and language processing. Our task here is to relate both to the central phenomenon of belief.

2.4.1. Speech Acts

Speech acts originated as a notion in philosophy (Austin, 1962) concerned with the peculiar logical property of utterances like 'I promise to come tomorrow.' They were said to be neither true nor false as sentences, but as acts, named by some word in the utterance, in this case 'promise.' In later work (Grice, 1969; Strawson, 1964; Searle, 1969) the notion of intention (in a sense requiring access to a speaker's 'mental acts') became central, together with the problem of disambiguating the variety of communicative functions of an utterance like 'I will come tomorrow,' which could be on different occasions a threat, promise, prediction, etc. This later work rested on a purported direct access to a speaker's intentions which could not, of course, be obtained. Although the later work of Grice and Searle acknowledged the dependence of communicative function on the beliefs and goals of hearers and speakers, philosophy had neither the tools nor the will to explicate these notions directly and in detail.

In linguistics, attempts to explicate speech acts had a difficult time within the Transformational-Generative paradigm. This is not surprising since Searle intended speech acts as a criticism of what he saw as Chomsky's deliberate separation of Transformational Grammar from any consideration of communication (Searle, 1974). Chomsky was in a way right about the solipsism of communication: it was no good Searle just writing speakers and hearers into his theories and assuming (as

he did) that that gave real access to other Gricean agents. As we saw, too, in discussions of SW earlier (2.3), a Chomskyan competence model without any mention
of other agents or believers (which is what SW's model is) is also unable to model
communication, and Chomksy himself never claimed to. The solution is the
solipsistic compromise of this book.

However, there were attempts to explicate speech acts within Transformational Grammar assumptions, broadly construed. These took the form of either (a)
the assumption that a given communicative function like *promise* is already marked
in 'deep structure' (Ross, 1970) so that all sentences have an a *priori* determinable
range of communicative forces; or (b) a set of 'conversational postulates' (Gordon
& Lakoff, 1971) whose overall relationship to the generative rules of a Transformational Grammar remained unclear.

One could say that work on speech act phenomena broke into a range of studies that were not clearly related, except in the general sense of being discourse
phenomena:

(a) a taxonomy of particular verbs, the so-called performatives, whose use did
not always result in sentences with truth values, e.g., "I hereby name this ship
'Titanic'."

(b) a consideration of the meaning of certain utterances with and without the
explicit presence of 'performative' verbs, e.g., "I promise to come" versus "I
will come." This class of verbs is almost certainly not the same as is captured
by (a).

(c) a study of the way in which the functions of utterances like the two in (b)
are determined at least in part by assumptions of the hearer about the beliefs
of the speaker etc.

(d) a study of "deep grammar" in which utterances that, for example, have the
form of questions such as "Can you pass the salt?" function as requests and
have to be so understood on the basis, again, of assumptions by the hearer
about the beliefs of the speaker.

Within AI, the first tool available for an original explication of speech acts
(SAs) was the modelling of the beliefs of one system (including itself) by another
(Minsky, 1968). There were also systems (e.g., Schank, 1972) that made similar
weak claims about intentions in that they required no postulation of access to inaccessible phenomena (although that fact was often obscured by the way such work
was described. In such systems, intentions were normally equated in practice to

'reasonable inference about another's intention based on what he says or does,' which is a far more defensible notion than one requiring real access to the intentions of others as was assumed in some philosophical accounts.

However, most early AI work on speech acts offered no distinctively AI explication of the phenomena, but settled for a discourse classification (utterance n is an example of speech act of type m) based on mutual following by conversation participants of an agreed technical information structure such as a frame about, say, repairing taps. That work drew upon structures from the frame, network and planning literatures in AI and was directed towards explication of only phenomena (c) and (d) in the list cited earlier. Yet, in order to assign that Speech Act of type m, it cannot be necessary to ascribe particular labels from the Speech Act literature (Searle 1969) such as THREAT or WARNING (unless, that is, one advocates some extreme version of the LOT view of the mind), although it is reasonable to assume that some process equivalent to that, at least in terms of the inferences to be drawn from an utterance, must be carried out. Hence, one might say that Speech Act ascription is an important special case of ascriptional reasoning; and because of what we are calling the nesting of belief environments, this reasoning. That speech act considerations make reasoning about propositional attitudes essential for the computational modeling of discourse has been established at least since the work of Perrault and his colleagues (e.g., Perrault and Allen, 1980). This work was truly original in AI, and broke completely from the weaker tradition of the AI explication of speech acts noted earlier. We shall describe it in more detail in (2.5.1).

2.4.2. Mutual Belief and Mutual Knowledge

Although work on computational speech acts is to be described in 2.5, it is worth noting here that such recent developments as Cohen and Levesque (1980, 1985) rest on an undefined notion of "mutual belief." This is a subjective variant of the notion "mutual knowledge" that was described originally from Grice through Schiffer (1972) and more recently by Clark and Marshall (1981). This approach accepts much of what has been set out so far and seeks to explicate a formal notion of "A and B mutually know P" as a solution. Although a great deal is idiosyncratically known or believed by individuals, communication is as successful as it is because we not only believe many things in common, but also believe ourselves to do so. The work of Clark and Marshall thus forms a middle case between SW's "uniform assumption space" approach, which does not attribute ownership of beliefs to individuals, and our own attempt to characterize beliefs more generally than by restricting attention to what can be "mutually known." Clark and Marshall's work has been discussed (in Smith ed., 1982) by SW and ourselves, and is not central to the concerns of this book, but it may be worth recapitulating briefly why that is so.

Their analysis is essentially of situations of actual or potential copresence, as when two people observe an object lying between them, or go to a cinema together. It is not only that each believes the other to have had such-and-such an experience, but believes (probably truly) that the other believes that of the first person, and so on indefinitely. Infinite numbers of steps like:

A believes *B* believes *A* believes..., etc

are possible, and it is not important for the sake of illustration which of the predicates "believe" or "know" are used here. Clark and Marshall have been misunderstood (not only through the faults of their commentators) as implying that understanders sometimes go through an infinite number of such steps. Of course they do not, and Clark and Carlson did not intend that, but only to claim that to know "*A* and *B* mutually know *P*" is to have the ability to apply a rule as often as is required in a particular case.

We believe that only very special cases can fall under this description, and that not much communication requires assumptions about real copresence. For all other cases, belief is a matter of cognitive solipsism: I truly believe you believe the world is round (rather than flat), just as I do. But this is MY belief not YOURS, and I am unlikely to have or have ever had any direct evidence of the matter. Even in cases of true copresence, as when two people went together to a cinema the night before and refer to the matter later in conversation, the ability to infer infinitely many propositions (cited earlier above) is either vacuous (in that there is a rule producing as many as are required for a case, and no evidence is relevant) OR in real cases, evidence is relevant at each stage, and may fail (e.g., on the sixth recursive application of the rule the evidence fails and it is not the case that *A* believes *B* believes...). It is hard to see real inference as much aided by the application of the trivial rule, although it might be handy to have it available for special cases, even though the mutual knowledge literature gives no clear guide as to which situations allow its application.

But in the case of real, fallible, applications, storage and effort considerations make it almost impossible that a truth value can reverse after a small number of consistent results (Steel, 1984). In sum, then, we find Clark and Marshall's analysis highly ingenious for extraordinary cases but little help in the everyday solipsistic world, where we have no guarantees of what it is both people know, and know each other to know, outside of intensive psychological experimentation. As we shall see, understanding does require assumptions about the knowledge of the other partner but they are always fallible, and hence, *ex hypothesi*, are not "mutual knowledge."

2.4.3. Metaphor

To consider metaphor at all in a study of belief might initially seem unmotivated or over-ambitious. However, we are amongst those who hold that metaphor is central to language use, and indeed essential to cognition in general (for related positions see, e.g., Carbonell, 1982; Hobbs, 1983; Johnson, 1987; Lakoff, 1987; Lakoff & Johnson, 1980). We feel, in particular, that metaphor is *inextricably* bound up with propositional attitude processing for two main reasons:

(A) The notion of a *metaphorical view* of "one topic as another" is, we suggest, procedurally related to the notion of an *agent's view* of a topic seen through another.

(B) Many if not most beliefs arising in ordinary discourse and reasoning are at least partly metaphorical in nature.

Consider, for instance, the beliefs that "terrorism is creeping across the globe," "Sally's theory is threatened by the experiment" and "Prussia invaded France in 1871." As an example of the difficulties that such beliefs raise, notice that the last one cannot be adequately represented on the basis of a literal sense representation for "Prussia", since it may be important to take into account exactly how the believer may be viewing the invasion as a matter of the army of Prussia doing something, of the Prussian government doing something, or of the Prussian people as a whole doing something, and so on. The simple predicate notations commonly used in belief research lead us to overlook such points.

The similarity in (A) is the main focus of this section. We shall exploit the similarity by seeking to extend, in a natural way, an existing belief-ascription system to cope with metaphor, although it was originally developed with no orientation towards it. Ultimately the system should deal with examples like those in (B).

In performing this extension we also wish, ultimately, to reconcile our proposition/belief-oriented approach to meaning and metaphor with a semantic net/dictionary approach with which one of us has been closely associated.

It should also be noted here that this brief introduction does no kind of justice to the huge area of metaphor studies outside the immediate cognitive science paradigm adopted here. We have chosen to discuss Davidson as a representative only because he holds some of the most striking and discussable views. Again, we shall not distinguish strongly in this book between analogy and metaphor; the relationship is subtle and complex (see Gentner et al., 1987) but for our simple purposes we shall not need that distinction. Another crucial issue to specialists in the field is whether the transfer in a "metaphorical act" from vehicle to tenor is of properties or of structural relationships (an issue discussed in some detail in Fass and Wilks, 1983. Although one talks of "property transfer," nearly all systems in AI that model analogy and metaphor actually deal in the transfer of complex structures (Falkenhainer, Forbus & Gentner, 1986; Fass, 1987 etc.).

Davidson (1978) said that metaphor is "simply false belief" and one of our aims in this work will be to show that that is correct, but in a surprising, computational way. In a moment we shall consider his views in some detail because, if we are interested in meaning, then we must also be interested in the phenomenon where meaning seems most obviously to extend itself, that is, metaphor, and hence in what philosophers of meaning have to say about it.

We should declare our hand, at least as regards the definition of the term "metaphor" (which is dangerous, bearing in mind scholarly history), and reveal that one of us is on record (Wilks, 1980) as identifying metaphor with virtually any breaking of semantic constraints. On such a view metaphor is not a rare utterance event, but is found everywhere. Just look:

". . . In her statement on the cuts last week, the Prime Minister gave a clear hint about the twin thrust of the **review kindled** by Sir Derek's paper. She said: 'It is the Government's job to ensure that the structure of the Civil Service, its working methods and the regard it offers for success **brings on the right kinds of** talent; gives it scope for personal initiative; and offers conditions which **promote loyalty and commitment...**' "

This is pretty much a random paragraph from *The* (London) *Times*, and yet at each point picked out in bold, the verb is plausibly boundary breaking (or "preference breaking" as it has been called elsewhere, e.g. Wilks, 1977) and metaphorical in form.   What is normally kindled is fire; what is normally brought on is an event; what is normally promoted is a person, and so on. Yet there is no problem of comprehension or correctness here (even if the nuances of the passage are not immediately clear to a reader unfamiliar with comment in British newspapers). Exactly the same phenomenon at work could have been located, and as frequently, on any front page of *The New York Times*.

2.4.4. Davidson on metaphor

Davidson has sought to bring metaphor within a general theory of meaning, but like almost all contemporary views of metaphor, his cannot be understood except by contrast to Black (1962) who plays in this field something of the role Katz and Fodor play in semantic representation. One always sets out one's theory in contrast with theirs, and Black plays a similar role in discussions of metaphor. He put forward what he called an "interaction view of metaphor" that in "X is Y" (the canonical form of metaphor) structural properties of Y are assigned to X's in such a way as to create metaphorical assertions quite separate from the literal assertion. This structural interaction view has been extended to the analysis of scientific theories by Hesse (1965) and others.

The plain weakness of this theory is how to specify what exactly are the structural properties that are *not* carried over. "Max is a pig" is taken to mean:

a) Max has unpleasant or aggressive personal habits.

rather than

b) Max is a four-legged porcine animal that sleeps on straw in a concrete pen.

Why a) rather than b) is the formal problem. On the common sense view, "Max is a pig" is literally false, but not asserted by the normal speaker of the sentence. Interpretation a) is asserted (no matter for the moment how firmly) and may be true or false. It is quite proper to reply to the above:

"No, he's not. He's kind and nice and I've known him for 50 years."

This denies a), not the "literal interpretation," which is not even asserted, nor believed by the hearer to be asserted by the speaker. All this is rather obvious, you may think, so let us turn to Davidson.

Davidson (ibid.) believes that such a sentence has only its literal meaning, which is almost always false. For him, truth and falsehood can only hold of literal meanings. This fits naturally into Davidson's general theory of meaning based on "T-sentences" (numbered sentences declaring the truth conditions of sentences quoted within the T-sentence). Moreover there is only one T-sentence per quoted sentence, hence he can never allow any pair like:

(Tn) S is T iff P

(Tn+1) S is T iff Q

where P and Q are different sets of truth conditions for the same sentence. He is at pains to point out that he is not against metaphorical truth, only that it "cannot be of sentences," which is no great consolation. The main plank of his platform is that metaphorical sentences do not have hidden meanings, nor any second any meanings at all:

> The central mistake against which I shall be inveighing is the idea that metaphor has, in addition to its literal sense or meaning, another sense or meaning... But if I am right, a metaphor doesn't say anything beyond its literal meaning (nor does its maker say anything, in using the metaphor, beyond the literal). (p. 32)

> For a metaphor says only what shows on its face, usually a patent falsehood or an absurd truth. (p. 43)

> We must give up the idea that a metaphor carries a message, that it has content or meaning (except, of course, its literal meaning). (p. 45)

> The theorist who tries to explain a metaphor by appealing to a hidden message, is then fundamentally confused. (p. 47)

These are bold claims, and a reader will either like them or not. Our response is that:

1) Davidson's false and only literal interpretation is not asserted by the user of a metaphor;

2) There is another interpretation that is asserted, and the proof of this is that it is taken to be the assertion by a reasonable, culturally appropriate hearer, and it can be denied, as we noted earlier in connection with the attack on Max;

3) We do have linguistic cues that we are in the presence of a metaphor and falsehood is not necessarily one of them. If someone utters either of the plain falsehoods "All elephants are green or dead," we do not look for metaphor.

Davidson offers the four following scenarios (2.4.5 to 2.4.8) to support his position, all of which seem to us irrelevant (even if true) or plainly false (though not metaphorical!).

2.4.5. Metaphor is not like ambiguity

Some words, Davidson notes, mean many things and we may be unsure which is appropriate in context:

> "A plausible modification of the last suggestion would be to consider the key word (or words) in a metaphor as having two different kinds of meaning at once, a literal and a figurative meaning." (p. 35)

> "This theory may seem complex, but it is strikingly similar to what Frege proposed to account for the behavior of referring terms in modal sentences and sentences about propositional attitudes like belief and desire. According to Frege, each referring term has two or more meanings, one of which fixes its reference in the special contexts created by modal operators or psychological verbs. The rule connecting the two meanings may be put like this: The meaning of the word in the special contexts makes the reference in those contexts be identical with the meaning of the ordinary contexts.

> Here is the whole picture, putting Frege together with a Fregean view of metaphor: We are to think of a word as having, in addition to its mundane field of application or reference, two special or super-mundane fields of application, one for metaphor and the other for modal contexts and the like. In both cases the original meaning remains to do its work by virtue of a rule which relates the various meanings."

(p. 36).

The Fregean point is exactly the one of noninnocence that was contrasted earlier (see 2.1) with Barwise and Perry's view. On the Frege/Davidson view we are to see that in the phrase:

John believes the murderer is blond

we cannot allow the sense-description of the murderer to select the referent Smith, even though we happen to believe Smith is the murderer, since John may not. This is very much like the phrase "the murderer," having another sense one peculiar to John, just as in "the mouth of the bottle," *mouth* has a sense that does not pick out human mouths. This is certainly ingenious, but it is not clear that it establishes that metaphor is different from word-sense ambiguity, as it is clearly intended to. John may also know a sense of "tap" that picks out plant roots and Jane may not; yet this is not on the face of it metaphor, only sense-ambiguity, although it seems just as open to the Fregean interpretation cited earlier. No firm distinction that might support Davidson here can be based on metaphor being a sense inferrable on the spot from the context, whereas ambiguity is between established senses, if only because established senses must have started life somewhere, presumably by some on-the-spot inference. At this point Davidson shifts to his major example.

2.4.6. The Saturn and floor story

How we learn a word, says Davidson, shows that there cannot be a special field of application of the word:

> "You are entertaining a visitor from Saturn by trying to teach him how to use the word 'floor.' You go through the familiar dodges, leading him from floor to floor, pointing and stamping and repeating the word. You prompt him to make experiments, tapping objects tentatively with his tentacle while rewarding his right and wrong tries. You want him to come out knowing not only that these particular objects or surfaces are floors but also how to tell a floor when one is in sight or touch. The skit you are putting on doesn't tell him what he needs to know, but with luck it helps him to learn it. Should we call this process learning something about the world or learning something about language? An odd question, since what is learned is that a bit of

language refers to a bit of the world. Still, it is easy to distinguish between the business of learning the meaning of a word and using the word once the meaning is learned. Comparing these two activities, it is natural to say that the first concerns learning something about language, while the second is typically learning something about the world. If your Saturnian has learned how to use the word 'floor,' you may try telling him something new, that there is a floor. If he has mastered the word trick, you have told him something about the world. Your friend from Saturn now transports you through space to his home sphere, and looking remotely at earth you say to him, nodding at the earth, 'floor.' Perhaps he will think this is still part of the lesson and assume that the word 'floor' applies properly to the earth, at least as seen from Saturn. But what if you thought he already knew the meaning of 'floor,' and you were remembering how Dante, from a similar place in the heavens, saw the inhabited earth as 'the small round floor that makes us passionate?' Your purpose was metaphor, not drill in the use of language. What difference would it make to your friend which way he took it? With the theory of metaphor under consideration, very little difference, for according to that theory a word has a new meaning in a metaphorical context; the occasion of the metaphor would, therefore, be the occasion for learning the new meaning. We should agree that in some ways it makes relatively little difference whether, in a given context, we think a word is being used metaphorically or in a previously unknown, but literal way." (p. 36-37)

The reader may reasonably feel here that a trick has been pulled on him, but is not quite sure how or why. Of course you cannot use a word in a "metaphorical" sense during the teaching of meaning by ostensive methods; if you do you will confuse, or produce a very odd meaning, etc. Hence it will make a great difference to the Saturnian if he thinks we are teaching the meaning, when we are actually assuming it and moving on to assume sense building rules for metaphor.

All Davidson has shown is that there cannot be "special field" of application during the learning of the first sense of a word. Whoever thought there could? His own distinction suggests this should be obvious to him too:

"Still it is easy to distinguish between the business of learning the meaning of a word and using the word once the meaning is learned." (p. 36)

The solution may lie in the following:

"We should agree that in some ways it makes relatively little difference whether, in a given context, we think a word is being used metaphorically or in a previously unknown, but literal way." (p. 37, 1978)

But all this misses the key point that if we predicate *Pig* of *Max*, who is of a different class, then we have done so because of similarities between Max and pigs that we wish to draw attention to, ones already known to our hearer. On the view expressed in the last quotation we would simply be starting up again and missing the whole point of what is intended, as in: 'When I call Max a pig, don't think of what you already know about pigs. This is just another learning situation, so sit back and find out what I mean.'

2.4.7. Dead metaphors

"Dead metaphors are not really metaphors because if they were metaphorical senses they would be paraphrasable and my whole case would drop to bits... The figurative meaning of the living metaphor should be immortalised in the literal meaning of the dead. But although some philosophers have suggested this idea, it seems plainly wrong. 'He was burned up' is genuinely ambiguous (since it may be true in one sense and false in another), but although the slangish idiom is no doubt the corpse of a metaphor, 'He was burned up' now suggests no more than that he was very angry. When the metaphor was active, we would have pictured fire in the eyes or smoke coming out of the ears." (p. 38)

"Finally, if words in a metaphor bear a coded meaning, how can this meaning differ from the meaning those same words bear in the case where the metaphor dies — that is, when it comes to be part of the language? Why doesn't 'He was burned up as now used and meant, mean exactly what the fresh metaphor once meant? Yet all that the dead metaphor means is that he was very angry — a notion not very difficult to make explicit.'" (p. 45)

These passages seem to us clearly wrong (elsewhere he admits that dead metaphor of "river/bottle mouth" did derive from mouth). The senses referred to are now independent senses, and can also lead to ambiguity. The important linking fact is that we who know English *but not these dead metaphors* could infer them on first acquaintance with the examples, and this is an excellent test for the reality of metaphorical processes. Davidson is just wrong about paraphrasability, too:

> "How can this be right? If a metaphor has a special cognitive content, why should it be so difficult or impossible to set it out? If, as Owen Barfield claims, a metaphor 'says one thing and means another,' why should it be that when we try to get explicit about what it means, the effect is so much weaker — 'put it that way,' Barfield says, 'and nearly all the tarning, and with it half the poetry is lost.' Why does Black think a Why inevitably? Can't we, if we are clever enough, come as close as we please?" (p. 44)

Of course it is possible, and Davidson denies it only because it suits his overall purpose.

2.4.8. Metaphors and lies

Metaphors are like lies, where lies of course are not just falsehoods, but falsehoods known also to the speaker.

> "The parallel between making a metaphor and telling a lie is emphasized by the fact that the same sentence can be used, with meaning unchanged, for either purpose. So a woman who believed in witches but did not think her neighbor a witch might say, 'She's a witch,' meaning it metaphorically; the same woman, still believing the same of witches and her neighbour but intending to deceive, might use the very same words to very different effect. Since sentence and meaning are the same in both cases, it is sometimes hard to prove which intention lay behind the saying of it; thus a man who says 'Lattimore's a Communist' and means to lie can always try to beg off by pleading a metaphor." (Davidson, p. 43)

Even if this is correct it is not clear how it helps his case. In fact, if the literal meaning is not asserted, as we contend, then a metaphor cannot be a lie. His two examples rest heavily on cultural belief problems, and given reasonable cultural uniformity, a lie and a metaphor could not be confused. Metaphorical interpretation like all linguistic interpretation rests on strong assumptions about similarity and goals between speakers and hearers. Davidson cannot claim any special rights for arguments *about* metaphors there.

Our case here has been that nothing Davidson says, elegant though it is, shows any convincing difference between the process of metaphor construction and comprehension when those two processes are used to give a word a new sense (and where the sense may not in fact be new but only new to the particular speaker or hearer). This last is important for us because the processes for metaphor manipulation in a belief environment that we shall propose later (6.1) rest on the continuity between metaphor manipulation and other more conventional processes. Davidson's arguments, like most arguments in cognitive science outside the connectionist paradigm, rest on there being some clear notion of what a word sense is, and how different senses of the same word are to be separated from each other. We, too, have assumed that in this book, even though a little reflection shows it is very hard to give any empirical basis to this almost universal scholarly assumption (although see Wilks et al., 1988).

Actually, some aspects of the Saturnian story cited earlier could be interpreted as showing that Davidson, too, has doubts about this conventional view: His story rests on our not being clear, and the Saturnian being totally unclear, as to whether or not the teaching of the initial sense of "floor" has ended. Indeed, if there were not the space trip in between, how could we understand that without falling back on arguments about "common and different features" of floors and planets? Later, as we saw, Davidson comes to himself and reasserts the conventional doctrine which, as we noted, further undermines his case. However, it is important to see that, even if there were no empirical basis to sense, and there were just more and more individual contexts of use with no evident taxonomy to them (and Wittgenstein certainly flirted with that view) then that would make no difference to our case against Davidson. Such lack of boundaries would apply both to new senses of words and to metaphorical use indifferently; both would still be in the same boat, as it were, and that is all we need to show here.

Chapter 2.5
Approaches to belief in NLP and linguistics

Belief is not a topic in modern linguistics whose focus, since well before Chomsky, has been on the phonetic and syntactic descriptions of languages. Semantic description has undergone development in more recent, post-Chomskyan years but consideration of belief and its linguistic relevance lies yet further on in pragmatics. But as we saw in the work of Sperber and Wilson (2.2), even some pragmatic systems lack the basic apparatus for representing the fact that different agents in a dialogue can have different beliefs, differences that underlie and determine the nature of their interaction.

As we also saw in that section, the Chomskyan competence paradigm remains important, even in areas so far from syntax, at least in the sense that it leads to the modelling of a notion of competence that is that of an idealized language user and therefore, curiously, a *lone* language user, but never one participating in an interaction. Perhaps the underlying error of that idealization was that there could not, within it, be more than one ideal speaker, yielding idealizations that differed from each other, as they inevitably would with respect to beliefs. Their differences would seem arbitrary and unmotivated within the Chomskyan view of things (e.g., speaker A believes p, and speaker B believes ~p, for some actual p). However, the error is the paradigm itself. Much later, Searle's speech act theory was taken into both linguistic pragmatics and into AI, but only in the latter was an attempt made to model the different beliefs of separate uttering agents, and that difference came from the AI commitment to "knowledge-based processing," since knowledge would, in the loose way the term is always used in AI, almost certainly be different for different agents. In Searle's own writing, before it got into AI hands, there is little or no recognition that the speaker and hearer will not only be separate, but also *differ* significantly.

More recently, and outside the Chomskyan paradigm altogether, Fauconnier (1985) and Dinsmore (1987) have developed the possibilities that arise from counter-factuals added to environment-like objects to see what consequences might follow; e.g., "If your husband had AIDS, would you leave him?." Someone who understands this and processes it is not strictly manipulating a belief at all, but a counter-factual possibility. Normal rules of inheritance and inference may well apply but not, we would maintain, our core notion of ascription.

Similarly, and much more generally, we cannot assume (at least in conversationally sophisticated societies) that speakers really believe all the things they say in normal dialogue situations. It is not that they are lying or being deceptive, but they are simply trying utterances out and seeing the consequences based on what happens. They are, in a sense, conversational mini-scientists, trying out hypotheses to see if they lead to conversationally acceptable truths. In terms of current fashion, it might then be said that the corresponding hypotheses would be "abduced."

2.5.1. Natural Language Processing

The history of belief notions in AI can go very far back if one includes all projects that were *intended* as models of belief. Colby's PARRY (Colby et al. 1971) gave the best performance of all dialogue systems in English, and was based on very efficient pattern recognition of English against about 3,000 stored word stem sequences. It was certainly said by its author to be a belief model, but on a stronger criterion for a belief system that it should model the beliefs of at least one other besides itself, then PARRY certainly fails.

Even among those in Natural Language Processing (NLP) who advocated the most wholehearted use of semantic and pragmatic information (e.g., Schank 1972, Wilks 1975) there was in the research of the seventies no representational device that allowed, or acknowledged the need for, representation of belief structures that differed from those of the host system itself. This lack was most striking in researchers of the Yale school who developed analysers and generators for stories with a number of participants such as Meehan (1981).

In his TALESPIN program, the beliefs and goals of a range of characters are considered and computed over. Yet the fundamental structure that controls the story being generated is a preformed "script," which is the structure (text grammar) of the story as a whole. It is true that the program knows about the goals/beliefs of various characters in it, but they do not form structures that are among the fundamental ones of the system, and which would have allowed a development in Yale theory in which the system could have detected when the characters differed about key aspects of their world.

This was a crucial missed opportunity, and left Yale structures with a curiously "flat" quality, one they shared (unknowingly or unwillingly if known) with text grammar approaches within linguistics (e.g., van Dijk 1979; Petoefi 1976; de Beaugrande 1980; Dressler 1978). In other Yale systems, such as Lehnert (1986) and Cullingford's (1981/1986) experiments with scripts for stories, the filled-in frame structures (see Minsky 1975) did indeed represent the beliefs and goals of a main character, but there was only one character and the contrast, essential to belief, was lost. Even Charles Martin's recent attempts to model the dialogue of economists with different beliefs and meanings for key words like "inflation" (1988) cannot properly represent any agent A's belief about agent B.

The root cause of the situation is that Schankian CD, always present at the heart of those systems, seems to have taken primitive representations of meaning to mean that they are the same for everyone, not only in the LOT sense, of a language, but also in the stronger, Leibnizian sense that some truths about the world when expressed as properly formed propositions are true and the same for everyone. Scripts or frames could well have been entities that corresponded not only to information about individuals, but also served as receptacles for their beliefs. That they did not was, as we noted, a lost opportunity in NLP.

The first important representational move in NLP for our present purposes was the notion of a "partitioned semantic network" due to Hendrix (1979). This was the device of drawing a closed partition on a conventional semantic network of nodes and links, and allowing that partition to impose certain interpretations on the nodes it covered. Thus, partition boundaries could overlap, and a node would be interpreted differently in one partition in which it fell, from the way it was in another. Thus in Figure 2.6 (where Hendrix-style figures appear in the SRI project, described by Grosz 1977) a node labelled "BOLTS" in a network underlying a program to assemble platforms with a robot is within two overlapping partitions, one that concerns "assembly parts" and the other "buyable parts." So, the links from the "bolts" node to nodes denoting "platform" etc., fall under the first topic, and the links to nodes with labels like a price in dollars fall under the second. This ingenious notation brings together two notions encountered previously: firstly, the partitions on networks have the same effect as frame partitions in Minsky (1975), in that they collect together entities and relations that fall under a topic.

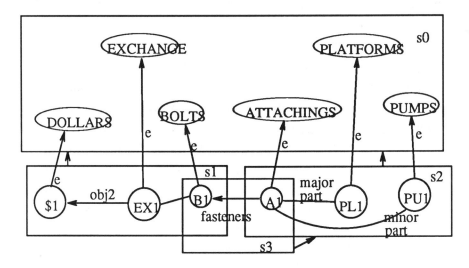

Figure 2.6. Partitioned network.

Secondly, and differently from standard frame and script notations, they display the equivalence of reference under differing intensional descriptions, the basic Fregean notion underlying all such logics. So, a given set of bolts corresponding to the "bolts" node can be considered under two quite different intensional descriptions: "what fastens platform parts together" and "what costs two dollars to replace."

Now this notational device is not equivalent to explicit belief, but it should be clear that it provides a mechanism by which belief environments could be introduced into NLP. The partitions could represent individual believers and the nodes and relations their beliefs: in that way entities could have different links between them in different partitions, and entities could be known under different descriptions to different believers. The opportunity was there even though it was not taken up within that particular project, yet, as we shall see, Grosz's metaphor of a "view" of partitions (ordering partitions in a chain) appeared exactly in Konolige's chaining of viewpoints in his logic for belief (Grosz, 1977, and see Section 2.6; cf. also Hayes, 1977.)

The direct introduction of belief representations and their attribution to different agents into NLP and AI came with the work of Perrault, Cohen and Allen. They adapted and refined (1969) Searle's speech act theory, separating out more clearly than he had the roles of speaker and hearer, attaching these to an explicit model of nested beliefs and setting the whole in an environment of goal-chaining so as to produce dialogues of the following sort:

Passenger at rail station: Do you know when the Windsor train arrives?

System: 9:30 at Track 6.

where the system does not give the foolish, but true, answer "Yes."

This was highly original work, unknown to us at the time of (Wilks & Bien 1979) and our brief description here in no way does justice to its complexity and sophistication. Here we shall simply draw attention to the key difference between their work and our own.

The emphasis of Perrault et al. is on speech acts and for that they assume a very simple theory of partitioned belief; our emphasis, by contrast, is on the latter and we assume that, if that is got right, a very simple theory of speech acts will follow, far simpler than theirs. In addition, they assume that all the nested beliefs required for any computation are laid out, as it were, in advance. Cohen (1978) uses a diagram of the form shown in Figure 2.7 to show nestings of beliefs:

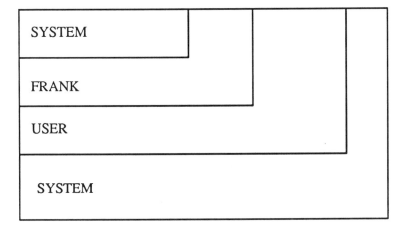

Figure 2.7. Cohen's form of belief nesting.

That space is an inclusion diagram in which individual beliefs, at any level of nesting, can be considered as elements in the space: a program simply accesses one when required in the appropriate partition. But this is neither psychologically nor computationally appropriate. Follow us through this *Gedankenexperiment*, if you will: Do you know what President Bush believes President Gorbachev believes about Saddam Hussein?

Of course, in a few moments, and believing what you do about the three individuals named, you can work out an appropriate nonempty belief set. But did you *already* know, and just access the partition? Surely not, for you took separate partitions and ascribed beliefs appropriately. That is the core of the idea behind *ViewGen*: the construction and maintenance of such ascribed objects. In their early work, Perrault et. al., were making a simplifying assumption so as to get on with what interested them. Perrault has recently reconsidered that position, (Perrault, 1990), leading to a position in terms of default logic much more like the one described here.

That their early position was no more plausible computationally than it was psychologically can be seen by considering what kind of information would be required to set up and maintain such a set of partitions in advance of any possible computations: you would need to perform the cross product of all the known beliefs of all believers known to your system! In one sense, what Cohen described in the figure was a formal semantics *in extenso* for the processes described in this book, and one's preference there may well be governed by one's taste as to formal semantics versus processes.

2.5.2. Noncomputational systems

Fauconnier's (1985) mental space theory uses environment-like entities to explore a number of the same issues as this book, but from a linguistic perspective. Although Fauconnier's account is not procedural in nature, there are certainly analogies between our default ascription mechanism and his notion (ibid. p. 91) of "maximising similarity" in a belief space, using notions like "in the absence of explicit contrary stipulation," etc. This is very similar to our own statements of the default rule (e.g., in Wilks & Bien, 1979), although it does not capture the sort of work we have described here and elsewhere on the strong limitations to the applicability of that rule in conditions of atypical belief (cf. 3.4.1). The main point to note is that Fauconnier makes great headway with difficult issues such as counterfactuals, presuppositions and ambiguities of propositional attitude reports by applying an environment-like "mental space" idea. Shadbolt's (1983) system is very similar, although psychological in style, and not worked out in as much detail as Fauconnier's. Dinsmore's work (1987) is also very much in the same tradition, although the center of his attention is always presuppositions and counterfactuals, which we do not consider a special topic within ascription to, and inference within, environments.

Of similar relevance is Johnson-Laird's (1983) use of explicit, nested groups of representational items in an application of his mental-model theory of human commonsense reasoning to propositional attitudes. In a different vein, there is a growing amount of work emanating from the modal-logic tradition that is conceding notion of belief "clusters" so as to make belief logics more accurately reflect commonsense views of belief. An example is Fagin and Halpern's (1987) local-reasoning logic. It is, however, strange that in this logic it is only in the *semantics* that any notion of clusters is made at all explicit as "frames of mind." What is important for *reasoning processes* is, of course, clustering made explicit in the representational expressions (cf. 3.1).

Chapter 2.6
Approaches to belief in AI

We shall now discuss the role that "belief" has played in artificial intelligence systems in general, outside the field of NLP proper. This section will not be highly critical, since virtually no work in AI has examined the problem of belief ascription. Most researchers have been interested in other problems, such as representation of belief sentences in various logics, resource-bounded reasoning, etc. These are all interesting problems in their own right, although some (such as representing *de dicto* versus *de re* belief sentences) are problems that disappear under the right conditions, or are fundamentally problems of interpretation of utterances, as we tried to show in 2.2. It will be clear from that remark, as well as previous sections, that we see belief processing by machines as firmly linked to the processing of natural languages, and not just as a detached representational issue. A side-effect of the position we adopted earlier (in the Introduction) that belief, to really be belief, requires a notion of nesting or the possibility of two differing believers, cuts us off from much excellent work in the field that calls itself belief: e.g., paradigms such as Pearl's (1987) and Truth Maintenance Systems (Doyle, 1979) which, on our view, are just inference systems.

2.6.1. Work of AI researchers on belief systems

In general our work has been (since that of Wilks and Bien, 1979) to construct a formalism and programs that capture the heuristic belief ascriptions that individuals actually perform in the process of understanding and participating in dialogue: that is to say, contentful, concrete beliefs and not merely meta-beliefs about the reasoning architecture of others, activities we suspect are rarely, if ever, undertaken. Thus our concern has been less with the powers of particular notations and proofs of their adequacy (the central feature of the work of Creary, 1979. Moore & Hendrix, 1979. Konolige, 1982; 1983; and Attardi & Simi, 1984 than

121

with the *content* of belief ascription.

The work of Maida (1983, 1986, 1988) is concerned with intensional representations and with the notion of simulative reasoning. His concerns are problems of shared reasoning strategies between agents, such as one agent's ability to decide that another agent is reasoning by *modus ponens*. Unfortunately, this problem could never be solved by means of a finite set of observations of a dialogue between the agents, since there will always be a range of plausible and possible strategies that another agent *might* use to reach the conclusions he does.

It seems much more natural to us to assume by default that the other's general strategies are like one's own, unless there is real information to the contrary. Concentration on such meta-issues that are not susceptible of proof seems to us only to delay the central issue, which is how to ascribe heuristically the actual beliefs of other believers. However, Maida (1983) is concerned with the very important, but we believe quite separable, issue of a heuristic rule for identifying intensional individuals under different descriptions.

Maida represents inexpressible items in beliefs (such as my belief that John knows his own phone number which cannot be expressed explicitly in my belief statement unless I, too, happen to know it) with two different methods: Haas constants and a form of Skolem function. In *ViewGen* this is done with lambda expressions, which are pretty much equivalent to the Skolem method (see 5.1.2).

Maida makes explicit, against conventional model theoretical semantics, that the objects under disussion and representation in belief spaces may or may not exist, and that there are correspondence problems between the objects in one believer's space and another's (for the system-believer, that is). Maida's own original work (1983) was on just this issue of ranking candidates as plausible referents of terms under conditions of belief.

Maida discusses the classic two-for-me-and-one-for-you confusions (see 2.2) under the term *compression,* and the reverse under the name *dispersion.* He holds the view that under dispersion, where you have two concepts I believe to be coreferential, as when the morning and evening stars for you are both Venus for me, then that requires that I believe you believe them to be coreferential (his principle is called Relative Denotation Identity or RDI). If he were right then Frege's key example could not be stated and Oedipus would inevitably know his mother and wife were the same person, and hence Greek literature could not have been written. As he puts it, if two symbols denote the same thing, then any believer, say Ralph, believes they denote the same thing:

$$All \; x,y. \; rel\text{-}den \; (Ralph, x) = rel\text{-}den \; (Ralph, y) <=> believes \; Ralph \; '(=x, y).$$

Maida seeks some interpretation of this statement (including weakening *rel-den*) so that he can continue to believe it! His principles of uniformity can be seen as closely linked to other very general notions. They are a form of Davidson's (1967) "principle of charity": Communication and understanding are only possible on the assumption that we ascribe our general principles to others. The same is true for *ViewGen* except that it explicitly allows special cases to override the default although, as we have noted, it is not easy to see what could be evidence for such overriding in the case of general reasoning principles.

Again, if Maida believes all believers adopt the principles of uniformity, then that effectively creates a notion of mutual belief at a much higher level than the standard "we see a candle between us" cases (see 2.4.2). However, our position remains that the default rule in *ViewGen* creates all that is needed of mutual belief without any need to make it a special category of belief in a calculus.

Although it might appear from the title of Martins and Shapiro (1983) "Reasoning in Multiple Belief Spaces" that they are concerned like us with nested beliefs, this is not the case. Their belief spaces do not correspond naturally to the beliefs of a particular individual, nor to one individual's beliefs about another's. They are concerned instead with sets of facts that enable mutual planning of tasks; hence their multiple belief spaces are closer to Weyhrauch's *contexts* (Weyhrauch, 1980) to the extent that both deal with the separation of facts from consequences, and of the justifications for individual facts or consequences.

Furthermore, Martins and Shapiro never need to consider BELIEVE or KNOW operators, so there seems little justification for naming their sets belief spaces, although they do concern themselves with belief revision (also known as Truth Maintenance, cf. Doyle, 1979, 1980; Reiter and de Kleer, 1987).

Huang, McCalla, and Greer (1989) have identified two forms of belief revision, which they term *evolutionary* and *revolutionary*. Their system for evolutionary belief revision is designed to institute and efficiently identify sets of beliefs whose removal reestablishes consistency in the system with minimum change. In other words, evolutionary change is designed to be the smallest change required to maintain consistency. This, they claim, is coherent with the idea of progressively

changing our views, as might be done by a tutor talking to a student. Revolutionary changes, on the other hand, correspond to "quantum changes" in comprehension
that are often observed in students' learning patterns when a threshold state is
crossed.

Rao and Foo (1989) present a view of belief revision that is similar to the
evolutionary method of Huang, McCalla, and Greer by advocating a *minimal
change* approach. They augment this by adding a principle of *maximal coherence*
by which they mean that as many coherent (consistent) beliefs as possible should
be maintained although to us these appear to be duals rather than separate principles (by minimizing the number of beliefs you change you must be maximizing
those that you do not change). They use their theory of belief revision as the foundation of a theory of action which they claim suffers from neither the *frame problem* (McCarthy and Hayes, 1969) nor the *ramification problem* (Hanks and McDermott, 1987). The work of Laskey and Lehner (1988) is concerned with unifying
Dempster-Shafer's approach to belief maintenance with assumption-based
approaches. They argue that significant advantanges may be gained by such a
unification including a greater number of control strategies to improve efficiency
and control of reasoning. So, defaults can be used to represent working assumptions, whereas degree of conflict between beliefs can be used to indicate when revision is required.

Induction is normally distinguished as a type of reasoning, one in which a set
of instances is to be generalized. This type of reasoning is obviously defeasible
(we are never sure that an induced generalization will not be proved wrong by the
next observation) and so is subject to revision when its generalizations are considered as beliefs. Rose and Langley (1987) propose a method by which the generalizations can themselves be used to guide the revision of beliefs (premises).
They propose a number of heuristics that can be applied to revision of premises.
The first is used to "prefer revision to premises that support relatively weak generalizations" (Rose and Langley, 1987: p. 750). So by this heuristic, weak generalizations are weeded out before stronger ones. Their second heuristic allows them to
select for revisions that confirm the predictions of stronger generalizations. These
two heuristics are based on the idea that scientific theories tend to become
entrenched, and that only an accumulation of evidence against them eventually
causes them to be overthrown.

The work of Konolige (1982, 1983, 1985, 1986, 1987) is concerned with logics of belief that permit a resource-bounded account of deduction that avoids the

assumption (found in many possible world models of belief, e.g. Moore, 1977) of deductive closure of belief; namely, that we believe all the conclusions of our beliefs. Konolige considers objects he calls views (e.g., $v=John,Sue,Kim$ is John's view of what Sue believes Kim believes); these views are exactly what we call nestings of beliefs. Konolige is not particularly concerned with the construction of these views although he does consider construction of purely introspective views (cited later).

The deductive model of belief describes an agent's beliefs as a set of sentences in a formal language known as the base set, and a deductive method for deriving consequences from those sentences. A belief subsystem is defined to be a base set of sentences, a set of inference rules and a control strategy for deducing consequences. A belief is submitted to the belief subsystem as a query of the form "is P believed?" and the subsystem will respond with YES or NO for an ideal agent, or UND for a real agent that can return *UNDecided* to a belief query.

Konolige further develops the notion of an *introspective belief subsystem*, capable of reasoning about its own beliefs by submitting the belief query to a nested belief subsystem. For example, if the query *"do I believe that I believe P?"* is submitted to a belief subsystem (M) then the query *"do I believe P?"* will be submitted by M to another belief subsystem (IM). Konolige's system allows for recursive operations of this form to belief subsystems $I^n M$.

Konolige has no construction for views, but is concerned with deduction within such sets and the problem of whether each individual has the same deductive system. This is better covered, we suggest (as does Maida), by some general rationality postulate. Konolige's main concern is to give a resource-limited account of a deduction schema so as to avoid the assumption (present in the possible world models of Moore and Hutchins, 1981) that one must believe all the consequences of one's beliefs.

McCarthy's work (McCarthy, 1979) is a first order theory of individual concepts and propositions (cf. Carnap, 1956). Individual concepts are similar to intensional concepts, and McCarthy's purpose is to give an explanation of individual concepts in first order logic without using modal operators such as POSSIBLE and NECESSARY. Logical formalisms often include the *extensions* of objects (i.e., the actual objects, not just representations of them), a drawback of McCarthy's system. McCarthy likens his work to that of Church (1951), which includes the notion of having concepts of concepts. McCarthy claims that all this can be handled within first order logic, which does not quantify over predicates and is without modal operators as are those cited earlier.

Moore's work (Moore, 1977); concentrates on the term "knowledge" rather than "belief," although as we have noted the use of the term *knowledge* in solipsistic AI is perhaps misleading. The information in AI systems labelled as knowledge frequently includes hypothetical objects and false statements. This type of information does not fit any standard notion of knowledge, and it is always less misleading to consider it as belief. A person does not necessarily know a fact because he asserts that he knows something; he knows something if he asserts a belief that is true (if we follow Russell, 1919), one for which he also has good reasons. But all this is normally beyond the scope of AI analysis. Moore's work is based on that of Hintikka (1962) and employs "rigid designators" that relate intensional concepts to their extensions. As with McCarthy, he is interested in first order representations.

On the other hand, Moore & Hendrix (1979) are explicitly concerned with computational belief systems and belief sentences, as well as such issues as disambiguating the use of indexicals (terms that change meaning depending on who is using them and when they are being used, e.g., "I", "he" and "now") in beliefs and how they should be represented. They discuss Perry's contention (1977, 1979, followed in Rapaport's account discussed in 2.2) that the indexical "I" is essential and cannot be replaced by a nonindexical description. They explain the use of "I" by assuming that the system has an individual constant in its internal language that intrinsically refers to the system itself, and that the system uses "I" in English translations of its internal language.

The work of Kobsa (1984, 1988) is concerned with representational issues in handling infinite-reflexive beliefs, the main type of which are *mutual beliefs* (see 2.4.2). Of particular concern to us is deriving mutual beliefs from user assertions, and Kobsa's approach to belief representation is one that partitions belief spaces according to the nesting of beliefs. In this it is similar to the approach taken by Maida (1986) and by ourselves. However, in order to increase the expressivity of partitions to represent mutual beliefs Kobsa introduces a notion he calls *acceptance attitudes*. These acceptance attitudes have the additional benefit that they eliminate the necessity of having a proliferation of partitions to represent disjunctive beliefs.

In this book we gloss over for the most part the distinction between knowledge and belief. One view often presented in philosophical literature is that of knowledge as "justified true belief": somebody has a piece of knowledge if it is both true *and* the person has a justification for believing it. This last part "coincidentally" eliminates true belief from being considered as knowledge; Russell's example of looking at a stopped clock at the same time at which it stopped gives you a belief in the time that is unjustified, even though true. Here would like to consider an alternative definition of belief: *belief as defeasible knowledge*, as proposed by Shoham and Moses, (1989). They claim that this is advantageous because it allows belief to follow from knowledge by one simple principle rather than a set of axioms. Although this approach has undeniable advantages from the perspective of simplicity of formalization, from the perspective of cognitive modelling this approach suffers from treating knowledge as a wholly objective phenomenon, a view that strongly conflicts with a cognitive view of knowledge.

Haas, like Konolige, is concerned with giving a resource-limited account of reasoning about beliefs, and aims to give such an account firmly within the confines of first order logic (1986). Furthermore, he is interested in relating belief and planning and in giving an account of time in first order logic. He presents a syntactic theory of belief involving quoted entities: quoting entities in a formula allows for first-order representations of propositional attitudes. Such theories have been developed by others (notably Quine, 1943, 1947). To see the motivation of quotation systems, consider the following: if we wished to represent that John believes that snow is white we might be tempted to represent it in this way —

(S1) (believe John (white snow))

This form has two separate problems, the first of which is that the representation of what John believes, namely "(white snow)" will, on the assumption that the whole expression S1 is truth functional, denote the truth value of the proposition that snow is white and not the proposition itself, which is what we want. In other words, (S1) represents that John believes some truth and **not** that John believes that snow is white. On such a view there is only one thing to be believed, which makes for an unsatisfactory account. A second drawback is that S1 is not a first order predicate expression because its form is equivalent to quantifying over predicates ("white" in this case) which is the defining characteristic of higher (non-first) order predicate logic.

A quotation system overcomes this problem and permits first order expressions of belief sentences, that allow for variables in the believed proposition, to be quantified outside the belief sentence. Thus (S2) expresses the proposition that John believes that Mary's phone number is some value n, and that n is the number 509-378-3425.

(S2) (some *n*
      (believe John ('= ('PhoneNumber 'Mary) *n*))
      &
      (Has-Value *n* 509-378-3425))

Levesque is interested in "attempting to characterize a kind of belief that forms a more appropriate basis for knowledge representation systems than that captured by the usual possible-worlds formalizations begun by Hintikka" (Levesque, 1984, p. 198; cf. Hintikka, 1962). As with Konolige and Haas, Levesque is particularly interested in an account that is independent of the need for deductive closure (that all the consequences of an agents' beliefs must also be believed by the agent). Levesque's solution is to characterize two forms of belief: explicit belief (the beliefs that an agent has) and implicit belief (the consequences of an agent's beliefs).

Following Barwise and Perry (1983), Levesque defines a *situation* to be a partial possible-world that supports the truth of some sentences (those relevant to the current circumstances) but do not deal with the truth of other sentences (those that are not relevant to the current circumstances). Explicit belief is then identified with a set of situations. The resulting logic **L** is both sound and complete; furthermore, it has reasonable computational properties. The intuitive difficulty with his original distinction, however, remains; there are (possibly infinitely) many things we believe when asked about them which we did not know we did, and yet which are not obviously consequences of other things we believe. "The wall behind us is red" on Levesque's view must be explicit if true, yet it was not made explicit in the normal sense of the word until we just made it so.

The work of Fagin and Halpern (1987) and Halpern and Moses (1985) extends the work of Levesque in developing logics for belief that do not require deductive closure. In Fagin and Halpern (1987), three logics are introduced: the first is an extension to Levesque's logic **L** to enable it to handle multiple agents and nested belief, the second is a logic that deals with the notion of "awareness" (the idea that an agent must be aware of a concept before having beliefs about that concept), and the third is a logic that partitions an agent's beliefs into clusters so the agent is a "society of minds" (cf. Doyle, 1983) that may contradict each other. One major lack in their work is that they are unable to handle quantified statements.

An investigation of various modal logics of knowledge and belief is given in Halpern and Moses (1985). In particular, they investigate the complexity of these logics, provide *worst-case* analyses for several of them, and claim that most interesting cases are not worst-case but closer to *best-case*. They note that for some of these logics (such as one-knower S5), a decision procedure for the satisfiability of formulae is an NP-Complete problem as it is for propositional logic.

In this book we make few commitments to representations for beliefs, but the subject of belief representation is an important one with much discussion behind it. Belief is often referred to as a "modal operator," since it is usually seen as a modifier of sentences. Work by Montague (1963) seemed to indicate that such operators could not be consistently represented in first-order logic (cf. also, e.g., Thomason, 1980); however, the work of des Rivieres and Levesque (1986) showed that by devising a weak version of first-order logic they could avoid many of the paradoxes. Perlis (1986), who has been concerned with devising a consistent treatment for self-referential contexts of propositional attitudes where one runs the risk of introducing paradoxes, concluded from this work that unqualified substitutive mechanisms present the same difficulties for modal treatments as they do for first-order ones, although it seems easier to "fix" the first-order treatments than the modal ones. Furthermore, he argues that even for an ideal reasoner, the belief "Bel x -> x" renders the system inconsistent. The last, he claims, means that belief cannot be equated with knowledge if consistency is to be maintained.

Koons (1988) further undermines the position of Montague (1963) and Thomason (1980) by showing that even in their systems, which disallow self-reference, there are still conditions under which paradoxes can arise. He suggests that a possible way out of the problem is to introduce a scheme of degrees of belief. Unfortunately, it appears that this will only work where we can explicitly express a greater degree of belief in one of the statements that leads to the paradox than the other — effectively eliminating the paradox by denying its existence as a real paradox.

There are two strong philosophical stands on the nature of belief that have been adopted by AI researchers: in one, a belief is a relation between an agent and a proposition and formal analyses of this often make use of *possible-world* semantics; in the other, a belief is a relation between an agent and a *sentence* that expresses a proposition. A problem of the first approach is that of *logical omniscience* whereby an agent is taken to believe all the logical entailments of his beliefs. A number of approaches to solving this problem have been proposed that incorporate elements of the second stand on the nature of belief, that of a relation between an agent and a sentence (Levesque, 1984; Fagin and Halpern, 1987).

However, Konolige (1986) and Hadley (1988) both claim that the proposed solutions do not work.

Konolige (1986) claims that the failure is not one of irreconcilable differences between the two approaches; rather, the possible-worlds semantics often used for the propositional approach is suspect and should be reconsidered. He does not, however, offer an alternative semantics. Hadley attacks the work of Levesque on the grounds that it cannot distinguish between incoherent situations, and the work of Fagin and Halpern on difficulties with their "awareness" operator. On the other hand, he goes further than Konolige, by offering an alternative approach: This approach is based on an intensional view of belief, where intensional equivalence is used in place of strict logical consequence.

Lesperance (1989) investigates the account of *de re* beliefs under a possible-worlds semantics and concludes that much knowledge required for planning actions does not depend on such beliefs, but rather on *de se* type beliefs which have received little if any attention in the possible-worlds literature. Furthermore, Lesperance claims that his analysis has shown that, although possible-world approaches can distinguish between *de se* and non-*de se* beliefs (as argued by Stalnaker, 1981), they are unable to characterize what he refers to as the "internal aspects of belief states": *"what two agents have in common when the world appears the same when viewed from their distinct perspectives"* (Lesperance, 1989: p. 869). To accommodate such characterization, Lesperance proposes a logic that is similar to the possible-worlds approach in which the accessibility relation characterizes both a world and a perspective from which it is viewed.

The work of Craddock and Browse (1986) is within a connectionist framework, and bases its reasoning on whether a proposition should be believed on a system of (a) measures of certitude for propositions and (b) endorsements of propositions by other propositions (i.e., having both beliefs p in which $p \rightarrow q$ is an endorsement for believing q). Heuristics are presented that evaluate the endorsements for propositions and give a value of certitude in the belief that the propositions are true. As opposed to many connectionist systems, they have nonnumeric representations of uncertainty in addition to numeric values.

Sidner and Israel (1981) propose two principles for ascribing beliefs, based on utterances and actions of individuals. The first (called the *Sincerity* rule) is that if some individual X is trying to convince another individual Y that X believes some proposition P, then we can assume that X believes P. The second (called the *Reliability* rule) is similar in intent to what we refer to as *percolation* (5.1.4): Y believes that X believes P, and further that X is "reliably informed" about P, then Y can believe P as well. Later, we give a more detailed account of reliability including when it fails.

Pollack (1986) is concerned with the differing beliefs that two agents have about actions in a specific domain, and the possible failure of communication because of these differences. This work is closely related to the work of Cohen and Levesque (1980, 1985) and Allen (1983). In particular, she is interested in plan inferencing and its relationship to beliefs, and contends that "Judgements that a plan is invalid are associated with particular discrepancies between the beliefs that the observer ascribes to the actor when the former believes that the latter has some plan, and the beliefs that the observer herself holds." (p. 208).

In other words, the observer can determine that an actor's plan is invalid based on the differences between the beliefs that the observer has, and the beliefs that the observer believes that the actor has. Pollack holds that not only must the observer ascribe a set of beliefs to an actor that would cause the observer to believe that the actor has some plan, but he should also ascribe beliefs that justify the plan (from the actor's perspective). This is a return within AI to an old Polish tradition of inference as in Bochenski (1961), who argued that we should assume others believe premises that make what they accept true, a tradition now claimed as part of the Piercean notion of abduction (1932).

A central issue in plan recognition and evaluation is in determining what would be the best plan ascription to make to another agent, given some observed actions of the agent; this issue is tackled by Konolige and Pollack (1989). However, although they discuss the significance of being able to ascribe beliefs, they do not offer a model for belief ascription; the model of plan ascription that they propose is one based direct argumentation. For example: "if the observer O can ascribe to the actor A a belief that another agent B has some object Obj that A wants, then the observer is justified in ascribing to A a plan fragment that involves asking B for Obj." Although this will work for cases such as those cited by Konolige and Pollack, we feel that a more general method of plan ascription could be achieved *through* belief ascription: that is, the system acts as if it is the agent (A in the above case) doing the planning. The system formulates the plan for itself and then attempts to ascribe the plan to the other agent in the same fashion as it would do for a belief. Such an approach, we argue, would allow the use of stereotypes for devising and ascribing plans such that agents are not attributed plans beyond their capabilities (i.e., a naive user of an on-line help system would not be attributed plans for using advanced features of the help system).

Appelt and Pollack's work (1990) is a continuation of the work of Konolige and Pollack (1989) which advocates the use of *weighted abduction* in selecting the "best" mental state to explain the observed actions of an agent. Weighted abduction is a method that applies costs or weighting factors to each of a set of literals and then in proving some goal seeks to establish a set of assumptions that lead to a lowest cost proof. Appelt and Pollack apply such weighted abduction to the argument procedures defined in Konolige and Pollack (1989), although it is not yet possible to determine the computational complexity increase that the former approach yields.

Sycara (1989) is concerned with working around uncooperative agents by using persuasion to modify the plans of the other agents. This requires negotiation with the agents in question, in turn requiring "the ability to (a) represent and maintain belief models, (b) reason about other agents beliefs, (c) influence other agents, beliefs, and behaviour" although how such models are derived is glossed over by saying that case-based reasoning on previously encountered agents can be used to derive the models. This work touches on the subject of deception, where other agents are uncooperative to the point of misleading the system.

The work of Taylor and Whitehill (1981) attempts to give an explanation of deception using models of the beliefs of agents. They describe a representation for complex nestings of beliefs that uses cyclic structures. For example, Figure 2.8 represents two sets of beliefs. The box marked **1** represents Andy's belief that Maggie is married. The box enclosed in box **1** represents a nested model, or rather a pointer to a nested model via the number inside it. The number is a reference to box **2** (Maggie's beliefs) so we can read this as Andy's belief that Maggie believes ... (whatever is contained in box **2**).

Box **2** represents Maggie's belief that she is married. It also contains the nested model of Andy's beliefs. From the structures in the above figure we can create any nested belief of the form "Andy believes that Maggie believes that Andy believes..." or of the form "Maggie believes that Andy believes that Maggie believes..." simply by chasing through from one box to the next via the pointers enclosed in the boxes.

Taylor and Whitehill propose a template to detect deception: suppose M represents Maggie's beliefs and MAM represents what Maggie believes Andy believes Maggie believes, they suggest that if comparing M to MAM results in a

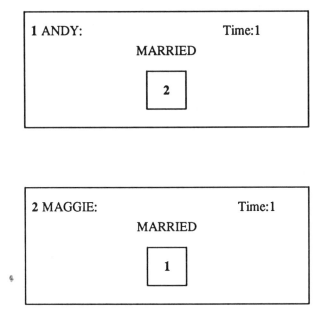

Figure 2.8 Cyclic Belief Structures for Andy and Maggie's Beliefs.

difference, then there is a deception. They claim that *MAM* not being equal to *M* represents the intention of the deception, and that *M* not being equal to *MA* represents the success of the deception. However, they fail to realize that the inequality of *M* and *MAM does not represent an intention to deceive*, but rather represents a difference in beliefs between Andy and Maggie, of which Andy is unaware. There are no Searle-like intentions to be inferred reliably from this state (Searle, 1969). It may have occurred because Andy is less informed than Maggie (Maggie might be expert about a topic that Andy is naive about), so rather than identifying deception, they are identifying belief mismatches.

It is generally assumed in the domains of comprehension and planning that the agents with which the system is interacting are not deliberately attempting to mislead it. Taylor and Whitehill (1981, cited earlier) proposed a template system for detecting deception although we argue that it, in fact, detects belief mismatches. The work of Rose (1985) uses a variant of the "three wise men" problem (see Konolige, 1982 and section 5.1) to explore deception. He proposes a categorization of deceptive behaviour into four classes: (a) intentional deception (misleading behaviour), (b) unintentional deception (misinterpreted behaviour), (c) unintentional self-deception (naive behaviour), and (d) intentional self-deception (irrational behavior). The first class is differentiated from the second by a deliberate attempt to deceive; in the first someone lies, whereas in the second their actions or statements are misinterpreted by another. The third and fourth classes deal with self-deception, again differentiated by intention.

Iterated propositional attitudes are nestings of propositions involving predicates such as *BELIEVE, KNOW, WANT,* and *DESIRE* and the work of Creary (1979) is an attempt to give an intensional theory for representing such nestings. Sentence (S3) is the type of sentence that interests us here:

(S3) Pat believes that Mike wants to meet Jim's wife.

Creary gives three possible semantic interpretations for sentence (S3): Pat believes that Mike wants to meet the person who is Jim's wife (whoever she is); Pat believes that Mike wants to meet somebody who incidentally happens to be Jim's wife (a fact that may or may not be known to Mike); Pat believes that Mike wants to meet a specific person who happens to be Jim's wife, although neither Pat nor Mike necessarily know this fact. Creary offers a system that allows for a different representation for each reading: however, his methods have been criticized as being unreadable (Maida, 1983) and suffering from more fundamental problems involving the use of concept functions (Barnden, 1983).

Barnden (1983, 1986), too, is interested in propositional attitudes and intensional entities. Barnden points out difficulties with Creary's "concept-functions" (functions that act on and produce concepts) and proposes, instead, a concept forming function that he claims "has a more primitive and natural notation base than Creary's ...[concept function system]... has" (Barnden, 1983, p. 280).

In particular, Barnden's system avoids problems involving the quantification of variables within propositions that are themselves the objects of propositional attitudes. He achieves this by transforming quantified expressions into expressions that contain no variables. He introduces two entities: ', a function that returns the *standard-concept-of* some intensional concept, and ¢, a function that produces a concept from a proposition.

Barnden (1986) emphasizes that a representational scheme can be used by a cognitive system as a basis for its cognitive processes, or as a means for describing the mental states of cognitive agents. These two separate uses can be mixed, as when one agent is reasoning about another agent's reasoning. Barnden claims that serious problems are encountered when these two uses are not separated clearly.

Reeves (1988) presents an interestingly different aspect of belief: namely, the use of conflicting patterns of belief to represent moral attitudes toward events in a story that presents moral problems. Reeve contends that strong attitudes are invoked by morally wrong situations and that such attitudes are a measure of *interest* in the story. Such attitudes, he proposes, can be represented by structures he terms Belief Conflict Patterns (BCPs), which serve a number of purposes, including indicating why a story is interesting, organizing reasons for a belief conflict, helping resolve coherency problems, directing attention towards aspects of a story that are important, and providing a framework for recognizing themes. The actual conflict they represent is that between a reader's understanding of a story and his ethical evaluation of the story. BCPs are classified into categories of good things happening to bad people, bad things happening to good people, good people doing bad things, and bad people doing good things. A problem with Reeve's classification of BCPs is that bad things happening to bad people, and bad people doing bad things, do not appear to generate moral conflicts in the reader except indirectly (bad people doing bad things may cause a bad thing to happen to a good person, etc.).

Among the works that have begun to appear in which defeasible inferences and beliefs are prioritized, is that of Konolige (1987). His method is based on autoepistemic logic, with the addition that evidence is divided into subtheories that are hierarchically organized. In this way, entire extensions form a priority hierarchy, rather than just individual statements (as is the case in prioritized circumscription: see Lifschitz, 1984). An added advantage is that extensions containing circular reasoning are rendered impossible, whereas in nonhierarchical autoepistemic logic, an elaborate characterization of the extensions was required to eliminate them. This hierarchic organization of extensions is particularly useful for conceptualizing taxonomic hierarchies with exceptions, for extension organization mimics that of the taxonomic hierarchy.

An interesting approach to default reasoning is the THEORIST system described in Poole's (1988) and Van Arragon's (1990) extensions to this system. The THEORIST system divides formulae into two sets: facts and defaults. If a logical consequence is derived from these facts and defaults, then they are said to explain the consequence. Addition of facts at a later time may mean that the consequence can no longer be explained. What Van Arragon proposes is an adaption of the THEORIST system. He extends Poole's formalism to allow for many agents, and, in particular, a nesting of the facts and defaults of agents. This extension allows the use of defaults for reasoning about other defaults, as well as the ability to do belief ascription. The Prioritized Theorist (Brewka, 1989) is a modified version of the THEORIST that reasons with degrees of certainty of belief by means of priority levels on defaults. In the same way as he extends the Theorist system, Van Arragon extends the Prioritized Theorist by adding the ability to reason about many agents and in particular, to reason about other agents.

Chapter 3
Belief Ascription

Chapter 3.1
Representational structure

In order to present the program *ViewGen* in this book, we have made few representational commitments: the clustering or partitioning of belief representations into environments, and the use of a simple form of first-order predicate expressions to represent the content of individual beliefs. That is all that is required to demonstrate the feasibility of the basic ideas underlying *ViewGen*, namely: the default ascription algorithm, and its modifications and extensions to questions of intensional identification and metaphor. The specific question of partitions, as opposed to what was earlier called the Heap-view-of-reasoning (by which we mean mental contents seen as an unorganized list of propositions), is defended in the next section (3.2).

Simple predicate logic formalism is convenient both to program in Prolog, and as a *lingua franca* of communication between AI researchers: everyone can read it and there is (more or less) a conspiracy to ignore the ways in which such a language cannot possibly express either the complexity of content of nontrivial beliefs or the relations between them (we return to real issues of complexity in the discussion of metaphor at the end of the book as well as the adaptation of our basic algorithm to deal with that phenomenon). But again, communication with the reader would be greatly hindered if we did not restrict ourselves (as we, in fact, do) to discussing even metaphor in terms of simple predicate expressions.

In this section we want to note the disastrous simplification involved in that choice, recall the representational choices and commitments made in earlier versions of the present work, and note two other representational commitments concerning the partition of environments to be made in what follows.

3.1.1. The problem of representational atoms

The discussion of earlier sections (especially 2.1.3) did not stress why so simple a representation is necessarily inadequate. A language of thought or belief cannot be anything so like English in its predicate content, and structured so like predicate calculus formulas. The evolutionary chances of that combination matching whatever code human brains process is simply too low.

A completely separate NLP and computational issue is that, leaving aside all issues of structural ambiguity, the word symbols of English are highly ambiguous and have no clear content when used in formal structures, beyond the content that we, as readers, impose on them. This presents few problems in simple examples but enormous ones if we step outside that very narrow area. If we take the (now widely accepted) position that metaphor is commonplace, then it follows that much commonplace English is metaphorical. As we shall see in the metaphor section later (6.1), it is by no means obvious how to represent metaphorical commonplaces like "Prussia attacked France in 1871." The statement is true, simple, and clear, but what is to be the representation of "Prussia" over and above using that English (or any other) atom, and keeping our minds shut to serious problems?

There are solutions to the problem on offer. Two current ones are connectionism and various versions of formal semantics, such as situation semantics. In the former (e.g., Smolensky, 1988), it is agreed that symbols are at some processing level unrealistic, and attempts are made to show that symbolic structures can be grounded or justified in nonsymbolic, quantitatively-based, networks that are plausible candidates for brain activities. This is an attractive theory, but one of us has argued elsewhere why this solution is as yet unconvincing (Wilks, 1990), and why we elect to stay within the "symbolic paradigm" with all its faults.

We discussed earlier (2.1.2.4) some of the solutions offered within the model theoretic semantics paradigm. In general, these come down to grounding certain key primitive arguments or predicates in abstract extensional entities, and reaching the others by meaning postulates that relate nonprimitives to grounded primitives. We have argued elsewhere (Wilks 1982) that the creation of such entities does not solve the problems it purports to: the entities remain symbolic, and do not take us out of the world of symbols to the real world as such semanticists seem to believe; and in no way does it touch the core problem of the sheer vagueness, ambiguity, and lack of clear reference of English words. Situation semantics (2.1.2.4) is said to avoid this criticism because it expresses a "relational view of meaning" with no such primitive symbols or extensions but, as we showed earlier, that is just not so.

What solutions are available within AI itself? Two standard ways of dealing with this problem are (a) to argue that there are, in some useful sense, primitive predicates for representation that do not need model theoretic semantic defenses for their use, and (b) that the ultimate grounding of predicates (primitive or not) is procedural in nature.

An early example of (a) would have been Schank's primitive actions (1972) in conceptual dependency, which he argued were not English in spite of their appearances, and needed only grounding in the human brain. This was, in essence, a reduced instruction set version of the LOT hypothesis. We argued elsewhere (Wilks, 1982) that there could be perfectly reasonable defenses of primitives on heuristic processing grounds, quite separate from the English-linguistic-imperialism of LOT approaches. On our view, there was no special English form of such atoms nor any special vocabulary of them. Moreover, although such primitives could still be so called, they could also appear in dictionaries and have definitions themselves. That may seem inconsistent with the use of the word "primitive" as "undefinable" but, in fact, all English words appear in dictionaries and have definitions, even though, as we all know, most of the definitions of those that are used to define other words (the "most primitive words of the language") are vacuous.

There was a debate (Bobrow and Winograd, 1977; Lehnert and Wilks, 1979) on primitives in relation to the language KRL, whose authors had strongly denied they made use of primitives. That consensus on KRL and primitives is consistent with (b) cited earlier: procedural semantics, a way of grounding predicates other than in extensional entities but rather by the procedures that use them. We have expressed a view elsewhere on this issue (Wilks, 1982), but basically some form of procedural semantics is an assumption behind this book: the entities used in the representations of a system complex enough to constitute an artificial believer, will be procedural in nature as opposed to some present or future form of model-theoretic semantics (a system not able to represent the complex behaviors of the symbols used to capture language and belief).

None of this will be needed to defend the program that forms the core of this book. Yet it is useful to set out our deepest assumptions, which are:

(a) justification is ultimately given by procedures rather than by model-theoretic methods;

(b) primitive predicates and arguments are a useful heuristic, provided one has determinate ways of linking them back into complex definitional representations such as those provided by a substantial dictionary or world model.

We cannot fulfill the promise of (b) here, but have shown in other work going on in parallel (Wilks et al., 1988, 1990) how we expect realistic meaning representations to be founded on network and predicate structures derived from large dictionaries. A reader may ask at this point: Why dictionaries rather than encyclopedic models of the world? We shall return to that matter later in connection to the relationship of meaning to world knowledge. The views on the representation of language and belief set out here could be parodied as: "you think meaning is just more words." And that may be a fair "slogan" version of our views, in so far as slogans are ever fair — one of us indeed attempted some while ago to set out a philosophical defense of just such a view (Wilks, 1971). Whatever its philosophical status, such a view is a practical one for anyone committed to the symbolic paradigm in AI, and anyone who denies the practical and metaphysical basis of model theoretic semantics. It might even be said to be a more complex and realistic version of the LOT hypothesis.

3.1.2. Granularity

Another dimension of representation is sometimes called grain, level, or alternative representations or perspectives. Suppose that certain institutional "facts" about the Xerox corporation differ from corresponding "facts" about IBM in certain structural ways, one of which might be that they have incomparable notions of "office" (different levels of description of a workforce grouping in the two organizations): this situation is commonplace, and was what the KRL designers (Bobrow and Winograd, 1977) originally intended to explicate with their notion of "perspective." That can be illustrated very simply with notions like "house": a house can be either a spatial point at a crossroads, say, or a container for living in, and quite different facts and inferences bear upon the two perspectives. But a major difference between our approach and that of KRL, is that the latter's designers had no notion of differing perspectives corresponding to different belief spaces.

However, their aim was much the same as ours in that this idea, whatever one calls it, widens one's notion of consistency because the differing perspectives on the house or office concept must not be thought of as contradictory, even though they are often formally inconsistent (i.e., one notion of "house" has volume, the other does not). The same notion of a wider consistency underlies more recent discussions under the heading "granularity" (e.g., Hobbs 1985). In *ViewGen*, this consistency is preserved by segregating beliefs within environments in the hope that consistency between or across environments need only be assessed under the kind of control given by the ascription mechanism. The underlying aims here go back a very long way to the closure of Leibniz's monads (1951), and to the insulation given in formal areas by the notion of "truth in a model," one that Tarski found ultimately unacceptable (1944) since there was only one objective world for him. If acceptance of that last statement is to be the criterion for the application of the term "realist" as it normally is, our approach is certainly not a realist one and we suspect no AI approach ever can be.

A striking example of Lenat's (Lenat et al., 1986) is appropriate here: consider the question, "Is there a large mass of blood near your steering wheel?" The answer should be "yes" if the person questioned is near the wheel since a person is undoubtedly a large mass of blood. The question would normally be answered negatively, because people do not store in their PERSON representation the fact that a person is, or contains, a large mass of blood (among other things), even though there is probably enough information in the representation to infer it via "Person has body "and" body contains 6 liters blood," etc. This is precisely what many would call a granularity issue: a preference for storing certain facts at certain levels, which for us means in some partitions rather than others.

3.1.3. Pseudo-texts and frame structures

In earlier versions of the work in this book (Wilks and Bien, 1983), we argued that sets of beliefs stacked in environments could be seen as simple versions of framelike entities called *pseudo-texts* (PTs). We are not asserting that here, but are recalling what the representational point of such entities was.

PTs were introduced as representational items designed to have the structure that would be produced by a parser parsing a text. Hence, the use of "text" in the name of the representation was deliberate, and under that lay the implicit claim that the structures of most representations were, in fact, more like the structures of text than their authors admitted. Current logic-based representations in NLP/KR were not English- (or natural language-) free in the way their authors pretended and we might as well admit that fact. The deepest assumption of that was therefore like Fodor's: that thought is language-like, but then differed from his in the ways we have set out.

PTs were thus unrefined (and in that sense unframelike) items of knowledge that had not been reclassified and checked against some permanent, semantic, memory. One could put this point by saying that the knowledge structure held by the system about Frank is in some sense only a narrative about Frank. It can be thought of as a text representation and an earlier paper (Wilks, 1977) argued that structures coming from a semantic parser of natural English could themselves be reasonable memory structures for certain well-defined purposes.

The PTs were considered as being packed into memory schemata together with topic-specific inference rules. The difference between pseudo-texts and inference rules may be often neglected, as it is in the environments of this book. Again, it was a strong assumption there that the representation of the system's beliefs about entities (humans, etc.), and the beliefs of such entities, are all in the same format as more structural beliefs of the system about itself and its own functioning. A further feature of that approach was the context-dependent nature of descriptions within PTs and their associated pointers (cf. Norman and Bobrow, 1975).

The context dependency of descriptions originally meant that they were never more precise than needed in the context of their creation. But we understand the feature in a broader sense: a given description in various contexts may refer to different items. For example (see 2.2.1), "the murderer" in the environment of John's beliefs may refer to Jones, but in the environment of Mary's beliefs to Smith. In other words, the context-dependent descriptions supply us with the power of intensional logic that is necessary for an adequate knowledge representation, as we have noted. Environments can properly be seen as a reversion to frames, in Minsky's sense of the representation of individual entities, as well as that of more generic entities, which is what the mainstream frame movement became.

PT's were also for general items such as groups of humans, objects, substances and classes as well as individuals like my car, a jury, a professor, a salesman, sulphur, and Germany. In Wilks (1977), their hierarchical relations and inheritance relations were discussed, and here we may assume these to be standard. In this book we concentrate only on structures for agents, a consequence of which is that when we consider nested environments, environments for agents will be the only ones that can be outer environments in nesting diagrams. We can consider computing, for example, Jim's view of the oil crisis, but we cannot consider the view the oil crisis has of Jim. We can do this for groups as well (to be able to consider Germany's view of the oil crisis, although never the oil crisis' view of Germany), but in the examples here, we shall confine ourselves to the names of individuals (rather than groups, states, or classes of individuals) as names on the "outside" of environments.

3.1.4. Beliefs about meaning and the world

The PT (Wilks, 1977) was considered separate from a semantic definition, as well as from a frame that was a permanent memory structure consisting largely of episodic information. Thus we expressed factual information about the generic concept of CAR separate from the definition of a car as a people-moving device. Other systems (e.g., KRL: Bobrow and Winograd, 1977) would not have accepted a separation which is, in the end, arbitrary and conventional. The simple illustrative PT for car of Wilks (1977) used the symbol "*" for "car" internally because it was not a pointer to another definitional PT or associated PT, as WHEEL would be, but to the PT itself in which it occurred. It was thus a special pointer, carrying as it were a warning against vicious self-reference.

When we come now to consider structures of representation for individuals that can themselves have beliefs, we must amend this. Suppose we ask where the system keeps its knowledge about Frank. Like the car, this will have a semantic definition (human, male, etc.) as well as beliefs the system has that it explicitly believes about Frank (e.g., that he is an alcoholic) as well as others that it relieves to be Frank's beliefs (Frank believes he is a robot and that he is a merely social drinker). Thus Frank's beliefs, as known to the system, can superficially contradict both definitional and accidental information about himself, if we may use an old-fashioned distinction here. Again, nothing crucial depends on it.

However, in the representational structures used in this book, we shall not assume any notational distinction between beliefs about facts about the world, and about definitions or meanings. The notational distinction in PTs that we noted was merely a matter of historical, commonsense, and lexicographical convenience. And since wider acquaintance with the arguments of Quine (1960) and Putnam (1960), most accept that there can be no fundamental difference between matters of meaning and of fact; nor is there clear agreement as to whether "A whale is a mammal" is a fact about the world or about English.

In the area of belief, where we now are, it is even more pressing that we make no such distinction of principle, and hence no notational one. The system may believe Frank is human but he may believe himself to be a robot. In matters of belief it is quite possible (without being mad) to contradict assertions of meaning and matters of "definitional essence." Frank cannot possibly accept that it is part of the meaning of Frank that he is human. More innocent cases are commonplace, and important for understanding belief-based communication, such as a difference between two persons, one of whom believes Thalassemia is a province in Greece and the other who believes (correctly) that it is a disease. Hence

John believes "Thalassemia" names a province of Greece

is for us, just another belief, which is false, in this case. Representational consequences, such as that word meanings should also be considered propositional in
form, follow from this. Hence, they, too, can take part in all the belief ascription
processes we describe. That is no more shocking than noticing that conventional
frame representations of meaning can easily be considered to consist of propositions like *Animate(human)*, as can any standard form of net representation, linked
by set membership and inclusion arcs. And such propositions are clearly about
meaning, since "humans are animate" is hardly a fact in the standard sense, and this
claim is usually defended on the grounds that it cannot turn out to be wrong as
facts can. Yet Putnam's argument to erode the distinction was that we could perfectly well imagine it turning out wrong, as in the case of Frank's beliefs about
himself cited earlier.

There would be considerable philosophical trade-off's if we could make do
with only a single representational form for meanings and facts: (a) a Quinean one,
in the sense of wanting to substitute talk about beliefs and sentences for talk about
word meaning as in (Quine, 1960), where he let the representation of meaning be a
function of belief representation (even though this is the inverse of the conventional
view) and (b) a neo-Quinean one, in the sense of aligning ourselves with those
current AI-oriented philosophers who have adopted the view that a self-contained
theory of meaning is vacuous and cannot be had independently of a theory of belief
and action (we shall return to this question in section 6).

3.1.5. Beliefs *about* and Beliefs *of*

A natural representational distinction to make is one between our beliefs
about someone and the beliefs *of* that individual. To put it simply, we can have
beliefs about Smith (that he is male, 45 years old, etc), and we can also have
beliefs about his beliefs: that Smith believes that, say, vitamin C cures colds. On
one general view of belief, these are all properties of Smith from the believer's
point of view but they are, of course, importantly different sorts of property for the
reasons we set out when discussing "primitive theories of belief" in 2.1.

On the other hand, we have adopted a general position in this book of not creating more segmented belief partitions than is absolutely necessary, a position that follows from our discussion of Perrault et al. in 2.5. There we argued that their system suffered from having all possible partitions inserted a priori, as it were, which was psychologically and computationally implausible. On the contrary, our intention is to maintain belief environments at the lowest possible level of nesting, which would imply not having initial internal partitions for beliefs *of* within beliefs *about* an individual.

Internal partitionings are created by new information which warrant such creations, typically when we find out that someone has a belief that we would not credit them with by default. For example, if we know that John is a doctor then we do not need to generate a special beliefs-of-John environment when we are told he believes Thalassemia to be a genetic disorder. On the other hand, it is quite likely that we would do so if we were told that Dave the postman believed the same thing.

Chapter 3.2
The argument for environments

In previous sections, the notion of *environments* was introduced. These environments fulfill two separate but complementary roles in our work: (a) they provide a means of organizing beliefs and (b) they facilitate certain processes, primarily the ascription process itself (in addition, they facilitate relevance determination, intensional identification, and metaphor processing). The first role is an extension of earlier work done by one of us (Wilks, 1977) on representing information for language processing. The second role is derived from the computer science notion of the "environment" of a procedure. The question naturally arises, "What is the status of environments? Are they elements of a theory of belief, or simply tools for implementing such a theory?" Environments are *explicit groups* of propositions and as such, we claim, a highly desirable tool for realistic reasoning. In addition, we claim that not only our theory of belief but many others, depend on a notion of environment. However, for others this notion is often hidden in "semantics" and only physically appears in the implementation machinery. We believe that for a clearer understanding, it is necessary to make entities of environments explicit.

What do we mean by "explicit?" We have made environments explicit in the diagrams of this book, but what does it mean for environments to be explicit in the system itself? The answer is that at least the following should be true:

(1.)   the environments are part of the top level of the system description;

(2.)   the contents of an environment are determined by the system itself through some sort of identifying name — it is not simply we as theoreticians who discern those environments; furthermore,

(3.)   the contents are *efficiently* determinable by the system.

Any practical system for reasoning about agents' beliefs will have to have some sort of efficient indexing for accessing beliefs belonging to specific agents and concerning specific topics; thus, there will be something analogous to our environments at *some* level of description in the system. Many approaches to belief representation leave that indexing purely at the implementational level. In contrast, we advocate the use of explicit environments at the *top* level of conception in the representation. (This is related to the idea that a semantic network makes certain types of indexing apparent at the top conceptual level, whereas traditional logic relegates such issues to implementation.) The following comments justify our stance:

First of all our stance has proven methodologically useful in guiding our research in specific fruitful directions. Most saliently, the explicitness of environments led directly to our consideration of the links between belief ascription, intensional identification and metaphor demonstrated in this book.

More technical benefits also follow from explicitness, however. In a realistic discourse, the system has to make rapid decisions about the sets of propositions believed by the agents. Now ascription can involve a significant amount of work in modifying an existing proposition before ascribing it, or in checking that there is no contrary proposition blocking the ascription (see 3.4; Wilks and Ballim, 1987); therefore, it is beneficial to minimize the number of propositions ascribed, as long as the techniques for minimization do not, themselves, eat up too much time. One technique for limiting ascription is to ascribe only those propositions that are deemed relevant according to some set of efficient relevance determination heuristics (see 3.4.2.3): the result of relevance determination is a group of propositions. Now we wish to argue that that group should be explicit in the above sense.

Suppose the system has already constructed its own topic environment B containing system beliefs about Bush. The "default ascription rule" used in *ViewGen* to construct or expand John's topic-environment JB concerning Bush requires us to push propositions in B down into JB. The pushing of a proposition may be blocked because, for instance, it is explicitly contradicted by a proposition in JB, or because it is political expertise that should not be ascribed to the politically inexpert John. Also, propositions may need to be modified rather than blocked (see 3.4). Therefore, the pushing process as applied to B does require separate processing of individual propositions in B. However, the explicitness of B as a *group* is nevertheless important because B is likely to be the result of a significant amount of knowledge-intensive relevance determination work, which may have involved processing system beliefs that are not about Bush in any explicit way. Once the system has created *B* for the purposes of its own reasoning about Bush, it is immediately available to help in constructing environments such as *JB* for the purposes of the system's reasoning about various other agents' reasoning about Bush. If beliefs were not parcelled into explicit environments, the ascription of beliefs about Bush to those agents would be likely to involve *duplicated* relevance determination work similar to that necessary to create *B*. In summary, one justification for environments (proposition groups that are explicit in the above sense) is that they reduce the amount of work dictated by considerations of relevance.

Also, pushing system beliefs about Bush down into John's viewpoint could involve the conjoint examination of several such beliefs rather than examination of them one at a time, which makes it especially important for the system to be able to *quickly* determine which of its beliefs are relevant to Bush. A similar observation holds for pushing beliefs at deeper levels of nesting, as in the attempted pushing of John's beliefs about Bush down into Bill's viewpoint, nested within that of John.

In our discussion of metaphor, we will make the point that the notion of explicit environments fits well into the widespread MIND-AS-CONTAINER metaphor (see, e.g., Lakoff, 1987: p. 450, also 383ff).[3] Now in the ordinary, common-sensical view, a container is taken to contain an explicit *group* of items: we do not normally have a collection of separate, *uncoordinated* beliefs, one that states that the container contains item A, another that states that the container contains item B, and so on. Analogously, to the extent that a real agent *X* does appear to view another agent *Y* metaphorically as a container of beliefs, we can plausibly regard *X* as viewing *Y* maintaining an explicit *group* of beliefs — that is, an environment. The contrast we are trying to show here is their *X* holds that *Y* believes *A*, and that *Y* believes *B*, and that *Y* believes C, and so on without representing any explicit grouping of these statements, as opposed to holding a belief that *Y* believes *A*, *B* and *C*. We owe this point to John Barnden, who has developed the notion independently (1989).

People often talk explicitly and implicitly about *sets* of beliefs and other propositional attitudes held by agents. For instance, someone might say "John's

---

[3] This metaphor is closely related to the CONDUIT metaphor for communication (Reddy, 1979; see also Lakoff, 1987: p. 450 and Johnson, 1987: pp.58, 59). Also, according to Lakoff (1987) and Johnson (1987) the idea of a CONTAINER is used metaphorically for understanding many abstract concepts, including — pertinently for us — the mathematical notion of a set.

beliefs about New Mexico are confused." This sentence is best interpreted as conveying that John's beliefs are as a set, inconsistent in some way, rather than conveying something about John's individual beliefs. Explicit topic-environments and viewpoints give us a handle for dealing with such cases, as work by other researchers tends to support (the work of Fauconnier, 1985 on mental spaces previously mentioned in 2.5 and that of Johnson-Laird, 1983 on human commonsense reasoning).

The propositions in John's Bush environment are not necessarily the ones about Bush that John is "aware" of in any sense to the ordinary notion of conscious awareness: here we are reacting against the use of the term "awareness" in Fagin and Halpern (1987). The propositions in a belief environment have no necessary relationship to "explicit beliefs" as used by say, Levesque (1984) because no clear idea is given by the authors using the term of what explicitness is meant to capture. However, in so far as other authors' explicit-belief notions get at the idea of beliefs that agents actually use in their reasoning, their's are exactly like our notion of propositions within a belief environment. Our orientation is different, though: We are not interested in massaging modal logic to extract from it an appropriate deductive logic of explicit and implicit belief, but in devising plausible commonsense reasoning mechanisms for constructing the explicit-belief sets in the first place.

In subscribing to a system that manipulates explicit environments, we are not *ipso facto* subscribing to a particular representational syntax: indeed, one could easily devise a representational syntax for belief environments that looked much like ordinary modal logic syntax. For example, a particular belief environment containing some beliefs P, Q, and R of John relevant to Bush lets say, could be expressed by means of a formula such as:

BE(John, Bush, P and Q and R)

where **BE** (Belief Environment) is analogous to a modal belief operator. Notice however, that we do not want an implication from an internally-conjunctive formula like the one shown to correspond to a partially-external conjunction such as **BE(John, Bush, P and Q)** and **BE(John, Bush, R)**. (If P, Q, and R form John's topic environment for Bush, then it is *not* the case that any proper subset of {P, Q, R} does so.) Analogous implications are standard in traditional modal logics (Chellas, 1980); however, in a nontraditional logic such as Fagin and Halpern's "logic of general awareness", (1987) they are not. It is therefore conceivable that **BE** could be a belief operator in a nontraditional logic not terribly different from correctional ones.

Assume then for the sake of argument, that a modal form of expression can be devised that allows explicit description and appropriate manipulation of environments. That would be perfectly acceptable to us however, the acceptability is confined to the form of *expression*: we are much less happy about the possible-worlds (even nonclassical ones) that are usually brought in to provide semantics of a modal logic. As has been frequently observed (e.g., Linsky, 1983), possible-worlds introduce as much mystery as they were apparently designed to dispel; not only mystery, but decided technical drawbacks such as logical omniscience which can only be avoided at the cost of elaborate manoeuvers that militate against the attraction of possible-worlds in the first place (Konolige, 1986).

Turning to nonmodal logics, it is similarly conceivable that a belief environment could be expressed in quotational logic by means of an internal conjunction of the lines in

BE(John, Bush, 'P and Q and R')

where **BE** is now a predicate symbol interpreted as: a predicate relating an agent, a topic entity, and a formula. Here, there is no necessary logical connection to corresponding partially-external conjunctions such as **BE(John, Bush, 'P and Q')** and **BE(John, Bush, 'R')**. Again, we would be happy if this lack of connection were to mean that belief environments could be adequately couched in a quotational logic and the same goes for other styles of representation such as the neo-Fregean, concept-denoting systems of Creary (1979) and Creary & Pollard (1985) developed from McCarthy, (1979), and situation/event-based styles (Barwise and Perry 1983; Hobbs 1985). Our general point is that we may be wholly neutral about a syntax of belief expression (provided we retain the benefit of explicit environment manipulation) while reserving judgment about semantics approaches usually associated with those syntaxes.

It has been pointed out that proposals based on belief environments can have expressive problems including, in particular, what we might call the "disjunctive explosion" problem (Moore, 1977). Suppose, for instance, we wish to state that either John believes *P* or he believes *Q*; that either he believes *R* or that he believes *S* (for simplicity's sake, assume that no other beliefs come into the picture). Then we would need a disjunction over four belief environments; one for each of the combinations (P,R), (P,S), (Q,R), and (Q,S). This objection ignores the fact that it would be possible to have an expression that represented a set of environments, without listing the environments in the set; one of several possibilities in this line would be to use the following representation:

```
┌─────────────────────────────────────────┐
│                                           │
│              P meta-or Q                  │
│              R meta-or S                  │
└───────────────────John────────────────────┘
```

Figure 3.1 Meta-beliefs

This representation acts as an environment *schema* standing in relation to a set of environments, much as an axiom schema stands in relation to a set of axioms. Each member of the set of environments is obtained by replacing each expression of the form *X meta-or Y* by either *X* or *Y*. The possible replacements in the present example give us the four environments mentioned earlier.

This suggestion has not yet been taken up in *ViewGen* and is raised merely to show that the disjunctive explosion problem, although serious in some cases, can in practice be sufficiently mitigated for the belief-environment technique to remain heuristically useful (more will be said on this in 5.1, where we consider a language for talking *about* environments).

Chapter 3.3
Construction of viewpoints

We now consider the simple proposal for ascribing beliefs to other agents in greater detail. We do so unless there is evidence to block the ascription. Such a description is deceptively simple, and this chapter points out some of the complexity of realizing an algorithm based it. (A word of warning is appropriate here for those readers who do not wish to get too far into the technicalities of belief ascription: some of those technicalities occur towards the end of this chapter and throughout the following one, so if you do not wish to have too much detail of belief ascription, we suggest that you read up to and including 3.3.2 and then skip through to 5.3. If you wish to know details of the program without knowing too much detail about belief ascription, then you can read up to and including 3.3.2 and then skip to 4). From our perspective, the purpose of belief ascription is to produce other people's viewpoints on given topics. Viewpoints are a particular type of environment, so let us begin by discussing the types of environment that are required for the system.

3.3.1. Types of Environments

The notion of an environment has been previously introduced (1) and defended (3.2). An environment is a small, explicit grouping of beliefs, collected under some form of indexing. The particular form of indexing is the initial basis for determining the *type* of any given environment.

There are two basic types of environment: (a) *viewpoints* (environments that represent a particular agent's point of view) and (b) *topics* (environments that contain beliefs that are relevant to a given subject). Viewpoints can contain either other viewpoints (the first agent's view of another agent's viewpoint), or topics (the agent's viewpoint on a particular subject). Topics can contain propositions (statements about the subject) or, in the case where the subject is an agent or class of agent, they can contain viewpoints. So for example, Figure 3.2 contains a viewpoint with a topic nested within it[4] and represents the system's view of atoms.

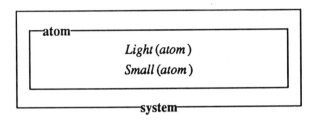

Figure 3.2 Nesting at topic and viewpoint.

The box labelled "system" at the bottom is a viewpoint. The box labelled "atom" at the top is a topic. A topic environment contains a group of propositions about the "topic." So for example, the above diagram conveys that the system believes that atoms are light and small. Topic boxes are motivated by concerns of limited reasoning (see 2.3 and 3.2 on relevance, and also Wilks and Bien, 1983). In short, it is envisaged that reasoning takes place "within" a topic environment, as if it were the environment of a procedure in a programming language.

We introduce the following notion as a way of referring to nested environments. A list of the form <*Bel System, Bel A_0, . . . , Bel A_n, About T*> indicates the system's view of A_0's view of , . . . , A_n's view of the topic T, so the innermost environment in the above diagram can be referred to as <*Bel System, About atom*>.

Within the system, environments are dynamically created and altered. The system's "knowledge-base" can be seen as one large viewpoint containing a large number of topic environments, each topic environment containing a group of "beliefs" that the system holds about the topic. Initially, each proposition in a topic environment has at least one symbol identical to the name of the topic.[5] Each such

---

[4] Note that all beliefs are ultimately beliefs held by the system (e.g., the system's beliefs about France, what the system believes John believes about cars, etc.) and so lie within the system's viewpoint.

[5] However, over time we may want to alter this as new beliefs become "relevant" to the topic. Also, we allow predicate names as valid topics. Where a topic is not a predicate name, we may wish to deem as relevant certain general beliefs that involve a predicate which predicates over the topic: so in beliefs about the Earth one might include a statement saying that spherical objects are not flat!

proposition is therefore *explicitly* about the topic. There are however, implicit ways in which a proposition can be "about" (or "relevant to") a topic. The simplest cases are generated by inheritance in the usual way: for example, if John is a man then any proposition in a "man" topic environment is implicitly or indirectly about John. However, we choose not to put such a proposition in the John topic box and justify that decision elsewhere in the section on relevance.

If the "topic" of a topic environment is a person (someone capable of having beliefs themselves), then the topic environment may contain in addition to the beliefs about the person, a viewpoint environment containing particular beliefs held by that person about various topics. Normally, this is only done for those beliefs of the person that conflict with the system's own beliefs about the topics. For example: suppose the system had beliefs about a person called John who believes that his cat is nice. This would be pictorially represented as in Figure 3.3:

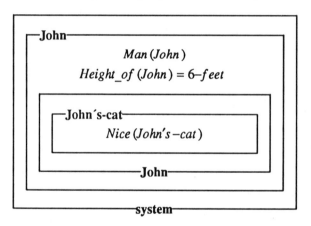

Figure 3.3 Nesting viewpoints.

The John viewpoint (shown as the box with "John" on the lower edge), is a *nested viewpoint*, as it is enclosed within the system viewpoint shown through an intervening topic environment about John (shown as the box with "John" on its upper edge). For the sake of simplicity, we often leave out propositions that are not in the innermost topic box in the diagram of a nested viewpoint; e.g., in the above we would leave out the beliefs that John is a man and that he is six feet tall. Further simplifying this, we often leave out all but the innermost topic box, leaving only it and the viewpoint boxes. Hence Figure 3.3 would be simplified as is shown in Figure 3.4:

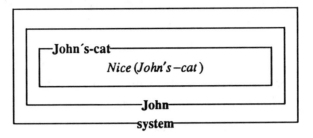

Figure 3.4 Compressed nesting.

In general, the only beliefs that the system stores on a permanent basis under other people's viewpoints are those that conflict with its own on the topic. Such beliefs form one type of "explicit evidence" against ascription. The process of generating a viewpoint can be regarded as an *amalgamation* mechanism that ascribes beliefs from one viewpoint to another by "pushing one environment down into another": ascribing certain beliefs, transforming some, and blocking the ascription of others.

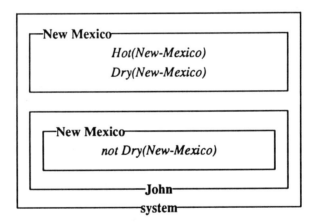

Figure 3.5 Differing beliefs in viewpoints.

3.3.2. The Basic Algorithm

The simplest form of the ascription algorithm, described in Wilks & Bien (1979, 1983), is that a viewpoint should be generated using a default rule for ascription of beliefs. The default ascriptional rule is to assume that another person's view is the same as one's own *except where there is explicit evidence to the contrary*. For example, suppose that at a certain stage the system believes that

New Mexico is hot and dry but that John believes that New Mexico is not dry. Before the system comes to consider John's reasoning about New Mexico, the system's state is represented pictorially as in Figure 3.5 (which has been simplified by "lifting" the John viewpoint out of the John topic environment).

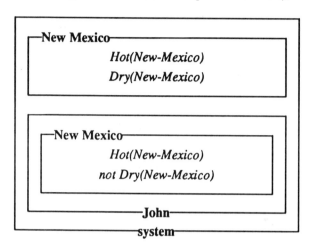

Figure 3.6 Ascription result.

The system can proceed to create a more complete environment for John's view of New Mexico by seeking to push the beliefs from the system's view of New Mexico (the upper New Mexico box in the diagram) into the topic environment for New Mexico within John's viewpoint. The belief that New Mexico is hot is successfully pushed into John's view of New Mexico because it does not conflict with any pre-existing belief in that viewpoint. However, the ascription of the belief that New Mexico is dry is blocked by John's contradicting belief that New Mexico is not dry. The result of the ascription is shown in Figure 3.6.

An important and special case of such examples is when the topic is the same as the agent. Suppose that the system is a medical diagnostician whose view of John is that he is not healthy and is six feet tall while John believes himself to be healthy. This is represented pictorially, as in Figure 3.7. The more complete environment for John's view of himself can be generated by ascribing the beliefs from the system's topic environment about John to the topic environment about John within John's viewpoint. Once again, one of the two beliefs survives the attempt but the other is blocked, giving the state in Figure 3.8.

This figure can then be simplified, to yield Figure 3.9.

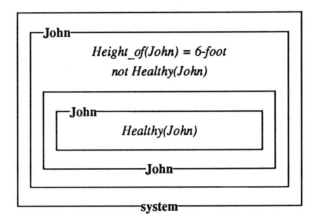

Figure 3.7 Topic and viewpoint the same.

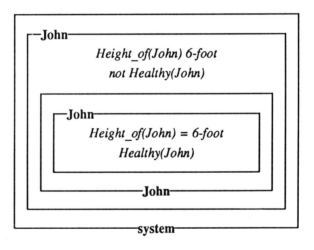

Figure 3.8 Result of ascription.

We see that in examples of this sort (where the topic is actually the agent an ascription is being attempted into), propositions in an outer topic environment *E* are *pushed inwards* into a topic environment for the same topic in a viewpoint nested within *E*. Such inward pushing is central to our later observations of intensional identification and metaphor.

The examples cited earlier demonstrate the basic ascription algorithm, and simple cases of ascription being blocked by explicit negation in the target environment to which they are being ascribed. Counter-evidence to ascription does not have to be as simple as that, however. For example, we would normally wish the

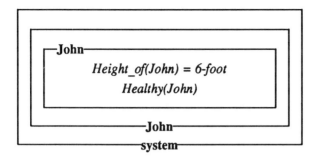

Figure 3.9 Compressed environment.

proposition "*Wet(New-Mexico)*" to block "*Dry(New-Mexico)*", if *Wet* and *Dry* are known incompatible predicates. Similarly, we later appeal to blocking that arises from incompatible function values, as in the blocking of "*Eye-color(Frank) = Green*" by "*Eye-color(Frank) = Blue.*"

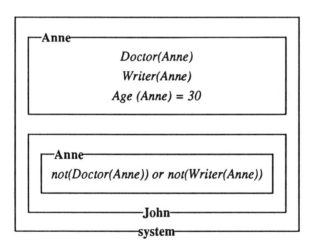

Figure 3.10 Views of Anne.

In general, only those beliefs from the environment being ascribed (the source environment) that are consistent with the target environment can be ascribed. So in the situation shown in Figure 3.10, the separate beliefs in the source environment that Anne is a doctor, and Anne is a writer are overriden by the belief of John in the target environment that she is either a doctor or a writer, but not both. Hence in generating John's view of Anne, we get the situation depicted in Figure 3.11.

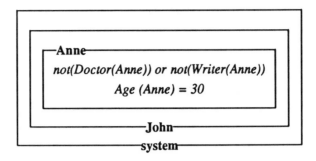

Figure 3.11 Resulting environment.

A more significant complication is that there is an entire class of beliefs that require the opposite of the default ascription rule given earlier: these are known as *atypical beliefs*, and include technical expertise, self-knowledge, and secrets. For example, beliefs that we hold about ourselves such as how many fillings we have in our teeth, are beliefs that we would not normally ascribe to someone else *unless we had reason to do so* (if, let's say, the person we were ascribing the belief to was our dentist). In fact, the notion of whether a belief is typical or atypical is relative to agents; what is a typical belief for one person or group of people may be atypical for everybody else — e.g., a typical belief of a physicist about atoms is most likely to be atypical for a layman. (These notions are explored in greater detail in 3.4.)

3.3.3. Issues in Constructing a Point of View

Two questions need to be answered about the use of nested beliefs: firstly, by when should a nesting of beliefs be constructed, and secondly, what determines the particular form of the nesting? In order to answer these questions, consider the form of the system in which the nestings are being used: assume the nested beliefs are being used in a dialogue system that is capable of performing the role of a participant in the dialogue; the obvious point at which to construct viewpoints is when analyzing an utterance by the other participant in the dialogue and when trying to formulate something to say. The question remains then, what environments should be constructed?

In Wilks and Bien (1979, 1983), a number of strategies for deciding when to construct an environment and what environment to construct are suggested. Two important strategies are discussed: the *presentation strategy* and the *insertional strategy*. The important question for a presentation strategy is, given incoming

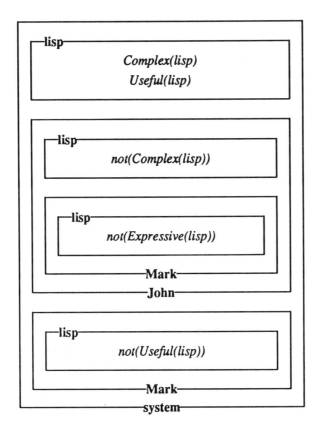

Figure 3.12 Multiple nested viewpoints.

information about an individual, how many levels of nesting should the system construct? Two forms of presentation strategy can be distinguished: the first is a *minimal strategy*, which corresponds to the shallowest environment with no level that corresponds to the speaker. Such a strategy would be used where one is not interpreting the input in terms of the speaker as where the speaker is a person delivering a lecture and the hearer is taking notes verbatim.

The second form of presentation strategy is the *standard presentation strategy*. The standard presentation strategy is to construct an environment corresponding to the speaker and then to construct appropriate levels corresponding to mentioned individuals.[6] This standard strategy allows a hearer to either disbelieve a

---

[6] Remember that an environment need not correspond solely to individuals. We have no qualms about constructing an environment to represent the beliefs of groups of individuals, such as the view of America on world terrorism.

speaker or cooperate with him as he chooses, in much the same way as that proposed by Taylor and Whitehill (1981) as described in 2.5.3.

The insertional strategy is designed to deal with the problem of how to handle the storage of a belief. (This problem is considered in 5.1.)

Another important question concerns the status of topics (discussed in 3.1) and how they correspond across viewpoints. In other words, how do I know what corresponding object someone else has for the object I am calling X, and which has a description (topic environment) indexed under that label?

Following the default rule for ascription, we employ a default that for every object X that I have beliefs about, other agents have an equivalent object also called X although of course, with possibly different beliefs about them. This question is bound up with questions about intensionality and reference. (They are discussed in detail in 5.2.)

Before leaving this chapter, more must be said about which beliefs are relevant for ascription. In generating what the system thinks is someone else's view of a topic — John's, for instance the system's beliefs about the topic are deemed relevant and hence are candidates for ascription; the special beliefs of John about the topic are also relevant, namely those that conflict with the system's own beliefs about the topic. In general however, for deeper nesting we must consider different environments as being relevant at different stages of the construction.

The above definition of ascription can be seen as encoding the assumption that other agents basically have the same beliefs as ourselves, or that we share a large number of common beliefs. So given the system's beliefs, it is not necessary to store all the common beliefs of agents, as they can be inferred through the ascriptional rule (although we may choose to store some common beliefs of another agent at any point, if deemed necessary). Rather, we generally only need to store those beliefs of other agents that we believe *a priori* to differ from our own.

This definition of ascription is often taken to entail a simple-minded recursive method for generating nested beliefs (see Wilks and Bien, 1979; 1983) whereby to generate what the system believes α_1 *believes*, ..., α_n believes we simply ascribe the system's beliefs to α_1 then those beliefs to α_2, and so on to α_n.[7]

---

[7] Note that the generation of such a nesting presupposes that the agents involved know about each other, i.e., we would not ascribe beliefs about Mark to John if we believed that John had never heard of Mark. Also, note that such "knowing about" need not be mutual: if John knows about Mark but Mark does not know about John, then we can generate John's beliefs about Mark but not Mark's beliefs about John.

Say we wish to construct *<Bel System , Bel John , Bel Mark , About lisp >*. Suppose that we begin with the situation depicted in Figure 3.12.

Now to generate the system's view of John's view of Mark's view of the lisp language, the environments that are relevant to the construction are: *<Bel System, About lisp>*, *<Bel System, Bel John, About lisp>*, *<Bel System, Bel John, Bel Mark, About lisp>*, and *<Bel System, Bel Mark, About lisp>*. Moreover, each of these environments are relevant to particular levels of the nesting that we wish to construct. Those environments that are relevant at say, level *i* , are also relevant at level *i*+1, etc. down to the bottom of the nesting. However, if the environments are taken into account in constructing the highest level in the nesting to which they are relevant, they need not be considered again.

The first level is simply the system's own beliefs about lisp. For this level only *<Bel System, About lisp>* is relevant. And so we get the first level of the nesting, shown in Figure 3.13:

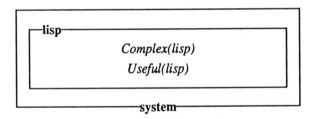

Figure 3.13 System's beliefs.

The second level is the system's view of John's view of beliefs. For this level, the relevant environments are the ones produced at the first level, and the environment *<Bel System, Bel John, About lisp>*. By pushing the first level into this environment, we get the second level of the nesting:

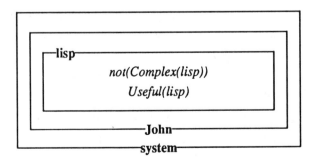

Figure 3.14 System's view of John's beliefs.

The third level is the system's view of John's view of Mark's view of lisp. For this level, the relevant environments are the ones produced at the second level: *<Bel System, Bel Mark, About lisp>*, and *<Bel System, Bel John, Bel Mark, About lisp>*. However, the question here is: In which order should we perform the pushing? The environment *<Bel System, Bel John, Bel Mark, About lisp>* should be last because it is the desired result of this level of nesting. But which should go first, the result from level two, or *<Bel System, Bel Mark, About lisp>*? We claim that the result from the second level should be pushed into *<Bel System, Bel Mark, About lisp>*, and the result of that pushed into *<Bel System, Bel John, Bel Mark, About lisp>* to give the desired result for level three. This order presumes that John knows whatever special beliefs Mark has about lisp, and that if John believes other than the system on this, that is captured by the final environment *<Bel System, Bel John, Bel Mark, About lisp>*. So we get the result shown in Figure 3.15.

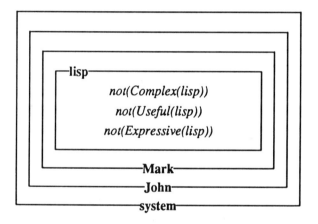

Figure 3.15 Innermost environment.

We can now define a general form of the algorithm which is that for each level of a nesting we wish to generate; we push the result from the previous level (if there was one) into the first of an ordered set of environments relevant to that level and then push the result into each subsequent environment from the ordered set until we have no more environments for that level. At that stage, we have generated the final environment for the given level.

For a given topic T, if we used the abbreviated notation $<Sys, A_1, \ldots, A_n>$ to indicate the environment that contains the special beliefs of the system's view of A_1's view of $,\ldots, A_n$'s view of the topic, $\rightarrow$ to indicate a pushing operation, and parentheses ( ) to imply that we are interested in the result of a pushing operation, then we can illustrate the procedure in general terms as follows: Say we are generating $<Bel\ System, Bel\ A_1, Bel\ A_2, Bel\ A_3, About\ T>$. Then the first level of nesting is generated (in our abbreviated notation) as:

$<Sys>$

The second level is:

$(<Sys>) \rightarrow <Sys, A_1>$

And the third level is:

$(((<Sys>) \rightarrow <Sys, A_1>) \rightarrow <Sys, A_2>) \rightarrow <Sys, A_1, A_2>$

To simplify things, let's call the result of the third level $<L3>$, in which case the final level would be:

$$((((<L3> \rightarrow <Sys, A_3>) \rightarrow <Sys, A_2, A_3>) \rightarrow <Sys, A_1, A_3>) \rightarrow <Sys, A_1, A_2, A_3>$$

As we can see therefore, the process of ascription must consider many environments (possibly empty) as relevant to each level of nesting as it is producing the level. The algorithm for automatically generating the ordered, relevant environments is given in section 4. Ascription cannot usefully be described as a form of unification, for our directionality assumption destroys that possibility; indeed, it may be an actual achievement in this area to find an algorithm that is not reducible to unification.

In the next chapter, we will discuss some further complications in ascribing belief, and a solution that rests on a notion of *competency* in having particular beliefs or beliefs about particular topics, i.e., in classifying beliefs according to agents' competency for holding them.

Chapter 3.4
Limitations to default ascription

The default rule thus presented relies heavily on defining explicit evidence to prevent ascription of beliefs, when necessary. One form that such explicit evidence might take is from environments we call *personae*[8]. Personae are environments that are used to represent the beliefs of typical classes of people; so we may have a *persona* that represents the beliefs that are typically held by an alcoholic, or someone who belongs to some profession or ethnic group, etc. As with all environments within the system, the only beliefs stored in an environment for a person are those that differ from the system's own beliefs.

Let us suppose we have a belief that Phil is a typical alcoholic. We may then use a persona for typical alcoholics in deciding to promote the belief that Phil is a typical alcoholic into *<Bel System, Bel Phil, About Phil>*. Suppose that the persona for typical alcoholics contains the belief that the typical alcoholic does not believe himself to be an alcoholic. If we allow the beliefs from the typical alcoholic persona to be promoted before the system belief that Phil is an alcoholic, the result is that the system believes that Phil believes he is not an alcoholic.

The astute reader will recognize that personae are basically objects for representing stereotypical beliefs. Stereotypes have played a strong role in AI, and in particular, *user modelling*. One might wonder therefore, what it would be like to base *all* belief ascriptions on such reasoning.

In such a scheme, the system would have prestored models of the beliefs of stereotypical individuals. Then, if we know that a particular stereotype applies to an agent under consideration, we may ascribe beliefs of the stereotype to the agent

---

[8] The name comes from McLoughlin (1986), but the structures which McLoughlin calls *personae* are more complex than our personae, as they include general information on stereotypical behavior of classes of individuals, not just the beliefs of the classes of individuals.

to form the hypothesis of the agent's beliefs. This requires a means of classifying individuals with respect to stereotypes. In work such as that of Rich (1979), the classifying is accomplished by asking the agents concerned what stereotypes they think might fit them: in general, this is not a fruitful approach. Agents may not be capable of answering such a question themselves due to lack of knowledge about beliefs of the range of stereotypes, or to an inability to apply stereotypes to themselves accurately.

A possible solution is to use an assumed, context-driven, basic stereotype (i.e., in a given context, a particular stereotype is most likely to apply to an agent). Another solution might be to home-in on the appropriate stereotype(s) from a selection on assortment by applying some evaluation criterion to a set of questions posed to the agent. Whatever the method, there is normally some subset of stereotypes greater than one that does apply to a given agent. This can lead to having too large a model of the agent and doing too much work in forming the model (for a medical specialist there could be a large number of medically-related stereotypes that apply to the agent with considerable overlap between their constituent beliefs).

In addition, where many stereotypes apply, beliefs from different stereotypes may clash with each other which gives rise to the problem of resolving the clash. Rich (1988) offers some possible solutions to the clashing information problem: in systems where beliefs have numeric attributes indicating confidence, support, etc., the values of clashing information could be averaged; it may be possible to get a least upper-bound of clashing information (effectively forming a disjunction over the clashing information); information from the longer established stereotype might be given preference, or information from the most recently established stereotype could be given preference; finally, information never before involved in a clash could be given preference.

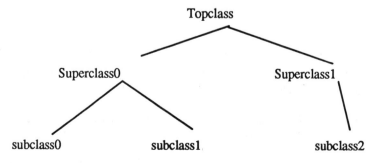

Figure 3.16 A taxonomy of classes.

An approach that helps with the problem of clash resolution although not solving it, is based on the notion of class taxonomies. The idea is that some classes can be considered to be subclasses of others (as in the case represented in Figure 3.16.

This allows for an efficient method of storing information by placing it in the most general class possible and allowing subclasses to inherit the information. In the case of a clash of information between that from a class and a subclass, the information from the subclass is given preference. Such *inheritance taxonomies* are a popular method of information storage in AI. However, in dealing with stereotypes a given class may be a subclass of more that one other class — such an example is shown in Figure 3.17.

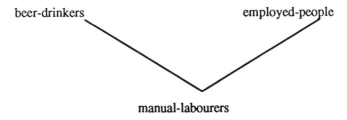

Figure 3.17 A partial multiple inheritance taxonomy.

It can be seen therefore, that a taxonomy of agents must allow for multiple inheritance from superclasses to classes, and exceptions must be allowed for. It is not unreasonable to expect that some manual-laborers are not beer-drinkers! Systems that allow multiple inheritance with exceptions are prone to a number of problems, most of which relate to clashing information (see Touretzky et al., 1987). Although solutions have been suggested to these problems (see Ballim, Candelaria de Ram, and Fass, 1989), the solutions are often computationally expensive — not a desirable trait of a system for forming hypotheses.

There are additional problems with using stereotypical information to ascribe beliefs: first of all, we must consider all the stereotypes that can apply to a given individual, even though in a given context most do not contribute useful information but increase the amount of "noise" in the model we are generating. Similarly, not all the beliefs of any *given* stereotype are useful in a particular context.

Furthermore, the actual taxonomy of agents is subject to variation between individuals. Specialists in a given area will have a more detailed stereotype taxonomy with respect to that area (possibly involving more diverse classes of stereotype) than non-experts. In performing for recursive (nested) belief ascription, we must allow for this. But, does this imply ascribing the entire taxonomy to the agent? And what of the beliefs within the taxonomy, must they also be changed?

The amount of "noise" generated by using stereotypes can be reduced by partitioning beliefs into topic-specific environments, which is precisely what we argue for in this book. Note that this does not prevent the same belief from occurring in more than one such environment. Also, the decision as to what beliefs belong to given environments cannot be based on simple logical notions such as *material implication*: not everything materially implied from a belief relevant to a topic will also be relevant to the topic! Of course, none of this should come as a surprise to the reader, as we have already seen (in section 2.3, for example) that stereotypes provide efficiency of storage and ease of description.

We can identify an entire class of beliefs (*atypical beliefs*) for which the opposite of our default rule is true — namely, we should only ascribe atypical beliefs to others *where we have evidence to do so*. Such beliefs include expertise, secrets, and the stereotype—beliefs derived from personae.

The difference between typical and atypical beliefs is not a simple dichotomy: what is a typical belief for one person may be atypical to another. In the system described so far, this could only be represented with explicit beliefs of the form "person X does not have belief Y". [9] Instead, a new representation is introduced, which allows us to capture the diversity of what we shall call *competency* in holding beliefs.

3.4.1. From Typical to Atypical Beliefs: Competency in Holding Beliefs

An atypical belief is a belief that is held by one agent, but would not generally be held by other agents. The class of atypical beliefs covers such areas as self-knowledge, secrets, expertise and knowledge of uncommon domains (such as the believer's hobbies, skills, personal medical history, etc.).

So for example, the belief that the Earth is flat is atypical. An important point must be made here: in terms of a specific agent, the foregoing definition of atypicality is insufficient. For a belief to be considered atypical with respect to an agent, the agent must hold the belief to be atypical, i.e., we may believe you to have an atypical belief. However, we may also believe that you think it is a typically-held belief; so although we believe it to be atypical, you believe it to be

---

[9] Note: this is different from person X believing NOT-Y.

typical. We can make this more general by saying that the notions of typicality and atypicality of beliefs are relative to the holder of the belief and the one to whom the belief is being ascribed (whether an individual or class of individuals). An agent would consider a belief to be typical with respect to some class of agents if he would ascribe it to the agents, and atypical if he would not. To adapt a well known expression *typicality is in the mind of the beholder*.

We might then characterize "Typical belief" (with a capital "T") by saying that, with respect to the agent holding the belief, the agent considers the belief Typical if he would ascribe it to the average man in the street. Conversely, the agent would consider the belief Atypical if he would *not* ascribe it to the average man in the street. These notions, *Typical belief* and *Atypical belief*, are specialized cases of the notions *typical belief* and *atypical belief*.

The astute reader will have realized by now that what lies at the heart of typicality and atypicality of beliefs is something we will call *competency* in holding beliefs. That is, who do we feel are capable of holding the same beliefs as ourselves and who do we feel are not?

Types of Atypical belief include beliefs that cover uncommon domains (a topic about which a particular agent has a very detailed set of beliefs that most other agents are not qualified to have; for example, beliefs about a particular agent's childhood). Beliefs about uncommon domains are similar to beliefs about expert domains because both types are uncommon.

Because uncommonly held, expert belief is a type of Atypical belief, one that exemplifies some special problems with regard to competency in believing. Consider the case of medical knowledge: It is possible to reason about a treatment for an illness without knowing the details of the treatment; we may discuss a cure for tuberculosis without knowing the cure. We can see from this example that preventing beliefs on expertise from being ascribed to an agent is often undesirable in itself, even though the agent is not believed to be expert on the topic of the beliefs.

For the class of Atypical beliefs, the rule is *not* to ascribe the belief unless one has explicit evidence to justify doing so. However, as we have seen from the medical example, competency is not simply a case of deciding whether or not to ascribe a belief it may involve ascribing some transformed version of a belief. What is needed is a flexible way of representing competency for believing that allows one to determine both a particular agent's competency in holding a belief *and* the form of the belief that they hold (thus the system as a medical expert can attribute beliefs to people about cures and treatments of medical problems that are naive, enabling it to formulate the best way of explaining cures and treatments to them).

3.4.2. A Representational System for Competency in Believing

McCarthy and others have suggested that λ expressions be used to represent knowledge of values. One of us (Wilks, 1986) has proposed that expertise may be expressed within a system using λ expressions with restrictions on their capable evaluators. Knowing or having the belief represented by the λ expression means that the agent is capable of evaluating the expression, so the representation for a cure for tuberculosis would look like:

$$\exists X \{ X = (\lambda L \ (cure\_for \ L) \ tuberculosis) <MDs> \}$$

The only capable evaluators of this are those agents known to be medical doctors (MDs). Competency in having the belief containing the λ expression is then dependent upon being able to evaluate that expression: an obvious first step along the road to representing competency in believing. However, as noted earlier it is not sufficient to merely say *who* has the competence to evaluate the expression: What of people who cannot evaluate such an expression and yet can at least *consider* beliefs involving it? And what about people who evaluate such an expression to differing values — a very real possibility?

3.4.2.1. Aspects of Competency in Believing

The above form of representation allows expressions that can only be evaluated by specific agents or classes of agents be the basis for representing competency in believing. However, it must be extended to cover various aspects of competency that we now consider.

λ expressions are used to encode functional descriptions, so it is appropriate here to consider some important forms of competency that one can have with regard to evaluating a function. Consider the taxonomy in Figure 3.18.

Let us consider a belief about John's phone number P and suppose that it contains a λ expression L, which is an abstraction of the phone number (i.e., the belief is that John's phone number is some value:

$$\exists X \{ X = (\lambda L_1(phone\_number\_of \ L_1) \ John) \} \qquad \text{(P)}$$

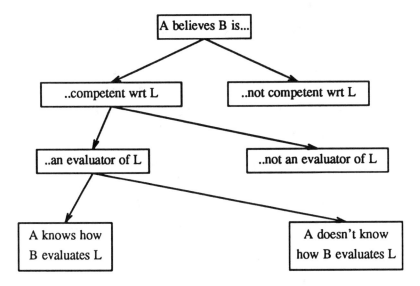

Figure 3.18 A Taxonomy of Competency in Believing

We would not want to ascribe this belief *in any form* to someone who has never heard of John, i.e., they do not have the competency to have beliefs about John because they do not even know of his existence! On the other hand, people who do know about John *will* have the competency to hold beliefs about John such as beliefs about John's phone number. So we could ascribe the belief P to them because they have the competency to have the lambda expression L, and hence the belief P.

However, it should be possible to have or to construct a λ expression such as the one that occurs in P without necessarily being able to evaluate it. That is, I can believe that you have beliefs about John's phone number; even though I believe you don't know what his phone number is, I may or may not hold you to be an evalutor of L.

If I *do* believe you know what John's phone number is (or rather, I *believe* you believe you know what John's phone number is), then I may or may not have an idea of what you believe it to be! So if I do not know John's phone number but believe that Mary does, I can use this to determine that I can find out John's phone number by asking Mary. We will now consider how λ expressions can be augmented with respect to such notions of competency.

3.4.2.2. *Lambda* Formulas

The original proposal for using λ expressions you will remember was to associate each one with a list of *capable evaluators*. In this section, we take this one step further by associating with each λ expression a complex relation that describes the competency of agents or classes of agents in evaluating the expression *and* specifies how they evaluate it[10]. In the original proposal, we might have:

$$\exists .X \{ X = (\lambda L_1(phone\_number\_of\ L_1)\ John)<John> \} \qquad \text{(P1)}$$

which is a proposition containing an expression that evaluates to John's phone number for John (supposing this is a belief of the System about John) but is unevaluable by any other agent. The imposition of John as a capable evaluator of the λ-expression is like adding an extra parameter to it, i.e., the agent performing the evaluation.

In the extended representation, we associate with each λ expression a possibly complex relation that describes the relationship between given agents (those who have the competency to evalute the expression) and how they evaluate the expression. These relations we refer to as *evaluation relations*. A λ expression and its associated evalution relation we call a λ formula. So, for example, from the λ expression that occurs in the belief *P1* cited earlier we might make the extended λ formula shown in (1):

$$
\begin{aligned}
&(\lambda\ L_1(phone\_number\_of\ L_1)\ John) \\
&[(\ System,\ John,\ Mary\,),\ 941662]
\end{aligned}
\qquad \text{(1)}
$$

In the λ formula shown in (1), [(System, John, Mary), 9414662] is used as a shorthand notation to express a simple evaluation relation between the System, John, Mary, and the number 9414662 with respect to the λ expression $(\lambda L_1(phone\_number\_of\ L_1)\ John)$: namely that the System, John and Mary are capable evaluators of the λ expression who evaluate it to 9414662.

Suppose an argument arises over John's phone number: Mary believes it to be 9414661, and we (the System) believe it to be 9414662. We represent this by

---

[10] It may appear that talking about the value of an expression is only valid for beliefs concerning values, such as phone numbers, etc., but not for propositions of the form: *"John is here"*. However, these propositions may be treated in one of two ways: (a) they may often be rewritten to reflect a value (e.g., location of John is x) or (b) the truth or falsity of the proposition may be treated as its value. Coupling the latter case with the notion of *unknown* values (see 3.4.XX) provides us with the power of a Kleene three-valued logic (see Kleene 1982; Haack, 1978).

introducing a complex evaluation relation that takes as arguments two evaluation relations, simple or complex. This complex relation (written as "comp (X,Y)" where X and Y are two evaluation relations) expresses the notion that there are two competing evaluations for the expression. We would then rewrite (1) as (2):

$$(\lambda L_1(phone\_number\_of\ L_1)\ John) \quad \rightarrow$$
$$comp\,([(System,\ John),941662],\ [(Mary),941661]) \tag{2}$$

(Note that the intention of using this relation is to capture those cases where there is argument over the evaluation, but each knows of the other's position on the argument).

We then introduce two more complex evaluation relations: An evaluation relation of the form "spec (X,Y)" is used to indicate that the evaluations derived from the evaluation relation X are considered "better" by those agents involved in X than the evaluations derived from Y. In addition, it indicates that the agents involved in Y do not believe the agents involved in X to have such "better" values. An example of how this might be used will make matters clearer: suppose John's phone number has just been changed from 9414661 to 9414662, and that John and the System know this but Mary does not, and John and the System know that Mary has not yet learned of the change. In that case, we could rewrite (2) as (3):

$$(\lambda L_1(phone\_number\_of\ L_1)\ John) \quad \rightarrow$$
$$spec\,([(System,\ John),941662],\ [(Mary),941661]) \tag{3}$$

A variant evaluation relation is "specK (X,Y)," which is the same as "spec (X,Y)" except that it states that the agents involved in Y believe that the agents involved in X have a better evaluation although they don't know the actual evaluation. This is used in expressing varying degrees of specificity in beliefs.

Suppose the System has medical knowledge that thalassemia is a type of hypochromic anemia, a genetically inherited blood disorder. Let's say the System believes that John (who is quite well-informed about medical topics) believes thalassemia to be a genetic disorder whereas Mary simply believes it to be a disease. Suppose further that Mary believes John and the System know more about thalassemia then she does, whereas John believes the System to know more about thalassemia than he does. A λ formula that represents this situation is shown in (4):

$$(\lambda L\ (immed\_type\_of\ L)\ thalassemia) \quad \rightarrow$$
$$specK\,([(System),hypochromic\_anemia], \tag{4}$$
$$specK\,([(John),genetic\_disorder],\ [(Mary,disease)]))$$

An important point to note about λ-expressions is that in the description above, we are presuming that the beliefs they occur within are in one of the system's topic environments. As those beliefs are ascribed to agents, we must transform the evaluation relations to reflect the capabilities of the agent to whom the beliefs are being ascribed in evaluating the expressions: this transformation is described in 3.4.2.5. First, however we will describe the process of evaluating a λ expression in a belief with respect to the innermost agent in the nesting, in which the belief occurs.

3.4.2.3. Competency, the Explicit and Implicit Mention of Agents, and Evaluating λ-Expressions

An outstanding question is: *how does one represent an agent as having the competency to have a belief involving a λ-expression?*

Our solution is this: An agent is said to have the competency to have a belief involving a λ-expression *if and only if* that agent is explicitly or implicitly mentioned in the evaluation relation of the λ-expression (by explicitly mentioned, we mean that the agent's name occurs in the evaluation relation; by implicitly mentioned, we mean that the name of a class of agents is mentioned in the evaluation relation and the agent is a member of that class of agents).[11]

An agent who is neither explicitly nor implicitly mentioned is deemed not to have the requisite competency to have the belief. If a belief involves a number of λ-expressions then for an agent to have the competency to have that belief, the agent must have the competency to have *each of the* λ-expressions *that are involved in it.*

If we define the class of agents "*average_person*," then we can determine whether a belief involving a λ-expression is typical by seeing if that class is mentioned in the evaluation relation of the expression. Similarly, a belief that involves a λ-expression whose evaluation relation does not mention the average_person class, is Atypical.

A recursive definition of the evaluation of a λ-expression (λ) with evaluation relation R in a nesting $N = <Sys, A_0, \ldots, A_n>$ is given in Figure 3.18. In this figure, the predicate *Mentioned* takes two arguments: an agent (or agent class) and a

---

[11] Determining if an agent belongs to a class of agents is performed by an inheritance reasoner (see Ballim, Candelaria de Ram, and Fass, 1989).

set of agents/agent classes. It is true only where the agent is either explicitly or implicitly mentioned in the set:

$$\varepsilon([A,V],N) = \begin{vmatrix} V \ iff \ Mentioned \ (A_n,A) \\ INCOMPETENT \ \ otherwise \end{vmatrix}$$

$$\varepsilon(spec \ (R_1,R_2),N) = \begin{bmatrix} \varepsilon(R_1,N) = V \ iff \ V \neq INCOMPETENT \\ \varepsilon(R_2,N) \ \ otherwise \end{bmatrix}$$

$$\varepsilon(specK \ (R_1,R_2),N) = \begin{bmatrix} \varepsilon(R_1,N) = V \ iff \ V \neq INCOMPETENT \\ \varepsilon(R_2,N) \ \ otherwise \end{bmatrix}$$

$$\varepsilon(comp \ (R_1,R_2),N) = V$$

where...
$\varepsilon(R_1,N){=}V_1$
$\varepsilon(R_2,N){=}V_2$
then $\ \ V{=}INCOMPETENT \ iff \ V_1{=}V_2{=}INCOMPETENT$
else $\ \ V{=}V_1 \ if \ V_2{=}INCOMPETENT$
else $\ \ V{=}V_2 \ if \ V_1{=}INCOMPETENT$
otherwise $\ \ V{=}ambiguous \ (V_1,V_2)$

Figure 3.19. Evaluation of a λ-expression from its evaluation relation.

It should be noted that the final case of evaluation for the *comp* relation permits of the possibility that there is no unique evaluation for the expression. (For discussion of how beliefs involving such a nonunique evaluation(— which can be represented by meta-disjunction over beliefs) — can be handled, see 3.2.

3.4.2.4. Viewpoint Variables and Constants

There are two outstanding questions with regard to λ expressions: one is how to represent an agent's having the competency to hold beliefs involving a λ-expression, even though the agent cannot evaluate it to anything meaningful. And the second is how to represent the case where an agent can evaluate an expression to something meaningful while how that agent evaluates the expression is not known to other agents within the nesting in which the evaluation is being performed.

The first question is answered by the introduction of variables that are scoped by the innermost viewpoint in which they occur. Hence they will be called *viewpoint variables* or *anonymous variables* to indicate that they stand for an anonymous value. These are similar in nature to existentially quantified variables, but are unbound within the viewpoint. Therefore, they convey the notion that the value of the expression is unknown.

Within the evaluation relation of a λ-expression, an anonymous variable is indicated by the value "*UNKNOWN*." For example, suppose that the system knows John's phone number, and Mary has been told this, but she does not know the phone number. This can be indicated by the λ formula (5):

$$(\lambda L\,(phone\_number\_of\ L)\,John)\,spec\,([(System,\ John),941662],\quad(5)$$
$$[(Mary),UNKNOWN])$$

In performing the evaluation of the λ-expression within a viewpoint, this unknown value will be replaced by an anonymous variable written as *EV_N_X*, where *N* is the nesting in which it occurs and *X* is some index.

To understand the second question where we know someone has better information than ourselves, consider the following situation: the System has some information about thalassemia, namely that it is a disease, but believes that a doctor would have a different, more detailed notion of what it is. Of course, the System cannot tell what a doctor's notion of thalassemia is: How can such a situation be represented?

The solution is to introduce constants (similar in nature to skolem constants), that stand for the actual value. Because these constants are dependent upon the nesting of agents, they are known as viewpoint constants and are written as *EC_N_X* where *N* is the nesting in which they occur, and *X* is some number. (These constants play much the same role in our system as bulleted constants play in various others: cf. Konolige 1983).

In an evaluation relation, a viewpoint constant is indicated by *EC*, and upon evaluation the *EC* is replaced by an actual viewpoint constant. So for example, the situation mentioned earlier could be represented by the λ formula shown in (6):

$$(\lambda L\,(immed\_type-of\ L)\,thalassemia)$$
$$specK\,([(doctor),\ EC],\ [(System),\ disease])\quad(6)$$

3.4.3. Transforming Evaluation Relations During Ascription

The use of λ-formulas poses a question: What effect does ascribing a belief involving a λ-expression to an agent have upon a λ-formula? Ascribing a λ-formula often requires altering the formula. Consider the ascription of the belief in (7) by the System to Mary. This belief involves a λ-expression whose λ formula is given in (8):

$$\exists X \{ X = (\lambda L \, (immed\_type\_of \, L) \, thalassemia) \} \tag{7}$$

$$
\begin{array}{l}
(\lambda L \, (immed\_type\_of \, L) \, thalassemia) \\
\quad specK \, ([(System), hypochromic\_anemia], \\
\quad specK \, ([(John), genetic\_disorder], [(Mary), disease]))
\end{array} \tag{8}
$$

Remember, the "specK" relation indicates that some agents have a more specific value than others, and that those others believe them to have a more specific value. For example, in (8) the System has a more specific value than John, who in turn has a more specific value than Mary. John believes that the System has a more specific value, but does know that it is "hypochromic_anemia." Mary believes both John and the System to have a more specific value than she does, and the System to have a more specific value than John (due to transitivity of "specK").

So in ascribing the belief (7) to Mary, the λ formula (8) should be transformed such that the particular values for the System and John are replaced by the viewpoint constant indicator (EC), yielding (9):

$$
\begin{array}{l}
(\lambda L \, (immed\_type\_of \, L) \, thalassemia) \\
\quad specK \, ([(System), EC], \\
\quad specK \, ([(John), EC], [(Mary), disease]))
\end{array} \tag{9}
$$

At this stage, we will introduce a variant on "specK," which we will call "specKn." The difference between "specK" and "specKn" is that "specK" implies a transitivity in knowing that some agents have more specific information than others. So in example (8), Mary holds that the system has a more specific value for the expression than John, who in turn has a more specific value than Mary (and Mary knows this); hence ascribing (7) to Mary transforms (8) into (9). With "specKn" this transitivity does not hold. So, if instead of "specK" in (8) we had "specKn," then in transforming (8) we would get (9a), below:

$$
\begin{array}{l}
(\lambda L \, (immed\_type\_of \, L) \, thalassemia) \\
\quad specK \, ([(John, System), EC], (Mary), disease]))
\end{array} \tag{9a}
$$

Suppose if the lambda formula for belief (7) was the formula given in (10) instead of that given in (8). How then should (10) be transformed in ascribing (7) to Mary? Or, to John?

$$
\begin{array}{l}
(\lambda L \, (immed\_type\_of \, L) \, thalassemia) \\
\quad spec \, ([(System), hypochromic\_anemia], \\
\quad spec \, ([(John), genetic\_disorder], [(Mary), disease]))
\end{array} \tag{10}
$$

The "spec" relation conveys the notion that some agents (call them group A) have a more specific value than the others (group B): however, those in group B do not hold this to be the case. The assumption is that they believe the group A agents to have the same value as themselves.

Consider ascribing (7) to John: John believes that he has a more specific value than Mary. However, he does not believe that he has a more specific value than the System would. So we obtain:

$$
\begin{aligned}
&(\lambda L\,(immed\_type\_of\ L)\ thalassemia) \\
&spec\,([(John,System),\ genetic\_disorder],[(Mary),disease\,])
\end{aligned} \tag{11}
$$

We define the *transformation of a* λ *formula* recursively as follows: let α be an agent from the domain of agents **A**, let λ be a λ-expression from the domain of λ-expressions Λ), and γ be an evaluation relation from the domain of evaluation relations Γ. The transformation relation (**Y**) is therefore of the form: **Y** : $A \times \Lambda \times \Gamma \rightarrow \Lambda \times \Gamma$ with definitions shown in (12). The predicate *"Mentioned_in"* is true of an agent or class of agents if that agent is mentioned in one of the agent sets that occurs in the given evaluation relation:

$$\mathbf{Y} : \alpha \times \lambda \times [A,V] \rightarrow \lambda \times [A,V] \tag{12}$$

$$\mathbf{Y} : \alpha \times \lambda \times comp\,(\gamma_0,\ \gamma_1) \rightarrow \lambda \times comp\,(\gamma_0',\gamma_1')$$

$$
\begin{aligned}
&where\ if\ Mentioned\_in(\alpha,\gamma_0) \\
&\quad then\ \gamma_0' = \mathbf{Y}{:}\lambda \times \gamma_0 \\
&\quad else\ \gamma_0' = \gamma_0 \\[4pt]
&and\ if\ Mentioned\_in(\alpha,\gamma_1) \\
&\quad then\ \gamma_1' = \mathbf{Y}{:}\lambda \times \gamma_1 \\
&\quad else\ \gamma_1' = \gamma_1
\end{aligned}
$$

In those parts of the definition of **Y** (cont. in 12a,b) in the function, *EC_all* replaces all values in an evaluation relation by the environment-constant indicator *EC* .

$$\mathbf{Y} : \alpha \times \lambda \times specK\,(\gamma_0,\gamma_1) \rightarrow \lambda \times specK\,(\gamma_0',\gamma_1') \tag{12a cont.}$$

$$
\begin{aligned}
&where\ \gamma_0' = \gamma_0\ if\ Mentioned\_in\,(\alpha,\gamma_0) \\[4pt]
&else\ \gamma_0' = EC\_all\,(\gamma_0)
\end{aligned}
$$

and $\gamma_i' = Y : \lambda \times \gamma_1$

$$Y : \alpha \times \lambda \times spec\,(\gamma_0,\gamma_1) \rightarrow \lambda \times \left[\begin{array}{l} spec\,(\gamma_0',\gamma_1)\ if\ Mentioned\_in\,(\alpha,\gamma_0) \\ \quad where\ \gamma_0' = Y{:}\alpha \times \lambda \times \overline{\gamma}_0 \\ \gamma_i'\ otherwise \\ \quad where\ \gamma_i' = Y{:}\alpha \times \lambda \times Merge\_agents\,(\gamma_0,\gamma_1) \end{array}\right. \quad \text{(12b cont.)}$$

The function *Merge_agents* collects all the agents from one evaluation relation, and unions that set with the agents in a second evaluation relation to produce a third evaluation relation, whose definition is given in (13):

$$Merge\_agents\,(\gamma_0,[A,V\,]) \rightarrow [A \cup All\_agents\,(\gamma_0),V\,] \tag{13}$$

$$Merge\_agents\,(\gamma_0,comp\,(\gamma_1,\gamma_2)) \rightarrow comp\,(Merge\_agents\,(\gamma_0,\gamma_1),\ Merge\_agents\,(\gamma_0,\gamma_2))$$

$$Merge\_agents\,(\gamma_0,spec\,(\gamma_1,\gamma_2)) \rightarrow spec\,(Merge\_agents\,(\gamma_0,\gamma_1),\gamma_2)$$

$$Merge\_agents\,(\gamma_0,specK\,(\gamma_1,\gamma_2)) \rightarrow specK\,(Merge\_agents\,(\gamma_0,\gamma_1),\gamma_2)$$

Examples of ascription of beliefs involving λ expressions will be given in chapter 4, although the elements of belief ascription are pulled together into a unified system, first.

Finally, we should note that one could believe the whole notion of default ascription to describe or create a situation in which there can be no learning, since inner beliefs cannot be overridden. But as we explained earlier, any such view would be a misunderstanding from the first, because ascription models the beliefs of others, and cannot in any straightforward way constrain basic belief acquisition or rejection of it by the system itself.

Let us think about the issue in the following way: the system is conducting a medical dialogue and is an expert. Presumably medical beliefs will be inherited into the "dialogue space" (at least if the dialogue partner is also believed expert) and they will include static, permanent medical knowledge like "measles causes spots" in the MEASLES environment. Suppose the System's interlocutor turns out to be a quack who denies this fact: What then stops the system's copy of the MEASLES environment from getting damaged by percolation, and how can we stop that without the system refusing to learn anything? The matter is simple, and is the same for the system itself as for any other belief system it is modelling: if the system decides to learn from another system X whose beliefs it trusts, then it allows ascription for a MEASLES environment. If the situation is a medical lecture by a reputable professor, this is fine and correct changes are made. Notice how this modelling will be done: the ascription will be from its own (possibly erroneous) MEASLES environment to the professor's environment, which it constructs during the lecture. The result is then copied by the system as its own, and that process is learning, i.e., ascription to the teacher environment followed by copying as its own. If the teacher subsequently turns out to be a quack, the process must be undone, which is why earlier copies of environments must be retained.

Chapter 4
Experiments in Belief: *ViewGen*

Chapter 4
Experiments in Belief: *ViewGen*

In this chapter, the various elements of belief ascription discussed thus far are brought together. The purpose of belief ascription is this: given a configuration of beliefs of the System, including those beliefs that the System believes others to have that differ from its own, how can a viewpoint about a particular topic be constructed? For example, given the System's beliefs about George Bush and the differing beliefs about George Bush that the System believes John to hold, how can we generate the System's view of John's view about George Bush (which we write as *<Bel System, Bel John, About George_Bush>* — the underscore used to make a single atomic symbol from the name)? The first question is: How beliefs are to be organized?

As previously discussed, beliefs are clumped together into environments indexed under topics (topic environments) and with respect to the agents who hold them. Minimally, a belief is indexed under a topic if the topic is a term in the belief.[12] This means of course that beliefs may occur in more than one topic environment.

Topic environments about other agents or classes of agents may contain a viewpoint of the agent about various topics. These will contain beliefs that are generally disparate from the System's own beliefs. The environments are therefore incomplete, in that they do not represent the entirety of what the System believes

---

[12] However, it should be noted that we do not plan this to be a restriction on the beliefs that may occur in a topic environment. Other notions of *relevance* may allow for the presence of beliefs in topic environments that do not explicitly mention the topic. For example, it is possible that beliefs brought in by inheritance or counter-factual beliefs could be deemed relevant to a topic.

the agent believes about the topics. For this reason, we refer to them as *degenerate environments*. (The general topology of the beliefs within the System is shown in Figure 4.1). Belief ascription is the process of producing more complete, *generate* environments from the System's topic environments and from *degenerate* ones for those to whom beliefs are being ascribed.

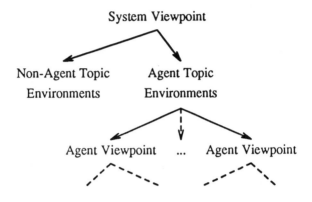

System Viewpoint

Non-Agent Topic   Agent Topic
Environments   Environments

Agent Viewpoint   ...   Agent Viewpoint

Figure 4.1 Topology of the System's Beliefs.

4.1. Generating Points of View

Suppose we wish to generate the viewpoint:

$$<Bel\ System,\ Bel\ \alpha_{0},...,\ Bel\ \alpha_{n},\ About\ T>$$

where T is some topic. The process of generation involves (a) for each level of the nesting, selecting the relevant degenerate topic environments, (b) ordering the relevant topic environments for each level, and (c) recursively generating a level and pushing the result down to the next level. At any level, we push the result from the previous level into one of the relevant degenerate environments, then push the result of that into another, etc., until all the relevant degenerate environments for that level have been used. Because the pushing process is asymmetric (the environment being pushed into has precedence over the one that is being pushed) it is necessary to determine the ordering of precedence of the degenerate environments. Let us now consider in more detail the selection and ordering of degenerate topic environments that are relevant to each level of generation.

4.1.1. Precedence Ordering of Relevant Degenerate Topic Environments

Can we determine any criteria for relevance? If we say (informally) that an agent is involved in a nesting only if the agent is one of the agents in the nesting, then we can specify a negative criterion as in **Criterion 1**:

Belief spaces that involve agents other than those agents involved in the requisite nesting, are not relevant to the nesting.

So in forming what the system believes Lisp-programmers believe about P, the System's beliefs about Bush's beliefs about P are not going to be relevant.

The trivial level of generation is the stage of generating:

$$<Bel\ System,\ About\ T>$$

because at this stage, the only relevant topic environment is the generate environment that contains the System's beliefs about T. So this generate environment can be used as the initial starting point of the next level of the nesting.

Suppose we have generated as far as:

$$<Bel\ System,\ Bel\ \alpha_0, \ldots, Bel\ \alpha_{i-1}>$$

with the result from this level being called R_{i-1}. The question for generating the next level of nesting (R_i) can be broken into two parts: (a) Which degenerate environments are relevant to generating the level of nesting? And (b) How should the relevant degenerate environments be ordered?

All relevant degenerate environments to the nesting are about the topic T. The relevant degenerate environments for generating

$$<Bel\ System,\ Bel\ \alpha_0, \ldots, Bel\ \alpha_i>$$

should be ones of the form:

$$<Bel\ System,\ Bel\ (someone),\ldots,\ Bel\ (someone\_else),\ Bel\ \alpha_i,\ About\ T>,$$

where possible intermediate agents are from the set of agents:

$$A = \{\alpha_j \mid 0 \leq j \leq i\}.$$

Why should this be so? First, the relevant degenerate environments should be nestings that end in α_i because at this stage, we are generating a view that ends in the agent α_i! Other degenerate environments will not be relevant because either (a) they are nestings that end in agents in **A** and hence would have been relevant at previous levels, or (b) they involve agents that are not in the nesting.

In addition, not all permutations of the agents of **A** are valid intermediaries for describing relevant degenerate environments. Only permutations that preserve the order of the level being generated are valid, so

$$<Bel\ System,\ Bel\ \alpha_0,\ Bel\ \alpha_2,\ Bel\ \alpha_i>$$

is relevant (where $i > 2$), but

$$<Bel\ System,\ Bel\ \alpha_2,\ Bel\ \alpha_0,\ Bel\ \alpha_i>$$

is not.

To simplify the following definitions, we will leave out of the environment descriptions the word "Bel" and the "About T" section. If we let "•" be an operator that concatenates two ordered sets, then the relevant degenerate environments for generating R_i are of the form $<System> • A^o • <\alpha_i>$, where A^o is an ordered subset (possibly null) of A such that it contains no subsequence of the form:

$$<\alpha_j, \alpha_k> \text{ for } 0 \leq k < j < i.$$

Let A^O be the set of such ordered subsets of A.

What about the relative ordering of these environments? Obviously, where they differ is in A^o, so the criterion for arranging their precedence will depend on this. We define the precedence on two criteria:

(1) If $A_{\hat{m}}$ is longer than $A_{\hat{\ell}}$ (where they are both elements of A^O), then the environment involving the sequence $A_{\hat{m}}$ takes precedence over the one involving $A_{\hat{\ell}}$.

(2) Sequences of the same length can be ranked by recursively applying the function *precedence* (defined in I) which determines which of two different equal length sequences of agents takes precedence.

$$precedence\ (<\alpha_m> • A_{\hat{m}}, <\alpha_n> • A_{\hat{\ell}}) \rightarrow \begin{bmatrix} <\alpha_m> • A_{\hat{m}} & iff & m < n \\ <\alpha_n> • A_{\hat{\ell}} & iff & m > n \\ precedence\ (A_{\hat{m}}, A_{\hat{\ell}}) & otherwise \end{bmatrix} \qquad \text{I}$$

So for example, if we were generating the environment:

<Bel System, Bel John, Bel Mark, Bel David, About dungeons_and_dragons>

At the trivial level, the generate environment *<Bel System, About dungeons_and_dragons>* is relevant. At the next level, the degenerate environment *<Bel System, Bel John, About dungeons_and_dragons>* is relevant. At the level after that, the relevant degenerate environments are, in order of increasing precedence:

<Bel System, Bel Mark, About dungeons_and_dragons>

<Bel System, Bel John, Bel Mark, About dungeons_and_dragons>

At the final level, the relevant degenerate environments are, again, in order of increasing precedence:

<Bel System, Bel David, About dungeons_and_dragons>
<Bel System, Bel John, Bel David, About dungeons_and_dragons>
<Bel System, Bel Mark, Bel David, About dungeons_and_dragons>
<Bel System, Bel John, Bel Mark, Bel David, About dungeons_and_dragons>

The process of generation takes these degenerate environments and uses them to form the required generate environment by recursively pushing environments into each other, from low precedence to high precedence.

4.2. Pushing An Environment into Another Environment

What of the process of pushing one environment into another? What is meant by saying that one environment gets pushed into the other? In essence, this means attempting to move the beliefs from one environment (the source) into another (the target). The beliefs in the target are taken to have precedence over those from the source. So in cases of conflict through contradiction, offending beliefs from the source that would lead to a contradiction are blocked from ascription.

To accomplish this, all λ-expressions must be transformed with respect to the level of nesting at which the pushing occurs (e.g., with respect to <Bel System, Bel John> after the trivial level in the above example) and then evaluated with respect to the same nesting. Beliefs from the source environment that contain λ-expressions that the last agent does not have the competency to have with respect to the nesting, are eliminated.

An assumption of the ascription process is that the particular choice of "packaging" for beliefs (i.e., how they are constructed) is important. So, there is a reason for having $P \wedge Q$ as a single belief as opposed to having P and Q as two separate beliefs. This means that an environment is *not* equivalent to the conjunction of all the beliefs within it. So for example, in Figure 4.2 the belief $((P \vee Q) \wedge R)$ is not ascribed from the source to the target because it conflicts with the two beliefs $\neg P$ and $\neg Q$ in the target:

However, in Figure 4.3 only the belief $P \vee Q$ is blocked from ascription; the belief R goes through unaffected.

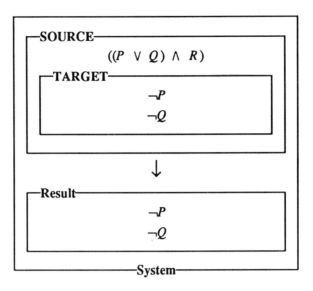

Figure 4.2 An example of pushing one environment into another.

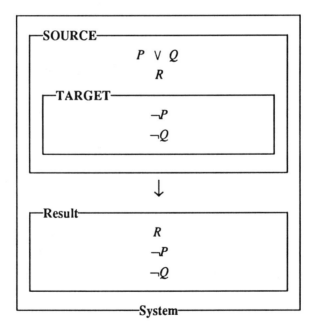

Figure 4.3 Pushing a disjunctive environment into another.

One last point to note about pushing environments: a question that has both practical and theoretical consequences is, Should all the source beliefs be ascribed to a target that does not contain beliefs? The process of ascription cited earlier acts as a filter for inconsistencies in the source environment, eliminating the source beliefs that are the cause of the inconsistencies. So there do not have to be any beliefs in the target for elimination of source beliefs to occur unless a short-cut is taken in the case of a target containing no beliefs. In the rest of this book we shall assume that this short-cut has been taken.

4.3. An Algorithm for Generating Points of View

The algorithm for generating viewpoints can now be easily described: firstly, a context is set up by selecting the System's view of the topic and all the relevant degenerate views of the other agents for each level of the nesting. The relevant degenerate environments for each level are then ordered in terms of increasing precedence. The algorithm may be stated as:

(1)   At the trivial level the result is the generate System environment about the topic.

(2)   At any other level, the result is obtained by

(i) pushing the result from the previous level into the lowest-precedence environment relevant to the level to form an intermediate result;

(ii) recursively pushing the intermediate result into the next lowest precedence relevant environment to form a new intermediate result, until all the relevant environments have had an intermediate result pushed into them.

(iii) pushing the last intermediate result into the highest precedence relevant environment, the result which is the generate environment for that level.

We can demonstrate this with an example. Consider the initial situation shown in Figure 4.4 (where dungeons_and_dragons has been abbreviated to DND) and presume we wish to generate:

<Bel System, Bel John, Bel Mark, Bel David, About dungeons_and_dragons>

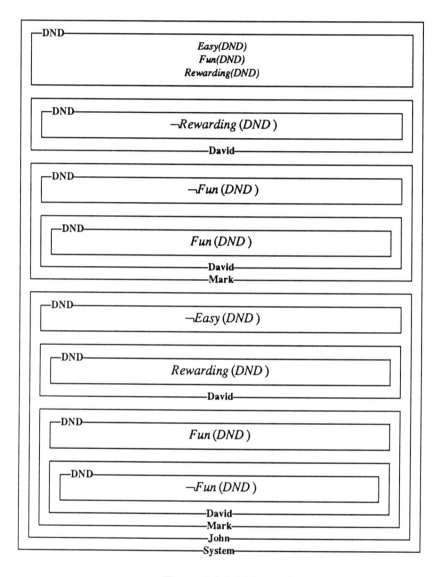

Figure 4.4 Initial situation.

The trivial level (*<Bel System, About DND>*) is precisely the topmost topic in Figure 4.4 containing three system beliefs: (a) that DND is easy; (b) that it is fun; and (c) that it is rewarding.

The next level of nesting (*<Bel System, Bel John, About DND>*) is generated by pushing the environment containing those three beliefs into the degenerate environment *<Bel System, Bel John, About DND>*. (The result of this is shown in Figure 4.5). The belief ¬*Easy* (*DND*) in the degenerate environment overrides the incoming *Easy* (*DND*), hence the resulting contents:

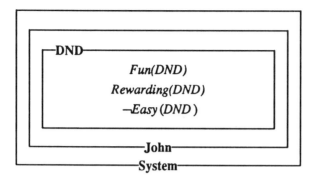

Figure 4.5 Generating <Bel System, Bel John, About DND>

The <*Bel System, Bel John, Bel Mark, About DND*> level is generated by:

(1) pushing the result in Figure BBB into the degenerate environment <*Bel System, Bel Mark, About DND*>, resulting in an environment containing the beliefs ¬*Easy* (*DND*), ¬*Fun* (*DND*), and *Rewarding* (*DND*).

(2) This result is pushed into the degenerate environment <*Bel System, Bel John, Bel Mark, About DND*> resulting in an environment containing the beliefs ¬*Easy* (*DND*), *Fun* (*DND*), and *Rewarding* (*DND*). This is the generate environment for the level of nesting (shown in Figure 4.6):

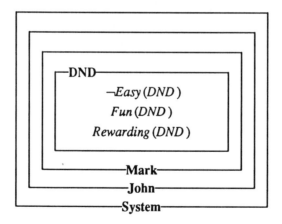

Figure 4.6 <Bel System, Bel John, Bel Mark, About DND>

The final level *<Bel System, Bel John, Bel Mark, Bel David, About DND>* can be generated by taking the resulting environment shown in Figure 4.6, and

(1)   Pushing it into the degenerate environment *<Bel System, Bel David, About DND>* resulting in an environment containing ¬*Easy (DND)*, *Fun (DND)*, and ¬*Rewarding (DND)*.

(2)   Pushing that result into the degenerate environment *<Bel System, Bel John, Bel David, About DND>*, given an environment containing the beliefs ¬*Easy (DND)*, *Fun (DND)* and *Rewarding (DND)*.

(3)   Pushing that environment into the degenerate environment *<Bel System, Bel Mark, Bel David, About DND>* resulting in an environment containing (in this case) the same beliefs ¬*Easy (DND)*, *Fun (DND)*, and ¬*Rewarding (DND)*.

(4)   Finally, pushing that result into the degenerate environment *<Bel System, Bel John, Bel Mark, Bel David, About DND>* to produce the generate version of it, with contents shown in Figure 4.7:

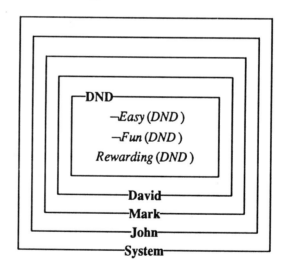

Figure 4.7

4.4. *ViewGen*: A Belief Ascription Program

We now describe *ViewGen*, a programmed implementation of the mechanisms and heuristics described in this book. This program is intended to be a subsystem of other systems which generates topic-specific nested points of view that can then be used by control programs in discourse analysis, planning, etc.

Figure 4.8 shows an example call to the *ViewGen* program to generate the System's view of thalassemia. The call to generate and display this viewpoint is given by typing *<Bel System, About thalassemia>* at the prompt "em:" — which stands for *environment manipulator*. The generated environment contains a belief that involves a λ-expression, so the binding of the existentially-quantified variable to the value of the λ-expression is given:

```
em: <Bel System, About thalassemia>


 [ <Bel System, About thalassemia>
   [
   E.Z{Z = (lambda.L (immed_type_of L) thalassemia)}
   ]
 ]
Z = hypochromic_anemia
  in: E.Z{Z = (lambda.L (immed_type_of L) thalassemia)}

em:
```

Figure 4.8 ViewGen: The System's View About Thalassemia

4.4.1. The Data Structures in *ViewGen*

ViewGen's database is a set of topic environments; where the topic environments are about agents or classes of agents, they may contain subviewpoints of those agents about various topics. Those subviewpoints will in general contain beliefs that differ from the System's own beliefs on the topics.

Associated with each environment are the λ formulas of the λ-expressions that occur in the environment. (If a λ-expression occurs in a number of different environments, then its λ formula will be associated with each of them.) Figure 4.9 shows the environment and associated λ formula used in deriving the viewpoint in Figure 4.8:

```
[ <Bel System, About thalassemia>
    [
    E.Z{ Z = (lambda.L (immed_type_of L) thalassemia)}
    ]
    [
    (lambda.L (immed_type_of L) thalassemia)
        spec(specK([(anemia_specialist,System),hypochromic_anemia],
                specK([(high_med_inform_person,doctor),genetic_disorder],
                    [(avg_med_inform_person),disease])),
            spec([(avg_educated_person),greek_province],
                [(avg_person),greek_place]))
    ]
]
```

Figure 4.9 ViewGen λ formula:
The Database Entry Used to Generate the Viewpoint in 4.8.

4.4.2. An Example of Viewpoint Generation in *ViewGen*

In the following example, assume that the system is a medical expert conducting a dialogue with a married couple who are seeking advice about thalassemia. The system has a λ formula for the intensional description *"immed_type_of(thalassemia)"* shown in Figure 4.9.

Hypochromic anemia is a genetic disorder. Suppose that the System has the view of genetic disorder as shown in Figure 4.10. (The point of view in Figure 4.10 contains the belief that the child of two people who both have a genetic disorder will suffer from the same genetic disorder as they do).

Suppose that the couple in question are called Paul and Susan and that the System has the beliefs about them shown in Figure 4.11a,b.

The important beliefs here are that the System believes Susan is a medically informed person, and that the couple both suffer from thalassemia. We presume that these reasoning mechanisms allow us to reason with the viewpoints in Figures em: <Bel System, About genetic_disorder>

[<Bel System, About genetic_disorder>
  [
    A.X1{A.X2{A.X3{
              {suffer_from(X2,genetic_disorder)
               ^ suffer_from(X1,genetic_disorder)
               ^ married(X1,X2)
               ^ child_of(X3,X1,X2)}
               -> suffer_from(X3,genetic_disorder)}}}
  ]
]

em:

Figure 4.10 The System's View of genetic_disorder.

em: <Bel System, About Susan>

[<Bel System, About Susan>
  [
    suffers_from(Susan,thalassemia),
    married(Susan,Paul),
    isa(Susan,high_med_inform_person),
    isa(Susan,female)
  ]
]

Figure 4.11a The System's Views of Susan and Paul: Susan.

4.9, 4.10, and 4.11a,b to form the hypothesis that any offspring of the pair will also suffer from thalassemia, something that they need to be warned about. If we presume that the System follows Grice's Maxims (1969), then we need to generate what the System believes each of them believes about thalassemia. (These points of view are shown in Figures 4.12 and 4.13).

em: <Bel System, About Paul>

[<Bel System, About Paul>
  [
  suffers_from(Paul,thalassemia),
  married(Paul,Susan),
  isa(Paul,male)
  ]
]

em:

Figure 4.11b The System's Views of Susan and Paul: Paul.

em: <Bel System, Bel Susan, About thalassemia>

[<Bel System, Bel Susan, About thalassemia>
  [
  E.Z{Z = (lambda.L (immed_type_of L) thalassemia)}
  ]
]
Z = genetic_disorder
  in: E.Z{Z = (lambda.L (immed_type_of L) thalassemia)}
em:

Figure 4.12 The System's View of Susan's View of Thalassemia.

In Figure 4.12, the belief that thalassemia is a type of genetic disorder has been ascribed to Susan. Because the system believes she is a highly medically informed person, and that such informed people believe thalassemia is a genetic disorder (see Figure 4.9). Paul however, is not believed to be a highly medically informed person. From the belief that he is a male (Figure 4.11b) it can be inferred through inheritance that he is an average person (avg_person) and for him thalassemia is a place in Greece (Figure 4.13).

    em: <Bel System, Bel Paul, About thalassemia>

    [<Bel System, Bel Paul, About thalassemia>
       [
       E.Z{Z = (lambda.L (immed_type_of L) thalassemia)}
       ]
    ]
    Z = greek_place
       in: E.Z{Z = (lambda.L (immed_type_of L) thalassemia)}

    em:

Figure 4.13 The System's View of Paul's View of Thalassemia.

To further complicate matters, in any dialogue between three agents, it is sometimes necessary for one agent to model what the second believes the third believes, or what the third believes the second believes about the topic; so we generate what the System believes Susan believes Paul believes about thalassemia and what the System believes Paul believes Susan believes about thalassemia. (These points of view are shown in Figures 4.14 and 4.15, respectively).

In Figure 4.14 using the beliefs about Susan and Paul, the System generates that Susan believes that Paul believes thalassemia is a Greek province. In Figure 4.15, the System generated that Paul believes that Susan also believes thalassemia is a Greek province.

Suppose however, that the System believed Paul to be medically informed. In that case, it would believe that Paul believes thalassemia to be a disease (see Figure 4.9). What would the System believe Paul believed Susan believed about thalassemia? Because he knows her to be highly medically informed and he believes thalassemia to be a disease, and because highly medically informed people have a more developed notion of thalassemia, he would believe she has a more developed notion of thalassemia than he does. (This is shown in Figure 4.16, where the binding of the existential variable is equivalent to the λ-expression ($\lambda.L$ (*immed_type_of L*)*thalassemia* .)

em: <Bel System, Bel Susan, Bel Paul, About thalassemia>

[<Bel System, Bel Susan, Bel Paul, About thalassemia>
  [
  E.Z{Z = (lambda.L (immed_type_of L) thalassemia)}
  ]
]
Z = greek_place
  in: E.Z{Z = (lambda.L (immed_type_of L) thalassemia)}

em:

Figure 4.14 The System's View of Susan's View of Paul's View
About Thalassemia.

em: <Bel System, Bel Paul, Bel Susan, About thalassemia>

[<Bel System, Bel Paul, Bel Susan, About thalassemia>
  [
  E.Z{Z = (lambda.L (immed_type_of L) thalassemia)}
  ]
]
Z = greek_place
  in: E.Z{Z = (lambda.L (immed_type_of L) thalassemia)}

em:

Figure 4.15 System's View of Paul's View of Susan's View of Thalassemia.

By using the environments generated in this example, a System could determine how much information would be necessary to inform each of them of the problems associated with their having children. This example merely indicated the use of nested environments in participating in discourse: in the following chapters, we will indicate ways of manipulating environments for purposes of reasoning, and generating new intensional descriptions from existent ones.

em: <Bel System, Bel Paul, Bel Susan, About thalassemia>

  [<Bel System, Bel Paul, Bel Susan, About thalassemia>
    [
     E.Y{Y = (lambda.L (immed_type_of L) thalassemia)}
    ]
   ]
  Y = EC_13
   in: E.Y{Y = (lambda.L (immed_type_of L) thalassemia)}

em:

Figure 4.16 4.15 Revised for a Hypothetical Medically-Informed Paul.

Chapter 5
Global Issues: Reasoning with Viewpoints

Chapter 5.1
Reasoning with viewpoints

In this and subsequent chapters, we speculate about various uses for belief ascription methods already outlined, in the context of various systems. This chapter deals with notions of reasoning with multiple viewpoints, as well as a language within that such reasoning can take place.

5.1.1. Forms of Reasoning with Viewpoints

We have already mentioned that our prime interest in viewpoints is as a means of explicating dialogue and facilitating participation in a discourse; for this purpose, viewpoints set up environments in which analyzing dialogue and devising plans for discourse participation can occur.

Consider the issues of which beliefs should be stored permanently, and how new beliefs may be added to the permanent environments: given our rules for construction of nested points of view, we can now see why the only beliefs not stored directly as beliefs of the System are those that the System believes other agents to hold, but that are different from those held by the System.

It follows from this that the way to handle new beliefs is to place them into the System's established set of beliefs. If this can be done without jeopardizing the consistency of the System's belief space, the belief is stored there permanently, as if the agent is more knowledgeable on the subject of the proposition than the System. The System must of course believe that the agent is truthful before accepting that agent's belief as its own. Otherwise, the belief is stored as a belief of the agent, who is the source of the proposition.

This sort of reasoning with viewpoints, which we call *percolation* (because beliefs can be seen to percolate out from nestings), is the one that interests us in particular. There are of course many ways for someone to reason with viewpoints; what we will consider here is a general language for facilitating the manipulation of beliefs, and how it can be used for the specific case of percolation.

To consider a language for reasoning with viewpoints, we must first at least outline what such a language would look like. We present a language similar in nature to Kleene's three-valued logic, (1952) using strong connectives and a special operator to express propositions having unknown truth values. This operator is similar in function to Bochvar's "assertion operator," which provides a mapping from three-valued to two-valued logic (see Bochvar, 1939).

Having defined our language for reasoning with viewpoints, we then introduce another language for expressing nested beliefs and viewpoints — similar to the "contexts" approach suggested by Weyhrauch (1980). (Their conjoint use is illustrated by the following famous puzzle).

5.1.2. A Simple Language for Viewpoint-Internal Reasoning

Let us represent beliefs within a viewpoint by propositions in a language (a valid proposition is any well-formed formula wff of the language, which we will call L_{int}). L_{int} is *three-valued* as well as many-sorted. In the semantic interpretation of classical logic there are only two truth-values (true and false) whereas three-valued logic adds a third value, the interpretation of which is the subject of much debate (see Haack, 1974, 1978; also Bochvar, 1939 and Lukasiewicz, 1930). In L_{int} the third value represents *"unknown,"* (a wff that has *unknown* as its truth value is not known to be either true or false); L_{int} has truth-value gaps as opposed to a genuine third value. Wff's are still either true or false in the real world, but the third truth-value is used to indicate a state of partial ignorance. (This is precisely the situation that can arise when a λ-expression is used to represent the truth value of a proposition, and on ascribing the proposition to some agent, the λ-expression evaluates to an environment variable; Within such a viewpoint that is, the value of the proposition remaining unknown).

A monadic operator **U** (pronounced "unk") is then introduced. This operator provides a mapping from three-valued to two-valued logic. Bochvar (1939) introduced a monadic operator known as the "assertion operator" that mapped true to true, false to false and the third truth value to false. His operator thereby "asserted" the truth of a proposition. On the other hand, the operator introduced here asserts that the truth value of a proposition is unknown. This operator is not fully truth-functional, because the mapping from a proposition to its truth-value is not a compositional function of the mapping from its components to their truth-values: just because the truth-values of p and q are unknown does not imply that the truth-value of $p \lor q$ is unknown.

Kleene (1952) developed his logic to facilitate reasoning about undecided mathematical statements, and it can be shown that the connectives are monotonic (i.e., no unwarranted inferences can be made: see Turner, 1984). Later we shall see, however, that for reasoning with beliefs it is necessary to allow belief revision, and thereby introduce nonmonotonicity into the language.

5.1.2.1. Elements of L_{int}

The vocabulary of L_{int} consists of the following: a set of individual terms, a set of n-place relational symbols (for each $n > 0$), a set of n-place functional symbols (for each $n \geq 0$), logical connectives ($\neg$ $\mathbf{U}$ $\land$ $\lor$ $\supset$ $\equiv$), quantification symbols ($\exists$ $\forall$), and parentheses ( ).

Well-formed formulae are constructed from atomic wffs by means of logical connectives, quantifiers, and parentheses. The atomic wffs are of the form $R(t_0, \ldots, t_{n-1})$, where R is an n-place relational symbol and each t_i is a term (either an individual constant or variable or having the form $f(t_0', \ldots, t_{m-1}')$ where each t_j' is a term and f is an m-place function symbol). For a given $R_k(t_0, \ldots, t_{n-1})$, each t_i $(0 \leq i \leq n-1)$ must belong to some domain D_{k_i} as prescribed by the semantics of R_k (the same goes for terms of $f_h(t_0', \ldots, t_{m-1}')$). Complex wff's are formed using the connectives, quantifiers, and parentheses. If p and q are wff's, then so are the following: $\neg p$; $\mathbf{U}p$; $p \land q$; $p \lor q$; $p \supset q$; $p \equiv q$; (p) and $\exists_x(p)$ and $\forall_x(p)$, where x is a free variable in p.

The rules of inference[13] for L_{int} that differ from those of first order predicate calculus are given in Figure 5.1, here p and q are wff's of L_{int}. (the rule of addition is given here to shed light on the example that occurs later in this chapter).

This is not an exhaustive rule set by any means. However, it will suffice for the types of reasoning we are to consider in this chapter. Notice that the given rules encode the assumption that if the truth of a proposition is unknown (within a

---

[13] The reason for the subscript i on the names of these inference rules is to distinguish them from inference rules of L_{ext} (the language for representing viewpoints).

Add: $\dfrac{p}{p \vee q}$, $I_i 10$: $\dfrac{Up \qquad \neg Uq \qquad p \vee q}{q}$,

$I_i 11$: $\dfrac{Up \qquad \neg Uq \qquad p \supset q}{q}$, $I_i 12$: $\dfrac{\neg Up \qquad \neg Uq}{\neg U(p \vee q)}$,

$I_i 13$: $\dfrac{\neg Up \qquad \neg Uq}{\neg U(p \wedge q)}$, $I_i 14$: $\dfrac{p}{\neg Up}$,

$I_i 15$: $\dfrac{\neg p}{\neg Up}$

Figure 5.1 Rules of Inference for L_{int}.

viewpoint, eventually), then the proposition can be proved neither false nor true from the assumptions in the viewpoint. So if $p \vee q$, Up, and $\neg Uq$ are true, then must be true; if q were false, this would contradict Up and $p \vee q$, because it would necessitate p being true, which contradicts Up, whereas if q were unknown, this would contradict $\neg Uq$.

5.1.2.2. Justifications and Assumptions of Formula

It is often necessary to retract previously held beliefs in light of new information; the retraction of one belief may necessitate the retraction of others that follow from it. Also, it is often necessary to simultaneously hold two or more contradictory beliefs, but not beliefs that follow from them: these are problems of *Truth Maintenance*. A method proposed by de Kleer (1984, 1986) for handling the problems is adapted for use here.

Each *ViewGen* formula has a Justification and an Assumption-set associated with it. The *Justification* consists of formulae that can be used to derive the formula in question by the application of a rule of inference or equivalences. The *Assumption-set* consists of the respective formulae whose (asserted) truth is necessary for the given formula to be true. By keeping a record of formulae that are inconsistent with each other, one can determine whether a new formula is valid by checking that there are no inconsistent pairs in the assumption set of the formula.

Formulae are written as triples of the form *name:(formula, Justification-set, Assumption-set)*. So, given the following:

α: $(p, \{\}, \{\})$ and β: $(p \supset q, \{\}, \{\})$

using *modus ponens* (MP) one can derive:

γ: $(q, \{(MP, (\alpha, \beta))\}, \{\alpha, \beta\})$

Two special Justifications are introduced. The first represents the fact that an agent asserts that he holds a formula (say p) to be true and this is written as:

α:$(p, \{(A)\}, \{\})$.

The second represents that a belief (say q) has been ascribed to an agent by the default ascription rule. It is written as:

β:$(q, \{(D)\}, \{\})$.

5.1.3. A Language for Viewpoint-External Reasoning — L_{ext}

Viewpoints state particular belief relations between agents and propositions. There are two basic types of viewpoints: generate and degenerate. An atomic, well-formed formula of L_{ext} is of the form:

(i)   *<Bel System, Bel a_0, ..., Bel a_n, About T>C* ;

(ii)   *<Bel System, Bel a_0, ..., Bel a_n, DAbout T>C* ;

(iii)   *<Bel System, Bel a_0, ..., Bel a_n, About T>P* ; or

(iv)   *<Bel System, Bel a_0, ..., Bel a_n, DAbout T>P*,

where C is a list of propositions of L_{int}, and P is a proposition of L_{int}. *DAbout* is used to indicate a degenerate environment or belief.

For example, the formula of L_{ext} given in (1) cited later represents the System's belief that agent a_0 believes that agent a_1 believes certain propositions about topic T, (represented by $p(T)$ and $q(T)$), and this is a degenerate viewpoint with $p(T)$ having been ascribed to a_i by a_0, whereas q(T) has been asserted by a_1.

<Bel System, Bel a_0, Bel a_1, About T>[α:$(p(T), \{D\}, \{\})$, β:$(q(T), \{A\}, \{\})$]   (1)

The formula of L_{ext} given in (2) represents that the System believes that a_0 (degeneratively) believes about topic T the proposition $p(T)$: [i.e., a_0 asserts q(T)].

*<Bel System, Bel a_0, DAbout T>*α:$(p(T), \{A\}, \{\})$ (2)

Definition: If E_1 and E_2 are atomic wff's of L_{ext} and p is a wff's of L_{int}, then the following are also wffs of L_{ext}:

(i) (E_1)

(ii) $E_1\ E_2$

(iii) $\neg E_1$

(iv) $E_1 = E_2$

(v) $\mathbf{A}E_1$

(vi) $\mathbf{P}E_1$

(vii) $\mathbf{C}E_1$

The formula $E_1\ E_2$ is used to indicate a disjunction over environments, e.g., (3) cited later represents that the System believes that John either believes about thalassemia that it is a Greek province, or that he believes it to be a disease: this is the meta-disjunction discussed in 3.2.

$$<Bel\ System\,,\ Bel\ John\,,\ About\ thalassemia >\alpha{:}(isa\,(thalassemia\,,\ Greek\_city\,),\{D\},\{\})$$
$$\vee \qquad\qquad (3)$$
$$<Bel\ System\,,\ Bel\ John\,,\ About\ thalassemia >\beta{:}(isa\,(thalassemia\,,\ disease\,),\{D\},\{\})$$

Similarly, $\neg E_1$ indicates a negation over a viewpoint (such as the System believes John does not believe $p(t)$ about t) which would be represented as:

$$\neg <Bel\ System,\ Bel\ John,\ About\ T>\ \gamma{:}(p(t),\{A\},\{\}).$$

The expression $E_1 = E_2$ indicates that the contents of the two viewpoints are the same. The two expressions $\mathbf{A}E_1$ and $\mathbf{P}E_1$ are expressions about consistency. (They are explained in detail later).

The expression $\mathbf{C}E_1$ is used to express competency in having beliefs. For example, C<Bel System, Bel John, About t~>α:(p,{D},{}) expresses the notion that *the System believes John to have the competency to have the belief p*.

In addition to the above wff's of L_{ext}, we have the following two functions that map from viewpoints to viewpoints:

(a) E_1/p

(b) $E_1\backslash p$

The function E_1/p produces the environment that has the same nesting as E_1, but with the contents of E_1 plus the proposition p. The function $E_1\backslash p$ produces the environment that has the same nesting as E_1, but with the contents of E_1 less the proposition p (if it occurs in E_1).

5.1.3.1. Contradictoriness, Contrariness and Consistency Across Viewpoints

In classical two-valued logic, if the propositions p and $\neg p$ are both true then they are contradictory. In the system discussed here, these two formulae are also contradictory if they both occur within one viewpoint. There is however, a special case to consider: namely, are they still contradictory if they occur in different viewpoints?

In this language, if p is not of either the form Uq nor the form $\neg Uq$ ($q \neq p$), then p and $\neg p$ are said to be contradictory across viewpoints. If on the other hand p is of the form Uq or $\neg Uq$, then p and $\neg p$ are said to be contrary across viewpoints. In this case, it is possible to draw valid inferences in one viewpoint using the propositions in the other, with certain restrictions.

Intuitively, having $\neg Up$ in one viewpoint and Up in another means that the truth value of p is known in the first viewpoint but unknown in the second. This is not contradictory, because it is possible for one person to know that p is true at the same time another does not. Furthermore, the person who does not know the truth of p may be able to deduce its truth value by simulating the reasoning of the other person, without that person asserting that p is either true or false.

If we are ascribing beliefs then, Up is inconsistent with p, $\neg p$, and $\neg Up$. If however, we are percolating beliefs outward, then a $\neg Up$, p or $\neg p$ being percolated into an environment containing Up is consistent, and overrides the Up, thus eliminating it. To consider how this could occur, suppose the System does not know whether it is raining out or not: John tells the System that it is raining. This statement of John's forms a belief of the form:

<Bel System , Bel John , About weather >α:(raining ,{A},{}).

This belief can be percolated out from the nested environment and adopted as the System's own belief, overriding the System's lack of belief in it either being rainy or not.

We can therefore define two types of consistency, and use two operators to denote them. AE asserts that the environment E is consistent under ascription (i.e., with reference to ascription, the contents are consistent). The expression PE asserts that the environment E is consistent under percolation.

We can use these two operators to define a rule for percolation. Suppose we have two environments:

    (1) <Bel System, Bel $a_0, \ldots , a_{n-1}$,About T>C_1
    (2) <Bel System, Bel $a_0, \ldots , a_{n-1}, a_n$,About T>$C_2$

such that C_2 contains a proposition p. We can percolate p if
$$P<Bel\ System,\ Bel\ a_0,\ldots,\ a_{n-1},About\ T>C_1/p.$$

That is we can define a rule for percolation $(I_e 1)$ of the following form:

$$\frac{<Bel\ System,\ Bel\ a_0,\ldots,\ a_{n-1},a_n,About\ T>p \qquad P<Bel\ System,\ Bel\ a_0,\ldots,\ a_{n-1},About\ T>C_1/p}{<Bel\ System,\ Bel\ a_0,\ldots,\ a_{n-1},About\ T>p}$$

This rule introduces nonmonotonicity into the language. It promotes a proposition of known truth value into an outer environment where the same proposition might exist, but with previously unknown truth value. In that case, the unknown truth value is replaced by the known truth value and hence belief revision has occurred. This rule does not mean that if an agent is ignorant of p, then adopting another agent's viewpoint will necessarily allow the first agent to know *that* p. Rather, it means that if one agent does not know the truth of p but is able to reason what another agent believes is the truth of p, then the agent can adopt that truth value for p as his own, given percolation consistency between the beliefs of the first and second agents.

How can this be put into practice? A favorite puzzle of researchers working on nested attitudes is the *Three Wise Men Puzzle*. Let us see how this system can cope with that puzzle.

5.1.4. Percolation — An Example of Reasoning with Viewpoints

Attardi and Simi (1984) state the *Wise Man Puzzle* as follows:

> "A king wishing to know which of his men is the wisest puts a white hat on each of their heads, tells them that at least one hat is white, and asks the first to tell the color of his hat. The man answers that he does not know. The second man gives the same answer to the same question. The third man answers that his hat is white." The puzzle is: How did the third man know that his hat was white?

Those authors then present a solution to the puzzle using viewpoints and a metalanguage called *Omega*. We feel that their approach is lacking, however, in that it makes use of a viewpoint of the real world. Such an omniscient viewpoint is unrealistic and fails to capture the reasoning of the third wise man in the puzzle.

Konolige (1982) presented a solution in a modal logic called K4 but (as Moore, 1984, pointed out) such a logic assumes that whatever is known to an agent is universally valid, which as Attardi and Simi admit (1984), makes it impossible to handle contradictory viewpoints.

The solution in this section does not depend upon an omniscient viewpoint on whatever is known to an agent as "universally valid."

The following abbreviations are used in the solution:

$$a_1 = the\ 1^{st}\ Wise\ Man$$

$$a_2 = the\ 2^{nd}\ Wise\ Man$$

$$a_3 = the\ 3^{rd}\ Wise\ Man$$

$$W_{a_1} = the\ 1^{st}\ Wise\ Man's\ hat\ is\ white$$

$$W_{a_2} = the\ 2^{nd}\ Wise\ Man's\ hat\ is\ white$$

$$W_{a_3} = the\ 3^{rd}\ Wise\ Man's\ hat\ is\ white$$

Let us consider the problem from the viewpoint of agent a_3 (the third agent to speak) and write beliefs in the form of L_{int} propositions within a_3's viewpoint. Assume that all three men are wearing white hats.

We begin by considering a_3's viewpoint before either of the other wise men has spoken, and again after they each speak in turn. Initially, a_3 believes that at least one of the hats is white; he knows that a_1's and a_2's hats are white because he can see their hats; he doesn't know if his own hat is white, as he cannot see his own hat. We then have an initial viewpoint for a_3 (shown in Figure 5.2) at time t_0:

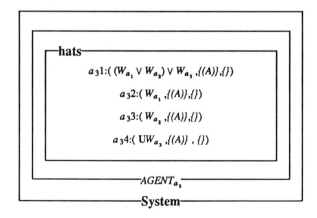

Figure 5.2 Agent a_3's view at time t_0.

At time t_1, the first wise man says that he doesn't know the color of his hat. We now consider what a_3 believes that a_1 believes about the color of the hats, and the inferences that a_3 may draw from these beliefs (Figure 5.3):

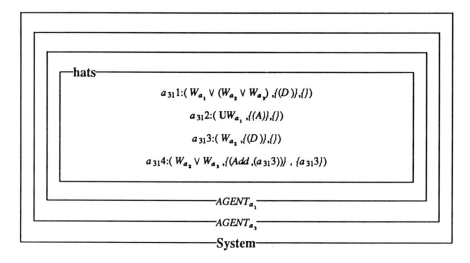

Figure 5.3. Agent a_3's view of a_1's view at time t_1.

Agent a_3 assumes that a_1 is aware that at least one of the hats is white (represented by $a_{31}1$). Furthermore, a_1 asserts that he does not know the color of his own hat ($a_{31}2$). Both a_3 and a_1 are able to see that a_2's hat is white, so a_3 can ascribe this fact to a_1 (formula $a_{31}3$). All the agents are *wise* men, so it is assumed by definition that they all reason perfectly with regard to the inference rules. Hence a_3 can reason that a_1 is able to infer that one or both of a_2's or a_3's is white (i.e., he can infer formula $a_{31}4$ by applying inference rule **Add** to formula $a_{31}3$).

At time t_2, a_2 says that he does not know the color of his own hat. Consider the viewpoint of what a_3 then believes a_2 believes a_1 believes about the color of the hats:

In Figure 5.4, we see how a_3 reasons about a_2's reasoning after a_1 has spoken, and how a_3 is thus able to reason that his own hat must be white and for a_2 to assert that he does not know the color of his hat.

Agent a_3 assumes that a_2 assumes a_1 believes that at least one of the hats is white ($a_{321}1$) and that a_1 knows the colors of a_2's and a_3's hats ($a_{321}3$ and $a_{321}4$). Agent a_1 asserted at time t_1 that he did not know the color of his hat, so agent a_3 assumes that agent a_2 believes that this is true ($a_{321}2$).

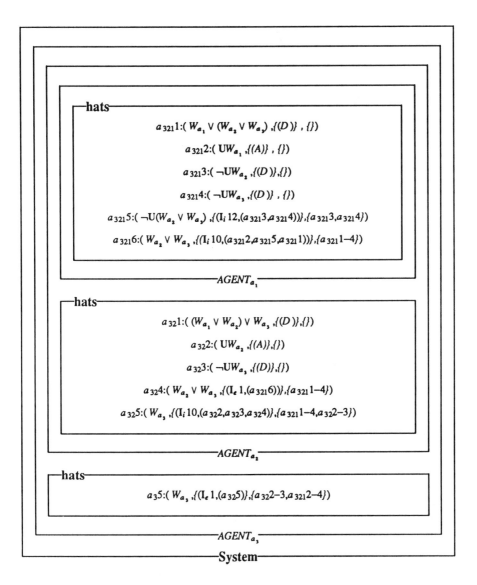

Figure 5.4. a_3's view of a_2's view of a_1's view at time t_2.

By reasoning with formulae $a_{321}1$–4, agent a_3 is able to simulate the way in which a_2 simulates a_1's reasoning. Thus, a_3 can derive that a_2 reasons that a_1 believes that at least one of agent a_2's or a_3's hats is white. (If they were both black, then a_1 could reason that his own hat must be white, but he has asserted that he does not know the color of his own hat).

Agent a_3 can simulate a_2's reasoning. First of all, a_3 assumes that a_2 believes that at least one of their hats is white (a_{321}) and that a_2 knows the color of a_3's hat (a_{323}). Agent a_2 asserts that he does not know the color of his own hat (a_{322}). Agent a_3 believes that the belief that one or both of a_2's or a_3's hat is white can be adopted by a_2 (a_{324}). Given a_{322}–4, agent a_3 can reason that a_2 must believe that a_3's hat is white (a_{325}). This belief can then be adopted by a_3, who has reasoned that his own hat is white.

(Thus far, we have been assuming that all beliefs are held with equal conviction; this makes life simple for us when describing ascription, etc., but is impractical for modelling real life situations in all but the simplest of cases.)

5.1.5. Speculations: Abstracting Quantitative Reasoning

There are a number of popular methods for reasoning with beliefs that are *not* held with equal conviction. Amongst these, numerical approaches are extremely popular. These involve attributing a probability value (as with Bayesian methods) or a range of probability values (Dempster-Shafer methods Shafer, 1976) to each belief.

Another popular method is *fuzzy logic* (Zadeh 1978) which has an ordered range of truth values. We consider this a pseudo-numeric approach because the range of truth values could in fact be mapped onto a number line. (Another method we consider pseudo-numerical is the approach to reasoning about likelihood proposed by Halpern and Rabin, 1987).

Nonnumeric approaches are, generally speaking, forms of default reasoning. Default reasoning is the ability to reason in the presence of incomplete or indefinite information. It has been described as "jumping to conclusions based on what is normally the case" (Konolige, 1987, p. 394) and as "the process of arriving at conclusions based upon patterns of information of the form *in the absence of evidence to the contrary, assume...*" (Reiter, 1978, p. 210), as well as that it involves reasoning that some property "is true of every [thing] for which it is not explicitly cancelled" (Fahlman, 1979, p. 16).

Approaches to default reasoning that typify the above descriptions include *default logic* (Reiter, 1980; Etherington, 1987), *autoepistemic logic* (Moore, 1985), conditional logic (Delgrande, 1987), and *nonmonotonic logic* (McDermott and Doyle, 1980), as well as the works of Nutter, (1987), and Sullivan & Cohen (1985). An associated area is that of reasoning about likelihood (Rich, 1983; Halpern and

Rabin, 1987).

In default logic, a reasoner has a collection of statements about the world that comprise a first-order theory. Default reasoning over this theory makes use of *default rules*, which have the following form:

$$\frac{\alpha: M\beta}{\omega} \qquad (1)$$

This rule can be read as: "if α is provable from the statements and β is consistent with all the assumptions, then assume ω." Statement α is the prerequisite for applying the default rule, β is the justification for the default, and ω is the consequent of the default. So for example, (2) is a default rule to allow the inference that birds, by default, fly:

$$\frac{Bird(x): MFly(x)}{Fly(x)} \qquad (2)$$

This language has a number of defects, as pointed out by Konolige (1987), chief of which is that default rules are not part of the language in which the statements are expressed. It would seem that a different meta-theoretic language is needed to describe and reason with the default rules, thus limiting their power.

An autoepistemic logic is a language for representing the reasoning that agents apply to their own beliefs. An agent's beliefs are compared to a set of sentences in a language, plus a modal operator L. If α is one of the agent's beliefs, then Lα means that α is indeed one of the agent's beliefs. Konolige (1987) has shown that default rules as in (1), can be rephrased as autoepistemic sentences of the form shown in (3):

$$L\alpha \ \wedge \ \neg L \neg\beta \ \rightarrow \ \omega \qquad (3)$$

This sentence can be read as: "if α is believed and $\neg\beta$ is not believed, then ω is true." Autoepistemic logic is capable of expressing the same statements as default logic, and provides the added bonus that defaults can be expressed as sentences within the language.

However, both approaches suffer from a number of problems: first of all, it is often necessary to include in the default rule, all counter-cases to the application of the default rule. So for example, the inference that birds can fly may have to be expressed as (4):

$$\frac{Bird(x): Fly(x) \ \wedge \ \neg Ostrich(x) \ \wedge \ \neg Penguin(x)}{Fly(x)} \qquad (4)$$

The above is an example of a *seminormal default*, a special type of default whose applicability is controlled to prevent the formation of certain undesirable extensions.

The second problem is that statements derived from defaults have the same status as any other derived statements within these logics. This is an undesirable trait, because nonmonotonic revision of statements derived from defaults is unnecessarily complex and considered to be equitable with the revision of statements normally derived from nondefaults.

Say we define a belief conviction to be a relative measure of belief in the truth of the statement. It seems intuitively appealing that statements derived by the application of default rules should have a weaker conviction value than statements derived by normal means. Certain models of reasoning can serve as a framework for capturing this notion, e.g., *belief functions* (Shafer, 1976), *fuzzy set theory* (Zadeh, 1978), or likelihood reasoning (Halpern and Rabin, 1987); however, these methods either explicitly attribute a numeric value to beliefs, or implicitly do so by placing the belief at some discrete point in an order.

One drawback that we see in this method is that *all* beliefs must be comparable. That is, in such a system any pair of beliefs can be compared to see which is more often believed. So for example, a belief that the CIA supply expertise to a Central American dictatorship could be compared to a belief that "GRUNDGE" is the best oven cleaner on the market! We feel that it would be advantageous for a belief reasoner if this were not necessary; that is, if beliefs could only be reasonably compared with beliefs that are somehow related to them.

However, the numeric approaches have an advantage in that they define a calculus that allows one to reason with uncertainty by aggregating uncertainty during a reasoning process. However, the uncertainty that they deal with is generally uncertainty of a probabilistic nature (i.e., there is uncertainty of an event happening), rather than uncertainty arising from incomplete information (an event definitely will happen in a particular way, but we may not have the information to predict the outcome). For reasoning with incomplete information methods such as default logic or methods based on endorsements (how beliefs endorse the plausibility of other beliefs: see Cohen and Grinberg, 1983) are more suitable. Unfortunately, they do not offer the same clean way of propagating uncertainty that the numeric approaches provide.

How, then, could we have the advantages of both methods (being able to reason with incomplete information, and propagate uncertainty, without recourse to numerical attributes and entailing that all beliefs are necessarily comparable)?

Suppose we begin by allowing all beliefs to be theoretically comparable, but not necessarily so (i.e., rather than placing beliefs at a discrete point or interval in an ordering, providing a language for saying — for instance — that p is believed more often than q, and for deriving such relationships from other ones). Then beliefs can only be compared if either an explicit comparison is given, or if it can be derived from existing ones. So for example, if someone believes p more than q, and q more than r, then we can say that person believes p more than q. On the other hand, if someone believes p more than q, and r more than q, then without other information the person couldn't compare p and r.

If the basis of ranking is relative conviction about the truth of a proposition, then we can introduce two concepts: *total commitment* in believing; and *noncommitment* in believing. Total commitment could be equated with the "folk" idea of knowledge (knowledge is beliefs that we hold so strongly that we are not willing to give them up, except in unthinkable circumstances, e.g., believing that the sun will rise tomorrow). Noncommitment in believing p implies that we have no basis for either believing or disbelieving p.

In such a system, deciding whether to believe p or $\neg p$ becomes a process of trying to find a way to compare the two based on the evidence for each, which in turn depends on how they relate to other beliefs.

We could consider different derivations of beliefs as generating a *manifestation* of the beliefs. The commitment to believing p is then the strongest commitment towards some manifestation of p, presuming that all manifestations are comparable. So for example, p as asserted by person X might be one manifestation, p deduced from some other beliefs a second, and p derived by application of default rules a third.

In such a system, inference should follow a *weakest link principle* whereby if $p_0, \ldots, p_n$ are antecedents for deriving p, then that manifestation of p should have the same commitment to it as the weakest of $p_0, \ldots, p_n$ (i.e., if a chain of evidence supports p, then the support for p can be no stronger than the weakest of the evidence). Note that in deriving a manifestation, the assumptions should be beliefs that have been determined to be more committed to than negated.

Default reasoning can easily be incorporated into such a system and one can also express relationships between various default rules, such as whether one provides better evidence (derives a stronger consequent) than another. By expressing such relationships, an infinite granularity can be developed between default rules.

A language that incorporates these features is currently being developed, and an initial version is reported in Ballim (forthcoming). In this language, statements of first order logic are embedded in a meta-language for commitment comparisons (e.g., $p > q$, $p \leq q$). A mechanism is provided that allows for new comparisons to be generated based on these comparisons. The deductive rules of first order logic are themselves expressible in this language, as are default rules.

Chapter 5.2
Environments, intensionality, reference, and speech acts

In this chapter, we discuss *Viewgen*'s treatment of certain fundamental phenomena at greater length. As hinted at earlier, our treatment of reference and speech acts remains largely programmatic, but we retain our fundamental assumption that if belief structures are properly outlined, then these other phenomena become more tractable, since they simply consist of bringing the belief environments of differing agents into some kind of consilience sufficient for normal communication.

5.2.1. An extended treatment of intensionality

We extend the default rule for belief ascription to cope with intensional object ascription by assuming (naturally enough) that intensional objects in one environment correspond directly to identically named or described intensional objects in another environment *unless there is evidence to the contrary*. This notion of correspondence of intensional objects between environments can be expressed in terms of beliefs, but these beliefs must be of a type different from those we have previously discussed.

There are two reasons for that: (a) they are beliefs about *intensional (mental) objects*[27] and (b) they express the believed relationship between intensional objects

---

[27] Similarly, beliefs about co-reference are also unique. Consider the following belief: "John believes tall(Mike)." This belief expresses that John believes about *the person Mike* that he is tall. However, the belief "John believes co-ref(Mike,Jim's-father)" expresses a relationship between two intensional descriptions, *not the things of which they are a description*. This difference remains even without commitment to a realistic view of reference: it succeeds in establishing a correction directly to objects, independent of the mind.

in one space and intensional objects in another space; they are beliefs about relationships between entities in different environments. We represent such beliefs by a predicate called *correspond*. Occurrence of such a predicate in an environment ABOUT an agent *X* indicates a correspondence between certain objects in the belief space of the believing agent *Y* holding beliefs about agent *X* on the one hand, and objects in agent *X*'s belief space on the other. The predicate expresses the notion that the intensional objects mentioned for the first person correspond as a set to the intensional objects mentioned for the second person. Here we only discuss one-to-one, one-to-many, and many-to-one correspondences; notice that by default we assume a one-to-one correspondence. The correspondence of intensional objects between belief spaces has been discussed previously by Fauconnier (1985), Maida (1986; 1988), Wiebe and Rapaport (1986), and Ballim (1987).

The reader will recall from section 2.2 that in CASE 1, Mary's viewpoint ends up containing a single intensional object (topic environment) *O* corresponding both to the System's Frank object (topic environment) and Jim's-father object. From the System's point of view, Mary does not realize these are two separate people. The question is how to decide what should be put inside the System's environment *O*: one possibility is to *symmetrically* combine the information in the System's Frank and Jim's-father objects, thereby removing any conflicting information. In the present case, this would result in *O* stating that Frank/Jim's-father is male and tall, but neither that he has blue eyes nor that he has green eyes, since the persons known to the system differ in that feature. However, we are claiming that *in realistic situations it will often be more appropriate to take an asymmetrical view*, one in which we choose to give precedence either to the information in the System's Frank object over the information in the system's Jim's-father object, or vice versa. The former choice reflects the assumption that there is a stronger, closer correspondence between Mary's idea of Frank and the System's idea of Frank than there is between her idea of Frank and the System's idea of Jim's father. This would be plausible for instance if the System regarded Mary's view of Frank as essentially the same as its own, except in making the mistake of assuming that Frank is Jim's father.

The second choice reflects the converse assumption that would most likely arise from a hypothesis that Mary is focussing on the person-description "father of Jim", and that she happens to believe this description identifies Frank. Our claim is that in realistic situations, there is more likely to be a reason for making one of these choices than to take the symmetrical, set union approach to the qualities of individuals.

Two-for-me-one-for-you

The way we handle the asymmetrical choices is as follows: for the first choice, the system constructs an intensional object O called "Frank-as-Jim's-father" inside Mary's viewpoint.[28]

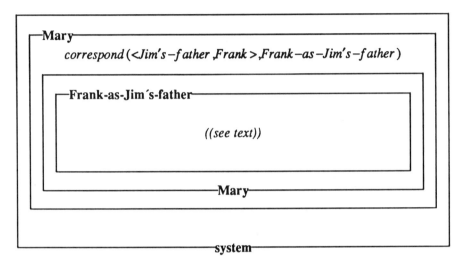

Figure 5.5. Frank-as-Jim's-father.

This object is so-called because it is (so to speak) "the Jim's-father view of Frank," according to Mary. Notice that this phrase does *not* state that the object is the view of Frank that Jim's father *holds* according to Mary; rather, the object is a view of Frank, colored by the idea that he is Jim's father. This way of regarding Mary's intensional object O is directly reflected in the proposed process for constructing O, as we shall see in a moment.

The diagram Figure 5.5 shows in outline what the system will produce, and the special correspondence belief that encapsulates the intensional correspondences (the contents of the Frank-as-Jim's-father environment are not shown).

Mary's Frank-as-Jim's-father object O arises in two stages as follows:

---

[28] An object containing prior information about Mary's view of Frank/Jim's-father such as that his eyes are brown may already exist. In such a case, the system will expand O rather than creating it, and the brown eyes attribution will block the green and blue attributions by the normal process of ascription blocking, as described previously.

Stage 1: The *System's* view of Frank as Jim's father is created; this view is created as a topic environment *O′* inside the System's viewpoint. The creation occurs in three substages (labelled 1a, 1b, and 1c):

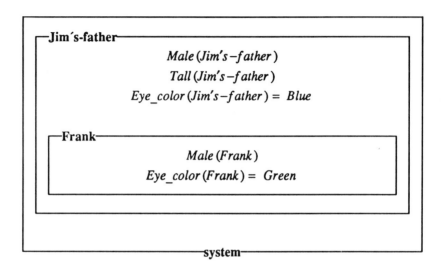

Figure 5.6. A stage before ascribing.

(1a) Initially, a copy of the System's Frank object (topic environment) is placed inside the Jim's-father object. The result is shown in the Figure 5.6.[29] Intuitively, we have not yet tried to identify Frank as Jim's father, but have merely established a view of Frank that is, so to speak, in the context of Jim's father. That context does not have an effect until substage (1b).

---

[29] We omit the System's Frank environment for brevity, and further simplify by omitting the Mary topic box.

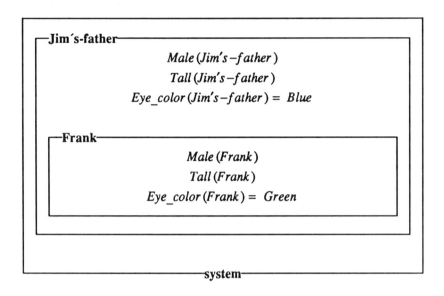

Figure 5.7. The environment with contents.

(1b) We now respect the required identification of Frank as Jim's father. We try to push the beliefs in the System's Jim's-father object into the Frank object embedded within it *using the ordinary default rule*, with the slight modification that *Jim's-father* is replaced by *Frank* in a pushed belief. Thus, the beliefs that Jim's father is male and tall are successfully pushed in (although the former happens to duplicate a belief already embedded in the Frank object), but the belief that Jim's father has green eyes is blocked by the blue-eyes belief already embedded in the Frank object. The result of sub-stage (1b) is shown in Figure 5.7:

(1c) The final substage in constructing O' the System's Frank-as-Jim's-father object, is to pull out the Frank object that is embedded within the Jim's-father object, making it into an object (topic environment) O' at top level within the System's viewpoint. In doing this, we replace the "Frank" topic-name by the name "Frank-as-Jim's-father," and similarly change the *Frank* symbols inside the environment to *"Frank-as-Jim's-father."* The diagram

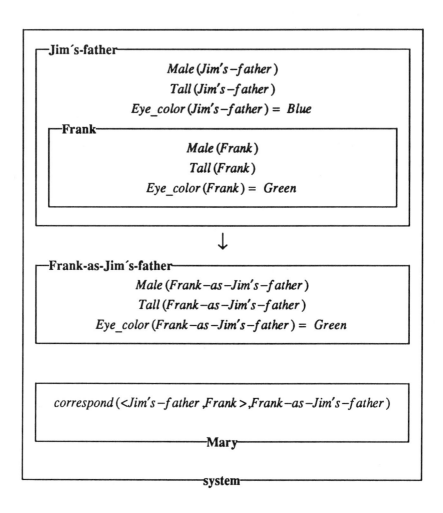

Figure 5.8. Ascription result.

Figure 5.8 shows the result, with the arrow notation indicating the pull-out process:

Stage 2: We now ascribe the System's beliefs about Frank as Jim's father — that is, the beliefs inside *O′* — to Mary, *once again using the ordinary default rule.* On the assumption that there is no prior information about Mary's view of Frank/Jim's-father (e.g., that his eyes are brown), all that will happen is that a copy *O* of *O′* will be created inside the Mary viewpoint, giving the revised Mary viewpoint shown in Figure 5.9:

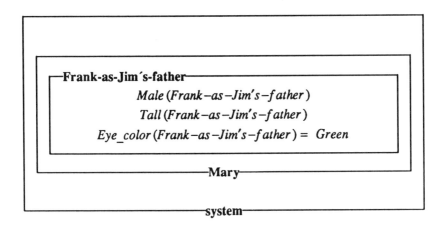

Figure 5.9. The result extracted.

If we had had prior information that Mary believes the person's eyes to be brown, then there would already have been a Frank-as-Jim's-father object (topic environment) O inside Mary's viewpoint, and the beliefs in O' would all have been pushed into that object, except for the green eye belief.

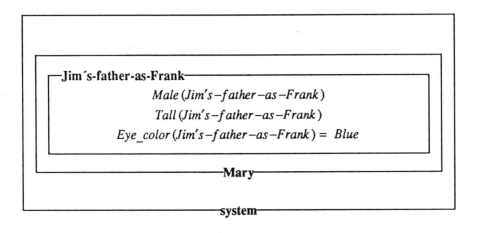

Figure 5.10. The inverse result.

If the System had decided to give precedence to the Jim's-father information rather than to the Frank information in doing the intensional identification (that is, if it had made choice (b), then it would have generated the following state by an analogous process, shown in Figure 5.10.

It might be thought that a symmetric intensional object with the feature differences appearing as disjunctions (e.g., Eye-color Blue or Green) would be appropriate as a construct for the Mary environment. But we are suggesting that this is in fact psychologically less plausible, and that subjects *do* construct stronger, more refutable hypotheses. A final important feature of the process described earlier is that the crucial pushing of information from the Jim's-father environment into the embedded Frank environment (or vice versa) is exactly the type of "inward" pushing used in a particular class of examples that we used to illustrate basic belief ascription in section 3 (the class where the topic was identical to the believer to whom beliefs were being ascribed).

One-for-me-two-for-you

In the (second) case where the System believes in the existence of one individual, but Mary believes in two, the natural computation of Mary's view of either Frank or Jim's-father simply duplicates the System's single representation, changing "Frank" to "Jim's-father" as needed. This is shown in Figure 5.11:

These are not merely aliases, but dual ascriptions, performed by making two identical copies. Further information about Mary's beliefs would cause the contents of the two environments to differ, since she presumably has different beliefs about those individuals she believes to be distinct.

In section 6.1, we seek to demonstrate that belief ascription (e.g., Jim's-father's-view-of-Frank), intensional identification (e.g., Frank-as-Jim's-father), and even metaphor, are distinct forms of a single computational process. In the present case, we argue that Frank-seen-as-Jim's-father is combined with the diagrammatic Jim's-father environment outside, and stands between us as observers, and the inner environment for Frank; whereas in the metaphor case, atoms-as-billiard-balls can be thought of as a metaphor in which "billiard ball knowledge" stands in front of existing "atom knowledge."

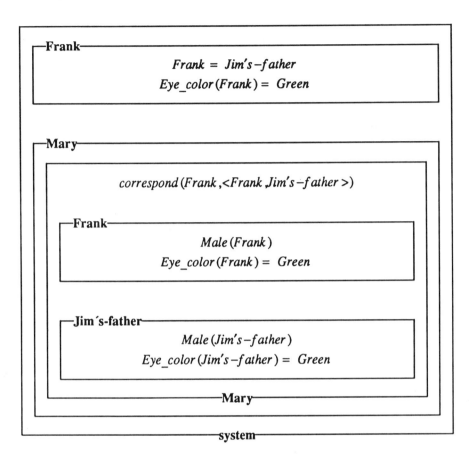

Figure 5.11. Treatment of CASE 2 on the Frank/Jim's-father example.

5.2.2. *De dicto* and *de re* issues

More difficult cases bring out the panoply of philosophical distinctions and discussion, and are conventionally grouped under the headings *de re/de dicto*. Take the following case: The System reasonably believes Feynman to be a famous physicist, but encounters Frank, who on the strength of a single appearance on TV, believes him to be a famous TV performer. (For the sake of this example, we must assume that the two occupations are incompatible.) Suppose the discussion now causes the System to construct its view of Frank's view of Feynman: there will be no point in performing that computation unless the System believes Frank's beliefs are *de re*. Frank no doubt considers his own beliefs *de re*, as we all do, but the crucial requirement is that the System believe this, too. The test of that belief would be some proposition in the Frank environment about Feynman, equivalent to *"Feynman" names Feynman.* If that, is not present, the System can infer that Frank has another person in mind (i.e., his beliefs are *de dicto* for the System, and hence any straightforward pushdown computation is pointless).

Consider the relation of this last case to simpler ones where the System can identify or separate distinct environments. In this last case, the System might know which individual Frank was confusing Feynman with (perhaps Johnny Carson), and could still perform a pushdown, even though it believed Frank's beliefs were *de dicto* as far as Feynman was concerned (they would be *de re* with respect to Johnny Carson). The System could then push Carson into Feynman, while changing the resulting environment's name to "Feynman" or more correctly, "Feynman-as-Carson."

To summarize, the absence of *"Feynman" names Feynman* in the Frank environment is the only reason for not straightforwardly pushing down Feynman, while it leaves open the possibility of some other *de re* pushdown.

5.2.3. Coreference versus equality

The issue of intensional identification and relevance of referents arises from the issue of equality versus coreference (the deeming of different intensional descriptions as coreferential). Our use of environments naturally corresponds to the use of intensional entities deemed coreferential, and hence to the implicit use of a coreference rather than an equality operator. In that sense, our assumptions are similar to those of the CASSIE group (Maida and Shapiro, 1982; Shapiro and Rapaport, 1986) except that we do not need to make the strong claim that only coreference will ever be used, and that all entities in the System are intensional, as they do. The unique part of our system is that the environment notation moves the coreference belief predicate from any level of nesting, out to the environment boundary or partition: Within a given environment, we have *precisely the conditions of a belief space that sanction substitution of coreferents without problems*, as in the *de dicto/de re* examples cited earlier.

5.2.4. The correct role of "mutual knowledge"

The issue discussed in section 2.3 of mutual knowledge can now be taken care of by the procedures suggested here automatically, without the need for special attention. If in the environment for X's beliefs there is a proposition p, where

p: X and Y both see a candle between them at t,

then any pushdown of the environment for Y into that of X (to construct the System's beliefs about X's beliefs about Y and his beliefs) to the required depth will always move belief p to the next inner environment (given the crude relevance heuristic proposed earlier).

This transfer of beliefs without direct supporting evidence, which we shall call *percolation of belief* (see 5.1.3.1 and 6.2.1) is equivalent to the establishment of a series of propositions:

(the System believes) X believes Y believes p

As a result of recursive nesting, the iterative percolation will produce in principle the infinite belief set found in "mutual knowledge" literature. In other, related papers (e.g., Wilks and Bien, 1983) we stress that it is just such recursive pushdowns that any system based on a "Principle of Least Effort" will seek to minimize, let alone the infinitely recursive.

Whereas for an "aboutness" belief of the system such as "X and Y are mafiosi," we expect ascription to the self's inner belief set, making it a candidate for iterative percolation, if only the predicate (becasue if you are one you know it!) or only the half of the conjunction drawn in by relevance. There is no reason that Y's being a mafioso should be promoted to the self-beliefs of X, just because the conjunction is entertained by the System. Clearly, it would be difficult to settle the issue of which predicates were so easily ascribed (a problem for Clark and his collaborators: e.g., Clark and Marshall, 1981).

Given such typing of predicates, the System's general inference rule does the rest without any explicit consideration of mutual knowledge phenomena; they have no privileged place, but are mere epiphenomena that have arisen in the literature because of an inadequate general characterization of beliefs and their computation.

5.2.5. Towards a general theory of speech acts

In recent years, much work has been done to develop natural language processing (NLP) systems that interpret sentences in terms of speech acts[30] (Allen and Perrault, 1978; Cohen and Levesque, 1987), sometimes referred to as "the Toronto work." As was noted earlier, the relationship between our basic belief ascription method and the work of others is that those authors assumed that partition of beliefs into viewpoints to any required depth of nesting was already in existence as a database, before speech act computations were performed. In our view, this is psychologically and computationally unrealistic and instead, the creation and maintenance of nested viewpoints is our primary computational and theoretical task. Furthermore, it is our belief that a study of systems using viewpoints to guide their interactions will lead to a more simplified, general theory of speech acts. (Perrault, 1990, has shifted to a more reasonable, default-oriented approach to speech acts with regard to both beliefs and their associated reasoning computations.)

Our approach can be understood as a demand for more realistic complexity in belief environment computation and simultaneously a reaction to the complexities of speech act analysis in the Toronto and other work. Put another way, if we treat belief less simplistically, we will be rewarded with a simpler treatment of speech acts.

Our main assumption in treating speech acts is similar to that of the other approaches mentioned, however: we locate a belief environment, usually of the System's beliefs of another agent's beliefs about the System itself, within which we reason to make sense of otherwise incomprehensible dialogue input. This very general assumption also serves to link the treatment of speech acts to that of metaphor; in both, a belief environment is created that makes sense of (otherwise anomalous) input.

As many commentators have pointed out, it is implausible to construct plans corresponding to speech acts on every occasion they are encountered. It would be inefficient to work out:

Can you give me your departure time?

as a request (rather than as a question) *freshly, each time it is encountered.* In our view, "speech act interpretation shifts" that do not undergo significant changes over time in a language are best stored as learned wholes, and treated as a special type of complex macro.

It is always necessary to assume that input like that above has an initial parsing phase, one that is capable of detecting that it is (superficially) a question about
an ability of the hearer, by whatever method. The crucial interpretation is that the
utterance in a certain environment is really a request; that is not arrived at wholly
independently of its surface form, for being an ability-question is one condition
(within a fixed stereotype for requests of a certain class) for being deemed a
request. Other conditions concern the System's belief that the above utterer believes
that the hearer/receiver/system is able to deliver such information, etc. Such stereotypical condition sets fit precisely into our notion of nested viewpoints, and it is
easy to check whether or not the environment within which the stereotype is filled
allows the conditions to be fulfilled.

Although these stereotypical structures resemble plans, they are in fact complex dictionary entries used in the process of mapping an input. For example:

There is no further information on thalassemia

must be mapped from its surface semantic representation which expresses a proposition about the world, to some underlying structure that expresses the content of
the communication in terms of an agent's belief and goals. This translation is subject to the context of beliefs and plans in which it is performed, and it is only
appropriate that this last example be translated into a goal for the hearer (at some
level of abstraction and with some level of priority) if he believed the speaker
believed the hearer knew how to find more information and would do so if asked;
and if the hearer believed that there was, indeed, more information and that he
knew how to locate it. There would be no point in forming such a goal if the
hearer believed the first part about the speaker's beliefs, but also believed that there
was no more information.

It is reasonable, when looking at any speech act model, to ask where the illocutions are; what (in a generated utterance) makes it more than merely an intended
effect? In the case of a warning, for example, the illocution is that the one who is
warned takes himself to have been warned over and above any *particular* effects,
on his goals and beliefs. A plan-based approach tends to deny illocution, independent of actual or intended effect. Earlier, Cohen (1964) went so far as to dismiss
illocution as a philosophical myth.

Illocution may have to be expressed as a completely unrunnable plan, whose
meaning is to be interpreted independent of its possible effects. We can think of
this in Fregean terms, by comparison with Winograd's SHRDLU (1972)

representations of objects: the *unrun* plan is intension, the run plan is extension. Suppose that in the case of speech acts, an unrun plan is an illocution, and run is perlocutionary effect (it is important to remember that an illocution is not wholly dependent on the particular belief states of hearer and speaker, because there is something general and conventional about, say, warning); "what would this have meant if I had said it to him" cannot be a test of the illocution of another's speech act. With that strong criterion, providing all current AI models of speech acts for distinctive illocutions is probably still defective.

Our proposal in this book is effectively neutral with respect to any system of inference, and any theory of plans based on it. However, there are constraints that would naturally have to be added, such as the notion of Strips-like plan segments for speech acts, noted earlier, and the intensional object in ascription (e.g., the "inexpert environment" for anatomy which the doctor ascribes to the lay patient, another sort of "unrunnable plan"). It must not be wholly unrunnable, since it allows the patient to answer some very general questions, like "Is Leukemia a disease?" it must also have runnable subplans. This notion refers to Bien's phrase (1976) "Running a belief in an environment": both beliefs and plans are partially runnable, evaluable functions. We suspect (although at this stage, without hard evidence) that partially runnable plans will explicate speech acts in this paradigm, just as partially runnable beliefs explicate belief and expertise.

In this section, we have tried to outline the way in which core ideas in the chapter on belief environment manipulation naturally extend to a specific stereotypical approach to speech act processing. We are not claiming, however, that that extension is worked out as fully as the extension to metaphor with which we now conclude. However, we expect that the intimate processing relations between intensional identification, relevance, and metaphor already discussed will become similar when speech acts (rather than metaphor) are made the center of attention.

Chapter 6
Further Extensions and Speculations

Chapter 6.1
Metaphor revisited

Metaphor is normally explicated (formally or computationally) by a process that transfers properties by mapping from one structure (the vehicle) to another (the tenor). A classic example in AI is the work of Falkenhainer, Forbus and Gentner (1986), and also the work of Fass (1987). Some would object here to raising the issue of transferring properties versus transferring structure, but we shall not enter into this argument, because although our examples transfer properties within propositional beliefs, it will become clear from our discussion later in this section that we consider our current representation to be merely illustrative; a fuller representation would display mapping of more complex structures. Indeed, in this section we shall play fast and loose with the metaphor versus metonymy and metaphor versus analogy distinctions; for our present purposes, these distinctions affect nothing.

We want to explore the possibility of applying our basic belief algorithm to metaphor as a means of seeking insight into the phenomenon. The attempt is not as surprising as it may sound: Metaphor has often been viewed in traditional approaches as "seeing one thing as something else" — a matter of viewpoints — just as we are presenting belief. We are proposing that propositions in the topic environment for the vehicle of a metaphor be "pushed inward" (using the standard algorithm presented earlier) into an embedded environment for the tenor to get the view of the tenor-seen-through-the-vehicle or the tenor-as-vehicle. (This process was already alluded to in section 5.2 on intensional identity).

The key features here are (a) the conceptual domain is viewed as a "pseudo-believer"; (b) the pseudo-believer has a metaphorical view of a topic or domain; (c) the generation of such a view is not dissimilar to ascribing beliefs by real believers and; (d) explicating this by pushing or amalgamating environments yields new intensional entities after an actual transfer of properties.

So in the classic case of atom-as-billiard-ball, given the environments for atom and billiard-ball shown in Figure 6.1:

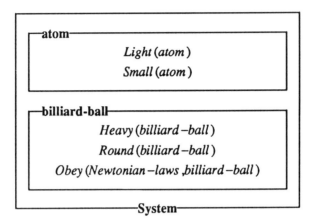

Figure 6.1. System beliefs about atoms and billiard balls.

we generate the environment for atoms-as-billiard-balls as follows. The environment for atoms is nested within the environment for billiard balls in Figure 6.2:

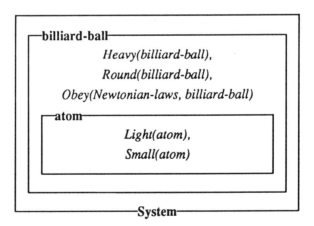

Figure 6.2. Nesting before ascription.

Then, the contents of the billiard-ball environment are pushed down into the nested atom environment, replacing the term "billiard-ball" by "atom" wherever it occurs in the propositions being pushed. The overriding of properties follows in the same way as for standard beliefs: e.g., **Light(atom)** and **Small(atom)** would not be overridden by the incoming **Heavy(billiard ball)**. However, **Round(billiard ball)** would survive as the property **Round(atom)** — correct for the original historical analogy — since there would be no preexisting shape property in the System's belief set for atoms.

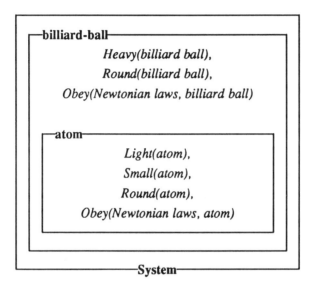

Figure 6.3. Environments with contents.

Then, the nested atom environment is pulled out to form a new environment — "atom-as-billiard-ball," replacing each occurrence of "atom" with "atom-as-billiard-ball." This new environment is the metaphoric view of atoms as billiard balls. As before, Figure 6.4 uses an arrow to illustrate the process.

Similarly, in the sentence

Jones threatened Smith's theory by reimplementing his experiments.

we recognize that we have a preference-breaking and potentially metaphorical situation from the object-feature failure on "threaten" which "expects" a person-object. In Wilks (1977), it was argued that metaphors could be identified (at least procedurally) with the class of preference-breaking utterances where in a broad sense, any assertion that two generic classes are identical, (e.g., "An atom is a billiard ball" or "Man is an animal") is also preference breaking. Awkward cases within that broad category are phrases like "Connors killed McEnroe" where no verb preferences are broken, although the utterance can be read metaphorically as "beat soundly at

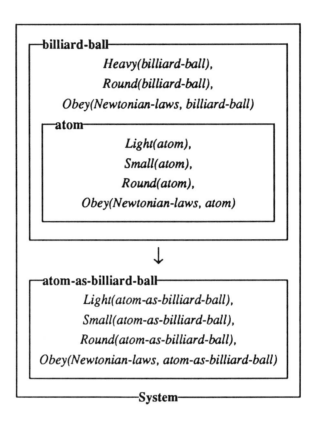

Figure 6.4. Forming the atom-as-billiard-ball environment.

tennis." Here one could take the classic Marcus-escape and rule the latter out of court (so to speak) as a "garden path metaphor," one simply delimited out of order by our procedural and preference definition. As we shall see in the following discussion, there is some independent motivation for linking together preferences and metaphor at a deeper level.

At this point, we could plausibly form a metaphoric view of theory-as-person using the same process as mentioned earlier. Figure 6.5 shows possible system environments for *theory, person*, and the resulting theory-as-person environment.

So by this maneuver, a new and complex metaphorical property of theories is derived. It may turn out of course that this procedure of belief-overriding as a basis for metaphor will produce a transferred set of plausible properties no different from that of any other system (e.g., "Structural" systems like that of Falkenhainer et al.), but that would again be an experimental question. The proposal's importance and originality lies in the fact that it applies an algorithm designed to explicate an

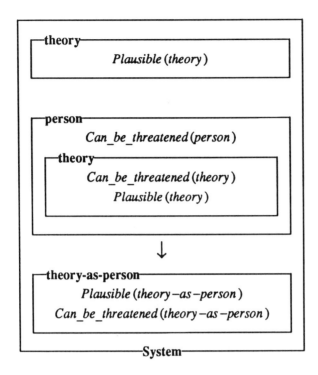

Figure 6.5. Forming a theory-as-person environment.

altogether different phenomenon (i.e., belief), yielding a procedural connection between two separate notions.

In principle, this method should be applicable to other phenomena considered by most to be metaphorical (e.g., Cohen and Margalit, 1972), but with a very different grammatical basis — such as "rubber duck." We can envisage the pushdown of environments *duck* and *rubber-object* after which properties like "animacy" from the *DUCK* environment would be cancelled out by the preexisting property (alias belief) "inanimate" within the *RUBBER-OBJECT* environment, so that we end up (correctly) with rubber ducks (alias *rubber-object-as-a-duck*) being inanimate. Cohen and Margalit themselves argued that there could be no principled basis for property transfer in metaphor explication but in a sense, all computational accounts including this one consider that to be a false empirical claim. The principled basis of this property ascription falls back on a relevance algorithm (see Section 2.3), supplemented by the old default-belief algorithm. Intuitive support for our proposal comes from a deep connection between belief and metaphor; one that takes metaphor-as-false-belief (Davidson, 1978) seriously, in that metaphors for a particular believer are merely special beliefs, ones that can of course become more generally believed (e.g., men are beasts!).

Thus far, we have stressed a procedural connection that may be improbable to some readers. But there is another aspect of the connection between belief and metaphor: the important but neglected phenomenon of the content of belief being inherently metaphorical itself, in a way that conventional theorists totally neglect by concentrating on simplistic belief examples like "John loves Mary" alone. A far more useful candidate for analysis might be an established truth such as:

Prussia threatened France before invading it successfully in 1871.

What are we to say of this historically correct belief? What are the entities referred to by "Prussia" and "France"? Simple translation into some first-order expression like **Invade (Prussia, France, 1870)** only obscures the real problem, and the semantics of first order logic are of no help at all here. Are the entities referred to (somehow metaphorically) the Prussian people, or its army, or some part of the army?

Following the approach described earlier, we might look for the breaking of linguistic preferences for the verb "threaten"; and perform a trial pushdown of properties of the "people" environment (given by the conventional preferences of "threaten") into an environment for Prussia (*a land mass*, would be its basic representation). An important safeguard we will merely hint at here is to examine our inventory of representations for the term "Prussia", which expressed the (dead) metaphor of a country-name-as-polity (some would call this a metonymy, but we have chosen not to stress this issue here). Another important safeguard would be to see how far a net-like, dictionary-derived (Wilks et al., 1988) representation of "Prussia" might guide property transfer and enrichment.

Notice also that there is asymmetry of available pushdown, as there was in the construction of intensional entities in a previous section. The construction discussed and illustrated in the last figure was that of a THEORY-AS-A-PERSON because we chose to push those entities; had we searched on the THEORY environment, we might well have found that a conventional relation of persons with regard to theories was one of *criticizing* the theory of another and based on a normal, stereotypical relationship, used that insight as a cue to attempt a pushdown of THREAT-AS-CRITICISM. As with the John-as-Jim's-father example, it might turn out to be a question of *which* inferences in *which* new environments produce the most satisfactory and coherent results. Such asymmetric duality of metaphor is also seen in the alternative treatments of the sentence:

My car drinks gasoline.

in Wilks (1977), where one can take the statement as a Car-as-drinker metaphor or a Drinking-as-using metaphor, and only overall coherence gleaned from a database of cases and knowledge structures can tell us which. In that project, the model was not one of beliefs but, in keeping with the *zeitgeist*, frame-like structures expressing dictionary information. But the underlying premise of the two approaches is the same: Determine preference violations trigger metaphorical processes, but do not determine which metaphor (regardless of the directionality of the preferences) will establish itself in that context. That is a matter for other more general inference processes and the coherence they produce to resolve. In the examples here, we have simplified the matter by considering only a single pushdown for each example.

In this chapter, applying notions derived for belief to explication and modelling of metaphor understanding has been presented as a crucial procedure. Before explaining the fundamental links between belief processing and metaphor, we will once again summarize our view of how we believe intensional identification relates to both belief ascription and metaphor.

6.1.1. Belief Ascription and Intensional Identification

Intensional identification of entities implies a combination of two or more bodies of information, that may or may not follow our environment-based approach. Consider Mary (see section 2.2), who thinks that Jim's father is someone she knows in another context: let us say, "Frank." In reasoning about Mary, we believe her to hold some person-idea that brings together two mental descriptions akin to the phrases "the father of Jim" and "the person called Frank." We also think it plausible that her person-idea incorporates other information, made more directly accessible perhaps by one of those descriptions. Moreover, it is typically the case that this auxiliary information is mainly an ascription to Mary of our own beliefs (when there is no evidence to the contrary). Therefore her person-idea combines two bodies of belief or information, both of which we possess. We must also allow for the possibility that because Jim's father is *not* Frank (according to us), these two bodies of information may partially conflict with one another.

This combination of two bodies of possibly conflicting information is similar to the combination that occurs in our environment-based approach to belief ascription (such as when the System attempts to ascribe to Mike its own beliefs about world hunger, but has to account for the possibility of conflicting information in an existing topic-environment for world hunger within Mike's viewpoint). This rough correspondence between intensional identification and belief ascription is further refined in our approach in two related ways:

First of all, we are claiming that intensional identification is likely to be asymmetrical in that one of the bodies of information being combined takes precedence over the others. In the context of the Mary example, this is because ordinarily, Mary's Frank/Jim's-father idea is likely to correspond more closely to one of our two person-ideas than to the other (either to father-of-Jim or person called Frank). This is not to exclude the possibility of more complex situations where there is no clear precedence, but in general, our approach is heuristically plausible. Thus intensional identification is asymmetrical at least by default, and corresponds still more closely to the belief ascription process that gives precedence to one environment over another.

Secondly, it is reasonable to take an asymmetrical identification of intensional objects A and B (with preference for the information indexed through A) as a matter of considering A *as* B, or taking "the B-ish view of A." Our final step then is to compare this to taking *agent B's* view of A. Both (a) the B-ish view of A and (b) an agent B's view of A involve the "coloring" of topic A with B-beliefs (beliefs *about B* in case (a) and beliefs *of B* in case (b)). Procedurally, the coloring manifests itself in similar ways.

6.1.2. Intensional Identification and Metaphor

We have just noted that the identification of intensional objects A and B (with a bias towards A) is a matter of taking A *as* B; this "*as*" is the equivalent of taking a metaphorical tenor A *as* the vehicle B of the metaphor (e.g., atom as billiard ball). In both cases, one view is imposed upon another (i.e., information about B is imposed on A), which does not amount to saying there are no differences between typical intensional identification and typical metaphor creation. It goes without saying that the latter is more likely to involve unusual, unexpected or category-crossing impositions of information; nevertheless, the two processes are similar both conceptually and from the (procedural) point of view of the detailed computational processes taking place. In cases where someone uses a phrase like "God the Father," we might not be able to say very definitely whether they are conflating two independent intensional entities, or using a metaphor. But this chapter suggests that if the basic computational technique for treating both is the same then we do not have to answer that question.

6.1.3. Belief and Metaphor

Here we return to our central idea that representational and processing notions derived for belief can be applied successfully to the explication and modelling of metaphor understanding. The force behind this notion comes from the fact that in the literature, metaphor has often been viewed as a point-of-view phenomenon: "seeing something as something else." But all that is quite vague. What is crucial here is the application of a precise notion of computational belief ascription to metaphor, and transferring properties (expressed as believed propositions) using our standard algorithm to create an entity's metaphorical viewpoint.

We also wish here to briefly touch upon what makes the converse notion compelling, as well; why belief ascription, as a fundamental psychological and computational process, is itself logically and empirically dependent on metaphor.

In one sense, that claim is trivial since all computational approaches to propositional attitudes rest on underlying metaphors in the final analysis (most commonly metaphors that bring in the idea of "possible worlds" or "situations" and others that depict the mind holding, possessing or being otherwise related to abstract objects akin to natural language sentences or logical formulae). Our approach rests on the class of metaphor known as the *MIND-AS-CONTAINER* in which the minds and belief sets of others are porous containers that can be nested like buckets or jars. This class of metaphors lends itself well to the explicit grouping idea we described in section 3.2.

But we are grasping at a more general principle here that is independent of any prevalent metaphor for mind and belief states. Consider the precept that in hypothesizing what some agent X believes about topic T, one begins by trying to ascribe one's own beliefs about T to X, perhaps failing to do so because of contrary beliefs about T that one already knows X to have. What we are suggesting is that this activity is parallel to a metaphor "ascribing" information from its vehicle to the tenor, perhaps failing to do so because of existing tenor information to the contrary that one wishes to preserve. That is, in a belief-ascription activity one uses one's current belief-state about topic T as the vehicle of a metaphor, the target being the other agent's belief state: *one uses one's own state of mind as a metaphor for others'*.

A second (very general) aspect of the dependence of belief processing on metaphor can be grasped by considering the assumption we have made throughout this chapter (one that virtually all AI researchers and logicians make when discussing beliefs): that beliefs can be conveniently expressed as simple propositions that contain predicates, that in turn (unfortunately) appear as words, but in fact univocally denote entities that are concepts or world-referents.

Everyone knows that this assumption, although it underlies all modern formal semantics, is highly dubious, particularly if we consider the frequently cited fact in Preference Semantics (see Wilks, 1975) that many if not most of English sentences in newspapers and the like are preference breaking. That is to say, the concepts contained in these texts are used out of their dictionary-declared constraint contexts, as in the phrase "Prussia attacked France". We are simply trying to underscore the now common observation that much normal discourse is broadly defined as "metaphorical," and also to point out, as few others have, that this has strong and destabilizing consequences for any formal semantic representation of language (cf. Johnson, 1987; Lakoff, 1987) and in particular, for belief ascription.

In light of such observations, the notion that univocal predicates are the basis of formal representations in a natural language (albeit freed from the contamination of natural languages like English) is hard to sustain, and the problem is in no way alleviated by allowing for nonunivocality (i.e., indexing predicates for particular dictionary word senses — e.g., POST1 means only a stick), because the very ubiquity of metaphor or preference breaking suggests that a natural language is normally comprehended even when no indexing of conventional senses occurs. Nor is this difficulty addressed by formalists who say things like "we do not use predicates — only axiomatic structures, or sets of *n-tuples*"... For them, the only way of knowing which set or axiom is which is by way of the associated predicate name, leaving the above problems unresolved.

Now, if we return to our central theme and consider that comprehensible sentences containing nonsense-indexable metaphorical uses are also the very substance of beliefs, and that they must be ascribed by believer to believer, then what trust can we put in the sort of naive representations used in this and every other work on the subject? In short, the answer is "none" — unless we can begin moving towards a notion of meaning representation for belief ascription that also takes into account the basic metaphoricity of beliefs and language.

At present, we can do little more than draw attention to this phenomenon (so as to avoid the future accusation of having been more naive than was necessary). However, we now feel we know what aspects of current research to draw on for further work on belief ascription. One essential task is to link the present work to work on meaning that is both dictionary-based, and is able to represent new usages, usually within networks of associations, as the basis of discrete senses (Fass, 1987; Wilks et al., 1990). Another essential task is for our exploration of the notion of metaphor via belief ascription to be bootstrapped back into the belief ascription process itself, so that we can ascribe a belief from believer A to believer B (e.g., "Smith attacked Jones' notion of continuity") in such a way as to assume that the metaphorical content (of "attack") transfers from environment to environment, assuming here that culturally-similar believers have the same metaphorical process- ing mechanism, as well as the same belief ascription mechanism. But even these assumptions may have to be relaxed in certain situations: such transfers are central to other work of one of our colleaques (Barnden, 1988a,b, 1989).

One interesting class of cases are those where a system believes another beli- ever to have *false* (rather than metaphorical) beliefs about word meaning. To return to the believer who confuses Thessaly and thalassemia (believing the disease to be a province of Greece); let us say he is confronted by the input phrase "The cure for thalassemia." A system might predict that faced with what should be a radical preference violation, the believer will give up and ask for help, and so it might "wait and see," and make no ascriptions at all. But a more plausible, more zealous strategy would be to ascribe the results of a metaphorical pushdown, based in the System's own view on wholly false beliefs about meaning. Anyone who considers this implausible should consider the locution (heard more than once on American TV): "the cure for Panama."

If we can free ourselves from the basic representational assumption made here and everywhere else (because it is so hard to think of alternatives!) that the predicates in an ascribed representation for belief are sense-determinate in a simple, denotational way, then the problem may be solved simply by a method of metaphor-processing, using belief-like methods such as those we have proposed here, during the belief ascription process.

An alternative, lazier possibility is moving a representational strategy in which we make no strong referential assumptions about the meanings of the predi- cates in beliefs ascribed from one believer to another; just as one can assume that if natural languages are very similar (like Dutch and German) we may not need to resolve words to word senses in order to transfer between them, and instead can allow the target understander to do the work. A process like the metaphor processor described here could be used only on demand when it is necessary to push an interpretation beyond its metaphorical expression. This again is consistent with certain highly plausible assumptions about human processing. Whichever of these alternatives is ultimately chosen, both require recognition of the intimate dependence of belief ascription on the metaphoricity of language and belief representations.

Chapter 6.2
Psychology and effort reviewed

At a number of points in this book we referred to what we propose as being broadly consistent with a "least effort" view of language processing. This is in no sense a well-worked out point of view, but rather a collection of anecdotal insights. Various other writers have paid lip service to it (Bien 1983, Sperber and Wilson 1986, etc.) as well as one of us in the promotion of a notion of Preference Semantics (Wilks, 1975), (according to which semantic structure in languages is to be assigned on a basis of the processor doing as little work as it can get away with). Such a theory clearly has evolutionary advantages over a theory that recommends maximum effort, a view that was sometimes thought to lie behind Rieger's (1975) theory of inference. It would also be easy to show that some such general assumption underlies Grice's principles of conversation (1975).

It is always dangerous in cognitive science to adopt such anecdotal hypotheses from other areas (in this case psychology). But one aspect of *ViewGen* does seem to invite connections with psychology: what we wish to call the percolation effect: namely beliefs ascribed within a system, and their remaining effects after ascription. This phenomenon is a side-effect of our processes and may correspond to real ways in which unsupported beliefs are propagated among real believers. The well-attested "sleeper effect" (Gruder et al., 1978) in which subjects come to hold beliefs for which they have no evidence as side-effects of other processes, is an obvious analogy for what we have in mind.

6.2.1. Percolation

A question that arises after any pushdown of environments in *ViewGen* is how the inner result is to be deconstructed. In the example I or section 1, we found that the proposition "Frank dislikes the system" appeared in the inner environment; but should it be retained there permanently, and if so, what would that imply? *It will be retained, if we adopt what we shall call the "percolation heuristic."* It will be remembered that it was this particular proposition that was ascribed into the innermost environment in the first (though not the second) nesting in the treatment of that example. The percolation heuristic is as follows: when a proposition has been ascribed to an inner environment and is not contradicted, it remains there in the standard copy of that inner environment *when that copy is subsequently re-established at the bottom level.* We shall say that the proposition "Frank dislikes the System" has *percolated* from the "outer" environment for the user, to the inner environment for Frank.

After the example dialogue has been dealt with, the inner environment is, as it were, pulled out, and remains as the System's view of Frank. The percolation heuristic's assert that "Frank dislikes the System" *stays in that copy,* which allows the possibility of multiple copies of an environment for Frank, and hence the problem that is most salient in later retrieval (see Bien, 1983). By iterative percolation, it will also have gone further into the innermost environment, which was the System's environment for itself in that example.

We are arguing that with a least-effort principle of belief manipulation, this percolation heuristic is justified. But let us first consider an immediate, potential counter-example. Supposing the user had said "Frank thinks you're crazy, but I don't" (the example was suggested to us by Dennett, personal communication); we might imagine a possible contradiction, achieved by ascription into the innermost environment. That would arise if we conducted two ascriptions, in parallel, as it were: one of the System's views of the speaker's view of itself, with the inner result "System is not-crazy," and one of the System's views of Frank's view of himself with the inner result "System is crazy." If we further allow that these ascriptions can be compared, it will become clear that one does not want to allow both to remain (by the process we have called percolation) in any permanent version of the System's view of itself where a contradiction will be evident, and potentially vicious.

However, this problem with percolation will disappear if we reconsider that nothing in the treatment of the example requires that it be done by comparing ascriptions. It could be treated more naturally with a single ascription, in which the views of the speaker and those ascribed to Frank simply coexist at different places in a single belief stack.

The worst that can happen on further ascription within this stack is a contradiction of the System's view *of the speaker's beliefs* after percolation. And none of us find anything disturbing about the idea that others (rather than ourselves) have contradictory beliefs. Nevertheless, although no contradiction follows here, we may wish to allow certain surface key words to inhibit multi-step percolations — in this case, "but":

The principal suggested here is that percolations remain for *all* future uses of a given environment, not just in relation to the environment from which they percolated. Another result of percolation will be that, say, Figure 6.6

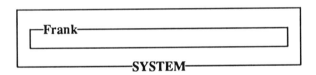

Figure 6.6. The Frank environment.

is no longer the *general* representation of Frank, for beliefs about him may percolate anywhere in the System's environments.

One argument for the percolation heuristic is based on the assumption that pushing down environments inside each other to create new environments requires considerable computational and psychological effort, and greater effort required for greater nesting depths. Allowing beliefs to percolate about the System in the way suggested avoids having to recompute the same environment by repeating a pushdown, should another dialogue be encountered that required the same environment. Before running a sentence representation in an environment, we can check the pushdown nesting required, and examine a flag in the innermost environment to see whether that inner environment had been constructed recently or not. The notion of recency would have to be firmly defined, but if the sentence representation had been run recently on any such definition, we would assume that percolations and settlings of consistencies had been done and would not need to be repeated.

An important point here is that the pushdowns are not in any sense topic-guided: that is to say, if the text required us to calculate Bush's view of Gorbachev's view *of a possible world oil shortage,* then we could not be sure that if we were to assemble the same order of nesting of outer environments for another topic (say, Bush's view of Gorbachev's view of Saudi Arabia) then the register of previous pushdowns would mean that all possible consistencies and percolations had already been achieved in the innermost environment, since they would have been directed by relevance to oil. However, our overall least-effort principle of comprehension requires that we do not repeat the *outer part* of that pushdown, which would already have been constructed.

It must be remembered that the pushdown metaphor is just that. The actual computation involved in computing the inner environments by ascription in *ViewGen* is a cross-product of environment contents. However, it might turn out experimentally that the assumption here about percolation is not suitable for all topics. We might on the basis of experiment wish to restrict percolation itself to certain topics or psychological modes, and in particular to that of *attitudes.* What is being suggested here in psychological terms, under the metaphor of percolation, is that it is essentially a side-effect that transfers beliefs for which one has no explicit evidence. As we noted earlier, there is a phenomenon called the "sleeper effect" (Gruder et al., 1978) which is well attested to, and yields experimental evidence about how people come to hold beliefs for which they have no direct evidence. We take this as indirect evidence that something along the lines we propose for percolation could in fact be experimentally tested, both as an effect on the individual's beliefs, and possibly as a model of the social propagation of beliefs.

We suggested that percolated beliefs might remain (with their source believer stripped away, as it were) and become beliefs of the System that it had merely inherited as a side-effect. It is clear that such persistence could not apply to beliefs that had migrated in and overriden inner beliefs in the way "Frank likes User" migrated into the Frank environment and contradicted "Frank dislikes User." For if that were to remain in a permanent copy, then further pushdowns might cause the System to randomly reverse its beliefs: e.g., having calculated Gorbachev's view of Bush and finding it the reverse of its own, it would not be likely to reverse its own beliefs on Bush only from having constructed that particular environment!

6.2.2. Personae and Self Models

Environments for the System's self have had a special role in this work from the beginning. The expertise involved in one's self-knowledge was one of the first examples that prompted limitations of the default rule for beliefs; we are all self-experts, and our knowledge of, let's say our number of teeth must not be ascribed to anyone else unless they have the necessary expertise — in this case, dental.

When reconstructing an environment after ascription, a system must decide how to retain the new ascribed beliefs without jeopardizing the consistency of the System's belief space. If that can be done then the belief is stored there permanently, as when the agent is believed to be more knowledgeable on the subject of a particular belief than is the system itself. The system must, of course, believe that the agent is truthful and qualified before deciding to accept that agent's belief as its own. But that rule will be interesting to consider in the case of models of the self: when should a system decide to accept new beliefs about itself? From doctors and dentists certainly, but from psychiatrists? From well-meaning friends? It may well be that there is no general rule here.

One way of looking at this issue is as a special case of what we could call "personal," following McLoughlin (1986) (although he used the term more generally to include features far beyond beliefs).

As was discussed in section 3.4, personae are environments that are used to represent the beliefs of typical classes of people. So we may have a persona that represents the beliefs typically held by a person who is an alcoholic, or belongs to some profession or ethnic group, etc. As with all environments within the System, the only beliefs stored in a personal environment are those that differ from the System's own beliefs.

For any system, natural additional personae will be a range of *public selves* (the System's view of its *public self, i.e., what it believes to be the public's view of it, including* what it is publicly believed to believe about itself). It might seem a pity to introduce a special entity here, one that ought to be constructible from the entities already available in the System, lest such entities have to be produced in some form for all other entities in the System. However, it may well be that one's public self cannot be generated (for oneself) by asking, and then ascribing, "What does X think of me?" That object is in not an individual's view (although that could be ascribed on demand in the normal way), nor simply a statistical average over one's acquaintances: it is a very special construct whose origins are unclear. If this object for the System were stored within the general system environment as the System's beliefs about the average man's view of its self, then all the *ViewGen* algorithms would run properly. (Figure 6.7.)

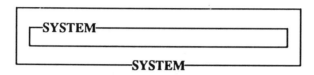

Figure 6.7. Autoepistemic system view.

6.2.3. Meaning transformed?

One outcome of what we have proposed is that belief is not just an addition to a meaning theory, as is conventionally thought (that you must know what a proposition means before you can tell if it is true, or believable). The present work suggests a more Quinean, or even Wittgensteinian view: that belief wholes and their manipulation support a very different theory of meaning, one in which a theory of meaning is empty (as Tarskian, denotational theories are for natural languages) if divorced from a theory of belief, plans, goals, and action. In saying this we are not falling back (as is often done in AI) on a "procedural theory of semantics or meaning," but hold that what something means is a function of the ascription processes and the action/utterance outcomes of which it forms a part. If we ask what "Prussia" means to one who truly believes that "Prussia invaded France in 1870," we cannot answer the question simply by using dictionary or denotational/referential processes, but only by applying an account of the interaction of metaphor, belief, and meaning structure.

In so far as there is a theory of meaning underlying all this, it is certainly not one that substitutes for a theory of formal semantics. It is our belief that these latter theories can only be useful for formal languages: that was Tarski's own position, and more recently, the (rather back-handed) compliment that Winograd (1987) offered to Situation Semantics.

Our view (Wilks, 1982) is that there is no "escape theory" for natural languages to another nonsymbolic domain of entities that somehow "justify" meaning: To search for such a solution is no more than a persistent illusion. Meaning remains to be found in other symbols, a position for which we argued (Wilks, 1971) when it was still madness to do so in AI, a position that nevertheless captured the basic intuitions of the AI researcher all along, if not the "man in the street." It is of course, as we just noted, a position that owes much to the views of Wittgenstein and Quine, as well as (on another cultural plane) the work of hermeneutic authors like Habermas who were the inspiration for Winograd and Flores' version (1986) of the same view. And as we have noted, it is a view consistent with the spirit, if not the substance, of Fodor's LOT theory.

To say that meanings are other words or symbols is, of course, not enough: our specific purpose in this book has been to show that among those symbols are essentially symbols for beliefs, goals, and plans.

Chapter 6.3
Practical and social matters

6.3. Belief and the evolution of responsible machines

In this concluding chapter, we turn to more general notions that follow naturally from the ascription of beliefs to machines, on the basis of programs and
behavior of the type we have described in this book. We have suggested that a
necessary condition for having beliefs in any serious sense is the ability to entertain
the beliefs of *others* (as part of a model of those others), and hence things that may
not be believed by an entity itself. All this is no more than a weakened version of
the notion (familiar in parts of linguistic philosophy) that languages, like selves, are
not wholly private matters but necessarily function as an interaction between selves.
We now wish to explore in conclusion the view that computational belief naturally
links through ideas like Speech Acts (cf. 5.1), to serious matters like responsibility
in computers. This idea is, after all, the one that the public naturally seize on when
talking of expert systems, not just as "Can they know about expert matters?" but,
"Will they be taking decisions (away from us)?" Researchers and salesmen often
try to mollify these concerns with talk of machine "assistance" and "advice," with
the implication that all decisions remain in human hands, but the issue of machine
responsibility (and its converse, consent in the decisions of others) is what really
interests people. We shall explore this concept here a little by continuing with the
example of computers in medicine, but any area of human interest and machine
capability could be substituted for that one.

6.3.1. Human attributes and machines

It is commonly observed that people now anthropomorphize computers in
their speaking and writing; and not only computers as such, but even their parts:
"What the color chip is telling you is that it's in the background mode," a vision
hacker said to one of us not long ago. That is no different from what we say of

251

human wholes and parts, as in "my stomach is telling me it's lunchtime," and so such attributions do not in themselves have any consequences or relevance, legal or general.

But they are nonetheless a necessary **precondition** for any attribution of legal or other responsibility beyond the human pale. Turkle (1987) has given the sociological *imprimatur*, if it were needed, to the claim that such usage is now commonplace, especially among small children.

More importantly, the fact that adults now talk and write that way has nothing to do with Turing tests and "being fooled by simulations," as some people acquainted with the historical AI literature might think. For the forms of words in questions are used by people who have never seen any plausible language or reasoning task performed by a machine, or rather have seen no such performances other than simulated versions on TV and in films. Given that TV viewers vastly outnumber computer scientists, it is those "performances" that are (we suspect) the driving force behind the language changes under discussion.

But those changes themselves are perfectly real, and for anyone of a Dennetist tendency in philosophy (if we may use that word to refer to one who gives theoretical priority to successful explanatory vocabulary, rather than to underlying or direct ontological evidence: Dennett, 1978), machines may therefore take on certain key human characteristics. If that is so, then it may become the peg on which to hang any possible legal responsibility of machines or programs. But before turning to that, let us take a different case for comparison.

6.3.2. Dogs

In English common law, there is already a well-established, operative precedent for a category of entities that are neither human, nor totally without responsibility. They are animals like dogs, which certainly pass the test of having appropriate attributions made to them, at least by a large part of the population. They are quite distinct from *ferae naturae* like tigers: if you keep a tiger and it does any wrong, you are responsible, for they are taken to be simple machines in your keeping. With dogs the situation is more complex, normally (though inaccurately) summed up by the cliche "every dog is allowed one bite;" the point being that a dog is not deemed savage simply because it bites someone once. It may (like us) be acting out of character, whereas to be a savage dog is to be a *habitual* biter, and in particular, to have a savage character known to its owner. Tigers are not to be thought of as having characters to act from: they are just machines that bite.

This notion of having a character one can act out is tightly bound up with the notions of moral and legal responsibility and blame.

Dogs are blamed and punished in analogous ways to people (in some countries both can be executed) and that is only because they share very similar, though crucially different, physiological structures. The problem with machines and their programs, even if we were to squeeze them into the same category as dogs, would be how to blame and/or punish them.

6.3.3. Responsibility

The difficulty can be avoided by always identifying the humans who are standing behind the machines and programs as it were, to carry the blame, in the same way as there are always real humans standing behind agents and companies that also have the legal status of nonhuman responsible entities ("anonymous persons" in much of European law). In the case of companies with errant machines, the companies themselves (i.e., not their individual directors or shareholders) are responsible for a broad class of failures of their products and non-criminal actions by their agents, acting within the general furtherance of company policy (see Lehman-Wilzig, 1981). In those cases the punishment/destruction of machines and software packages would be merely a matter of internal company discipline, and of no outside interest.

In most situations now imaginable, it would not be too hard to identify individuals, if there is a need to do so, behind programs and machines. However, things may become more tricky as time goes on, and the simple substitution of responsible people for errant machines, harder to achieve. There are two obvious possibilities here: first, there are already in existence enormous bodies of software such as major bank and airline programs, that are the work of large numbers of individuals, that have been constantly edited and updated over many years, and are probably now without any adequate documentation. Those who could have written the documentation may well be dead. Such gigantic kludges function, up to a point, and it would be difficult and expensive to replace them. However, those who work with them are often unsure why they do what they do, or what they might do in the future. Errors committed by such software will be very hard to attribute to particular responsible individuals.

Secondly, it is a small step from that present reality to a future situation when we will accord the machine itself greater authority over the state it is currently in than we now do to information gained from diagnostics, traces, or even looking in its cabinet (see Wilks, 1984). The complete print-out of the program run by such a machine may be horrendously long, unannotated, and effectively structureless. This situation approximates, as closely as you like, that of the human brain where a print-out is pretty useless in establishing what "state" a person is in; we tend therefore to give great authority, in courts and elsewhere, to what people say about their own states of mind, particularly for the attribution of a "guilty" state of mind-the **mens re**. That movement through impenetrable software to ultimately inadequate diagnostics is, we think, the progression by which blame for machines might creep in, despite the attempts by advocates of more perspicuous programming styles to keep it out.

6.3.4. Punishment

But what can we say of "machine punishment?" A machine can be turned off and smashed,[17] and the software will either go with it or can be burned separately, provided we know we have **all** the copies! Only if some notion of computer blame had already crept in by the route we mentioned earlier, could we consider any of this destruction (or, more moderately perhaps, compulsory court-ordered edits to a program) as punishment. And then the issue for a court might be to decide whether to punish the software or the hardware, which would be in keeping with the speculations of the many philosophers who have toyed with the analogy hardware:software::body:soul-or-mind. But the weaknesses of that approach are well known by now in an era of machines that are practically hardwired for special software languages.

Anyone who finds something lacking in Joan of Arc's cry at the stake, that they were punishing her body but not her soul, will tend towards a position that persons are **embodied minds-or-souls** and that perhaps only these can be punished, even in principle. It would then be a short step to a position that if we were ever to talk of punishing intelligent machines, given that they could be blamed, it would have to be as *machine-embodied software*. It is a long way from the Lisp and Prolog machines of today, together with a little specialized speech and vision hardware, to the notion of a fully and ineluctably machine-embodied program. But that is the technicological road we are going down, and it may also be the only one down which machine crime and punishment can possibly lie...

---

[17] "Reprogramming with a large axe" (Adams, 1989). We are grateful to Nigel Shadbolt for reminding us of this crucial reference.

6.3.5. Obligation

In conclusion, let us return to the issue of "obligation," seen as it were from the machine's point of view, and not only as a matter of "Under what circumstances do we attribute responsibility and hence blame, to machines?", what we have called the Dennetist question; but also how would we introduce into programs the notion of "obligatory" or responsible action? This matter is far less speculative than the former, and one might say that current work in AI gives us a fairly clear view of the way forward.

The issue is not just one of representations, as many AI issues are, but of certain actions by the machine being the acceptance of obligations, marked internally as such. Searle (1969, cf. 5.2) set out bodies of rules for such notions as "acts of promising": conditions that must obtain, in terms of beliefs and goals, for a promise to have been made by an utterance.

What is worth noting here is that such work has normally been treated in AI as analyses of, say, "promising": as a linguistic mapping task from utterances such as "I'll give you US$5 next week" to inner entities such as **PROMISE**.

But what is often ignored is that Searle intended his work not solely or even principally as a linguistic task, but as an exploration of the foundations of moral obligation (i.e., of promising, not of "promising"). One of the successful adaptations that Speech Act work has made in AI, rather than in linguistics or philosophy, has been to show the intimate connection between such analyses and planning theory. Such work can now go one step further towards Searle's original goal within the theory of obligation (whether or not he would concede it), by incorporating, within the planning aspects of Speech Act representations the notion of actions deemed obligatory by a system for itself, and the tight connexion between such deeming and the external "social acts" that express the taking on of obligation (e.g., "I, robot, swear....").

6.3.6. Consent in computers

Consent is in a clear sense the inverse of liability: we are liable for what we do to others, but we consent to what they do to us.

Let us explore a little an immediate extension of the notions embodied in *ViewGen*, applied to examples like the thalassemia and pneumonia cases discussed in detail in the body of the book. Consider, as a domain of practical application, the medical notion of informed consent: in consenting to a medical procedure, a patient relieves the doctor of legal liability for known side-effects of the procedure. However, the patient's signature on a consent form is not wholly adequate for releasing the doctor from these liabilities; it is the doctor's responsibility to see that the patient is supplied with enough information he can understand to make a reasonable decision about consenting to the procedure. In this case, the patient is said to have given his *informed consent.*

Now, consider a computational belief system that can be used to construct two views relevant to establishing informed consent:

1) the patient's view of a medical procedure and its side-effects;

2) the physician's view of the patient's view of the procedure and its side-effects.
The System can be used after the fact to determine whether informed consent had been established, and whether the physician believed that it had been established. The System can also be used during consultation as an aid for the physician to determine whether he has supplied enough information for the patient to give his informed consent.

The *ViewGen* techniques of expertise representation, along with the default and inheritance mechanisms for ascription, form a natural experimental test-bed for such an application especially since, as we noted earlier, the key to much lay-medical interaction is not only expertise, but the construction (by the automaton in this case) of structured but totally false hypotheses (as would be appropriate for a patient in pain with a false view of where his stomach is, when he says "The pain is in my stomach"). This is the representation of vague and false theory/knowledge as much as expertise, yet it is exactly what an automaton would need as the basis of a belief and decision system that could judge when a patient was giving informed consent.

A patient would be deemed to have consented to therapy X if the System, in its model of the patient, has sufficient believed propositions which taken together justify X. A nice touch here from the point of view of the history of AI, is that this would amount to a classic Turing test in reverse: the *machine* would be judging whether or not the human understood, rather than vice-versa. In our view, it is interesting and nonobvious applications of this kind, far from the popular image of "expert systems," that artificial believers (deciders, consenters, and responsible actors) lead to.

Chapter 6.4
Conclusion

A feeling some readers may have at the end of this book is that a great variety of related pragmatic phenomena have been ignored; in particular, the vital contents of environments that are not straightforward beliefs, but are plans, goals, and other structures essential to the artificial believer if it is also to act. We freely acknowledge this. Our claim has been that belief ascription is an essential prolegomenon to all that, and that much that seems difficult about the theory of plans for cooperating agents becomes much simpler when belief ascription has been made clear. So for example, much multi-agent planning has been vitiated by the fact that the agents have not agreed on what constitutes a precondition for a given action: this step had simply been omitted. All that difficult, complex work can only begin once belief ascription has been tackled.

Our slow, sleep-walking steps have taken us from a simple idea of belief to a system for ascribing belief, and onwards to the consideration of more general questions concerning language: How can we understand it when it is uttered by someone else? How can a representation be said to have "meaning"? And how are these ideas interwoven with notions of beliefs, and ascribing beliefs to others?

We hope that a general reader of this book will come away with some notion of the complexity of the issues involved, as well as an understanding of why belief ascription (and *attitude* ascription, in general) is particularly important, as well as a view of how we might begin to model such ascriptions usefully on a computer.

Chapter 7

References

Adams, D. (1989). *Dirk Gently's Holistic Detective Agency.* New York, NY: Pocket Books.

Allen, J. F. (1983). Recognizing Intentions from Natural Language Utterances. In *Computational Models of Discourse.* Edited by M. Brady and R. C. Berwick. pp. 107-166. Cambridge, MA: MIT Press.

Allen, J. F. and Perrault, C. R. (1978). Participating in Dialogues Understanding via Plan Deduction. *Proceedings of the 2nd National Conference of the Canadian Society for Computational Studies of Intelligence.* Toronto.

Anderson, A. and Belnap, N. (1975). *Entailment: The logic of relevance and necessity.* Princeton, NJ: Princeton University Press.

Appelt, D. and Pollack, M. (1990). Weighted Abduction as an Inference Method for Plan Recognition and Evaluation. *Second International Workshop on User Modeling.* Honolulu, Hawaii.

Arragon, P. van (1990). Modeling Default Reasoning Using Defaults. *Second International Workshop on User Modeling.* Honolulu, Hawaii.

Attardi, G. and Simi, M. (1984). Metalanguage and Reasoning Across Viewpoints. *Proceedings of the ECAI-84,* pp. 315-324.

Austin, J. L. (1962). *How to do things with words.* Oxford: Oxford University Press.

Bach, K. (1982). *De Re* Belief and Methodological Solipsism. In *Thought and Object.* Edited by A. Woodfield. pp. 122-151. Oxford: Oxford University Press.

Bach, K. and Harnish, R. M. (1979). *Linguistic Communication and Speech Acts.* Cambridge, MA: The MIT Press.

Ballim, A. (1986). Generating points of view. *Memoranda in Computer and Cognitive Science,* MCCS-86-68. Computing Research Laboratory, New Mexico State University, Las Cruces, NM.

Ballim, A. (1987). The Subjective Ascription of Belief to Agents. In *Advances in Artificial Intelligence.* Edited by J. Hallam and C. Mellish. pp. 267-278. Chichester, England: John Wiley & Sons.

Ballim, A. (1988). A language for representing and reasoning with nested belief. *First Annual Irish Conference on Artificial Intelligence and Cognitive Science.* Dublin, Ireland.

Ballim, A. (forthcoming). *Belief convictions, quantification and default reasoning.* (manuscript in preparation.).

Ballim, A., Candelaria de Ram, S., and Fass, D. (1989). Reasoning using Inheritance from a Mixture of Knowledge and Beliefs. In *Proceedings of the Conference on Knowledge Based Computer Systems.* Edited by S. Ramani, R. Chandrasekar, and K. Anjaneylu. pp. 387-396. Delhi: Narosa Publishing House.

Ballim, A., Wilks, Y., and Barnden, J. (1991). Belief, Metaphor, and Intensional Identification. In *Belief Systems in Language: Studies in Linguistic Prototypes.* Edited by S. Tsohadtzidis. London: Routledge. Also in *Cognitive Science,* 16.

Barnden, J. A. (1983). Intensions as such: An outline. *Proceedings of the IJCAI-83,* pp. 280-286. Los Altos, CA: Morgan Kaufmann.

Barnden, J. A. (1986). A viewpoint distinction in the representation of propositional attitudes. *Proceedings of the AAAI-86,* pp. 411-415. Los Altos, CA: Morgan Kaufmann.

Barnden, J. A. (1988a). Propositional attitudes, commonsense reasoning, and metaphor. *Proceedings of the 10th Annual Conference of the Cognitive Science Society,* pp. 503-509. Hillsdale, NJ: Lawrence Erlbaum Associates.

Barnden, J. A. (1988b). Propositional attitudes, polysemy and metaphor: initial report. *Memoranda in Computer and Cognitive Science,* MCCS-88-139. Computing Research Laboratory, New Mexico State University, Las Cruces, NM.

Barnden, J. A. (1989). Belief, metaphorically speaking. *Proceedings of the 1st Intl. Conf. on Principles of Knowledge Representation and Reasoning*, pp. 21-32. San Mateo, CA: Morgan Kaufmann.

Barwise, J. and Perry, J. (1983). *Situations and Attitudes*. Cambridge, MA: Bradford Books.

Bien, J. (1976). A multiple environments approach to natural language. *American Journal of Computational Linguistics*, 54.

Bien, J. (1983). Articles and Resource Control. *Proceedings of the IJCAI-83*, pp. 675-677.

Black, M. (1962). *Models and Metaphors*. Ithaca, NY: Cornell University Press.

Blakemore, D. (1987). *Semantic Constraints on Relevance*. Oxford: Basil Blackwell.

Bobrow, D. and Winograd, T. (1977). KRL: Another Perspective. *Cognitive Science*, 3, pp. 29-43.

Bochenski, I. (1961). *A History of Formal Logic*. Indiana: Notre Dame University Press.

Bochvar, D. (1939). On three-valued logical calculus and its application to the analysis of contradictions. *Matematiceskij Sbornik*, 4.

Braithwaite, R. B. (1962). Models in the Empirical Sciences. In *Proceedings 1960 International Congress on Logic, Methodology and Philosophy of Science*. Edited by E. Nagel, P. Suppes, and A. Tarski. Stanford, CA: Stanford University Press.

Brewka, G. (1989). Preferred Subtheories. *Proceedings of the International Joint Conference on Artificial Intelligence*, pp. 1043-1048. Los Angeles, CA: Morgan Kaufmann.

Carbonell, J. G. (1982). Metaphor: An Inescapable Phenomenon in Natural Language Comprehension. In *Strategies for Natural Language Processing*. Edited by W. G. Lehnert and M.H. Ringle. Hillsdale, NJ: Lawrence Erlbaum Associates.

Carnap, R. (1956). *Meaning and Necessity*. Chicago, IL: The University of Chicago Press.

Chellas, B. F. (1980). *Modal logic*. Cambridge: Cambridge University Press.

Chomsky, N. (1964). Current Issues in Linguistic Theory. *Janua Linguarum*, 7.

Church, A. (1951). A Formulation of the Logic of Sense and Denotation. In *Structure, Method & Meaning: Essays in Honor of H.M. Sheffer*. Edited by P. Henle, H. Kallen, and S. Langer. pp. 3-24. New York, NY: Liberal Arts.

Churchland, P. (1979). *Scientific Realism and the Plasticity of Mind.* Cambridge: Cambridge University Press.

Clark, H. and Marshall, C. (1981). Definite Reference and Mutual Knowledge. In *Elements of Discourse Understanding*. Edited by A. Joshi, B. Webber, and I. Sag. pp. 10-62. Cambridge: Cambridge University Press.

Cohen, L. (1964). Do Illocutionary Forces Exist?. *Philosophical Quarterly*, 14.

Cohen, P. (1978). On Knowing What to Say: Planning Speech Acts. *University of Toronto, Computer Science Department Memorandum*.

Cohen, P. and Grinberg, M. (1983). A Framework for Heuristics Reasoning About Uncertainty. *Proceedings of the IJCAI-83*, pp. 355-357. Los Altos, CA: Morgan Kaufmann.

Cohen, P. and Levesque, H. (1980). Speech Acts and Recognition of Shared Plans. *Proceedings of the Third Biennial Conference, Canadian Society for Computational Studies in Intelligence*, pp. 263-271.

Cohen, P. and Levesque, H. (1985). Speech Acts and Rationality. *Proceedings of the 23rd Annual Meeting of the Association for Computational Linguistics*, pp. 49-60. University of Chicago.

Cohen, P. R. and Levesque, H. J. (1987). Intention = Choice + Commitment. *Proceedings of AAAI-87*, pp. 410-415. Los Altos, CA: Morgan Kaufmann.

Cohen, J. and Margalit, A. (1972). The role of inductive reasoning in the interpretation of metaphor. In *Semantics of natural language*. Edited by D. Davidson and G. Harman. Dordrecht: Reidel.

Colby, K. (1975). *Artificial Paranoia: A Computer Simulation of Paranoid Processes*. New York, NY: Pergamon Press.

Colby, K., Weber, S., and Hilf, F. (1971). Artificial Paranoia. *Artificial Intelligence*, 2, pp. 1-25.

Craddock, A.J. and Browse, R.A. (1986). Belief Maintenance with Uncertainty. *Proceedings of the Eight Annual Meeting of the Cognitive Science Society*, pp. 607-612.

Creary, L. G. (1979). Propositional attitudes: Fregean representation and simulative reasoning. *Proceedings of the IJCAI-79*. Tokyo.

Creary, L. G. and Pollard, C. J. (1985). A computational semantics for natural language. *Proceedingss of the 23rd Annual Meeting of the Association for Computational Linguistics*. University of Chicago.

Cullingford, R. (1986). SAM. In *Readings in Natural Language Processing*. Edited by B. Grosz, K. Sparck-Jones, and B. Webber. pp. 627-649. Los Altos, CA: Morgan Kaufmann.

Davidson, D. (1967). Truth and Meaning. *Synthese*, XVII, 3, pp. 304-323.

Davidson, D. (1978). What Metaphors Mean. *Critical Inquiry*, 5, pp. 31-48.

de Kleer, J. (1984). Choices without Backtracking. *Proceedings of the 22nd Conference of the Association for Computational Linguistics*, pp. 79-85.

de Kleer, J. (1986). An Assumption-based TMS. *Artificial Intelligence*, 28, pp. 127-162.

Delgrande, J.P. (1987). A First-Order Conditional Logic for Prototypical Properties. *Artificial Intelligence*, 33, 1, pp. 105-130.

Dennett, D. (1978). *Brainstorms*. Cambridge, MA: MIT Press.

Dennett, D. (1982). Beyond Belief. In *Thought and Object*. Edited by A. Woodfield. pp. 1-95. Oxford: Clarendon Press.

des Rivieres, J. and Levesque, H. (1986). The consistency of syntactical treatments of knowledge. In *Theoretical Aspects of Reasoning About Knowledge*. Edited by J. Halpern. pp. 115-130. Los Altos, CA: Morgan Kaufmann.

Devlin, K. (1991). *Logic and Information*. Cambridge: Cambridge University Press.

Dijk, T. Van (1979). *Macro-structures*. Hillsdale, N.J: Lawrence Erlbaum Associates.

Dinsmore, J. (1987). Mental Spaces from a functional perspective. *Cognitive Science*, 11, pp. 1-23.

Donnellan, K. S. (1966). Reference and Definite Descriptions. *Philosophical Review*, LXXV, 3, pp. 281-304.

Doyle, J. (1979). A Truth Maintenance System. *Artificial Intelligence*, 12, pp. 231-272.

Doyle, J. (1980). *A Model for Deliberation, Action, and Introspection (Ph.D. Dissertation)*. Massachusetts Institute of Technology: Artificial Intelligence Laboratory.

Doyle, J. (1983). A Society of Mind. *Proceedings of the IJCAI-83*, pp. 309-314. Los Altos, CA: Morgan Kaufmann.

Dressler, W. (Ed.) (1978). *Current Trends in Text Linguistics*. Berlin: de Gruyter.

Dretske, F. I. (1981). *Knowledge and the Flow of Information*. Cambridge, MA: MIT Press.

Dreyfus, H. (1972). *What Computers Can't Do: The Limits of Artificial Intelligence*. New York, NY: Harper & Row.

Etherington, D. W. (1987). Relating Default Logic and Circumscription. *Proceedings of the IJCAI-87*, pp. 489-494.

Fagin, R. and Halpern, J. Y. (1987). Belief, awareness and limited reasoning. *Artificial Intelligence*, 34, pp. 39-76.

Fahlman, S. (1979). *NETL: A System for Representing and Using Real-World Knowledge*. Cambridge, Massachusetts: MIT Press.

Falkenhainer, B., Forbus, K., and Gentner, D. (1986). The structure-mapping engine. *Proceedings of the AAAI-86*. Los Altos, CA: Morgan Kaufmann.

Fass, D. C. (1987). Collative Semantics: An overview of the current Meta5 program. *Memoranda in Computer and Cognitive Science*, MCCS-87-112. Computing Research Laboratory, New Mexico State University, Las Cruces, NM.

Fass, D. C. and Wilks, Y. (1983). Preference Semantics, Ill-formedness and Metaphor. *American Journal of Computational Linguistics, special issue on ill-formed input*, 9, pp. 178-187.

Fauconnier, G. (1985). *Mental Spaces: Aspects of meaning construction in natural language*. Cambridge, MA: MIT Press.

Field, H. (1978). Mental Representations. *Erkenntnis*, 13, pp. 9-16.

Fodor, J. A. (1975). *The Language of Thought*. New York, NY: Thomas Y. Crowell.

Fodor, J. A. (1980b). Methodological Solipsism considered as a research strategy in Cognitive Psychology. *The Behavioral & Brain Sciences*, 3.

Fodor, J. A. (1980a). *Representations*. Cambridge, MA: The MIT Press.

Fodor, J. A. (1987b). Information and Association. In *Language and Artificial Intelligence*. Edited by M. Nagao. Amsterdam: North Holland.

Fodor, J. A. (1980b). Methodological Solipsism considered as a research strategy in Cognitive Psychology. *The Behavioral & Brain Sciences, 3.*

Frege, G. (1892 & 1949). Ueber Sinn und Bedeutung. In *Readings in Philosophical Analysis (English translation)*. Edited by H. Feigl and W. Sellars. New York, NY : Appleton-Century-Crofts.

Gazdar, G. and Good, D. (1982). On a Notion of Relevance. In *Mutual Knowledge*. Edited by N. Smith. London: Academic.

Gentner, D., Falkenhainer, B., and Skorstad, J. (1987). Metaphor: the Good, the Bad and the Ugly. *Proceedings of 3rd Workshop on Theoretical Issues in Natural Language Processing (TINLAP-3)*, pp. 155-159. Las Cruces, NM.

Gordon, D. and Lakoff, G. (1971). Conversational Postulates. *Papers from the Seventh Regional Meeting of the Chicago Linguistics Society*, pp. 63-84.

Grice, H. (1969). Utterer's meaning and intentions. *Philosophical Review*, pp. 147-177.

Grice, H.P. (1975). Logic and Conversation. In *Syntax and Semantics 9: Pragmatics*. Edited by P. Cole. New York, NY: Academic Press.

Grosz, B. J. (1977). The representation and use of focus in a system for understanding dialogs. *Proceedings of the IJCAI-77*. Los Altos, CA: Morgan Kaufmann.

Gruder, C. et al. (1978). Empirical Tests on the Absolute Sleeper Effect Predicted from the Discouting Cue Hypothesis. *Journal of Personality and Social Psychology, 36.*

Haack, S. (1974). *Deviant Logic*. Cambridge: Cambridge University Press.

Haack, S. (1978). *Philosophy of Logics*. Cambridge: Cambridge University Press.

Haas, A. (1986). A syntactic theory of belief and action. *Artificial Intelligence, 28*, pp. 245-292.

Hadley, R. (1988). Logical Omniscience, Semantics, and Models of Belief. *Computational Intelligence, 4, 1*, pp. 17-30.

Halpern, J. Y. and Moses, Y. (1985). A guide to the modal logics of knowledge and belief. *Proceedings of the IJCAI-85*, pp. 480-490. Los Altos, CA:

Morgan Kaufmann.

Halpern, J. Y. and Rabin, M. O. (1987). A Logic to Reason about Likelihood. *Artificial Intelligence*, 32, pp. 379-405.

Hanks, S. and McDermott, D. (1987). Nonmonotonic Logic and Temporal Projection. *Artificial Intelligence*, 33, pp. 379-412.

Harman, G. (1973). *Thought*. Princeton, NJ: Princeton University Press.

Hayes, P. J. (1977). In Defense of Logic. *Proceedings of the IJCAI-77, Cambridge, MA*. Los Altos, CA: Morgan Kaufmann.

Heidegger, M. (1962). *Being and Time*. New York, NY: Harper & Row.

Hendrix, G. G. (1979). Encoding knowledge in partitioned networks. In *Associative networks*. Edited by N.V. Findler. New York, NY: Academic Press.

Hesse, M. (1965). The Explanatory Function of Metaphor. In *Proceedings of the 1964 International Congress on Logic, Methodology and Philosophy of Science*. Amsterdam: North Holland.

Hintikka, J. (1962). *Knowledge and Belief*. Ithaca, NY: Cornell University Press.

Hintikka, J. (1973). *Logic, Language-Games and Information*. Oxford: Clarendon Press.

Hobbs, J. R. (1983). Metaphor interpretation as selective inferencing: cognitive processes in understanding metaphor (Part1). *Empirical Studies of the Arts*, 1, pp. 17-33.

Hobbs, J. R. (1985). Ontological promiscuity. *Proceedings of the 23rd Annual Meeting of the Association for Computational Linguistics*. University of Chicago.

Huang, X., McCalla, G., and Greer, J. (1989). Belief Revision: An Evolutionary Approach. *ARIES Technical Report*. Saskatoon, Canada: Department of Computer Science, University of Saskatchewan.

Johnson, M. (1987). *The body in the mind*. Chicago, IL: University of Chicago Press.

Johnson-Laird, J. N. (1983). *Mental models*. Cambridge: Cambridge University Press.

Katz, J. (1972). *Semantic Theory*. New York, NY: Harper & Row.

Kleene, S. (1952). *Introduction to Metamathematics*. New York, NY: Van Nostrand.

Kobsa, A. (1984). Three steps in constructing mutual belief models from user assertions. *Proceedings of the 6th European Conference on Artificial Intelligence*, pp. 423-427.

Kobsa, A. (1988). A Taxonomy of Belief and Goals for User Models in Dialog Systems. In *User Models in Dialog Systems*. Edited by A. Kobsa and W. Wahlster. Berlin: Springer Verlag.

Koestler, A. (1959). *The Sleepwalkers: A History of Man's Changing Vision of the Universe*. New York, NY: MacMillan.

Konolige, K. (1982). Circumscriptive Ignorance. *Proceedings of AAAI-82*, pp. 202-204. Los Altos, CA: Morgan Kaufmann.

Konolige, K. (1983). A deductive model of belief. *Proceedings of the IJCAI-83*, 2, pp. 377-382. Los Altos, CA: Morgan Kaufmann.

Konolige, K. (1985). A Computational Theory of Belief Introspection. *Proceedings of the IJCAI-85*, pp. 502-508. Los Altos, CA: Morgan Kaufmann.

Konolige, K. (1986). What awareness isn't: A sentential view of implicit and explicit belief. In *Theoretical Aspects of Reasoning about Knowledge*. Edited by J. Y. Halpern. Los Altos, CA: Morgan Kaufmann.

Konolige, K. (1987). On the Relation Between Default Theories and Autoepistemic Logic. *Proceedings of the IJCAI-8*, 1, pp. 394-401. Los Altos, CA: Morgan Kaufmann.

Konolige, K. and Pollack, M. (1989). Ascribing Plans to Agents. *Proceedings of the IJCAI-89*, pp. 924-930. Los Altos, CA: Morgan Kaufmann.

Koons, R. (1988). Doxastic Paradoxes without Self-Reference. In *Theoretical Aspects of Reasoning About Knowledge II*. Edited by M. Vardi. pp. 29-41. Los Altos, CA: Morgan Kaufmann.

Kripke, S. (1972). Naming and Necessity. In *Semantics of Natural Language*. Edited by D. Davidson and G. Harman. Dordrecht: Reidel.

Kripke, S. (1977). Speaker's Reference and Semantic Reference.. In *Contemporary Perspectives in the Philosophy of Language*. Edited by P. French et al. pp. 6-27. Minneapolis, MN: University of Minnesota Press.

Lakoff, G. (1987). *Women, fire and dangerous things: what categories reveal about the mind*. Chicago, IL: University of Chicago Press.

Lakoff, G. and Johnson, M. (1980). *Metaphors we live by*. Chicago, IL: University of Chicago Press.

Langley, P. (1980). *Descriptive Discovery Processes: Experiments In Baconian Science*. Carnegie-Mellon University, Computer Science Department, Technical Report.

Laskey, K. B. and Lehner, P. E. (1988). Belief Maintenance: An Integrated Approach to Uncertainty Management. *Proceedings of the National Conference on Artificial Intelligence (AAAI)*, pp. 210-214. Los Altos, CA: Morgan Kaufmann.

Lehman-Wilzig, S. (1981). Frankenstein unbound: towards a legal definition of Artificial Intelligence. *Futures*, 13.

Lehnert, W. (1986). A Conceptual Theory of Question Answering. In *Readings in Natural Language Processing*. Edited by B. Grosz, K. Sparck-Jones, and B. Webber. pp. 651-657. Los Altos, CA: Morgan Kaufmann.

Lehnert, W. and Wilks, Y. (1979). A Critical Perspective on KRL. *Cognitive Science*, 3, pp. 1-29.

Leibniz, G. (1951). *Selections*. Edited by P. Wiener. New York, NY: Scribner.

Lenat, D., Prakash, M., and Shepherd, M. (1986). CYC: Using Common Sense Knowledge to Overcome Brittleness and Knowledge Acquisition Bottlenecks. *The AI Magazine*, 6, (4), pp. 65-85.

Lesperance, Y. (1989). A Formal Account of Self-Knowledge and Action. *Proceedings of the IJCAI-89*, pp. 868-874. Los Altos, CA: Morgan Kaufmann.

Levesque, H. (1984). A Logic of Implicit and Explicit Belief. *Proceedings of the National Conference on Artificial Intelligence*, pp. 198-202. Los Altos, CA: Morgan Kaufmann.

Lifschitz, V. (1984). Some Results on Circumscription. *Proceedings of the National Conference on Artificial Intelligence*. Los Altos, CA: Morgan Kaufmann.

Linsky, L. (1983). *Oblique contexts*. Chicago, IL: Chicago University Press.

Lukasiewicz, J. (1930). Many-valued systems of propositional logic. Edited by S. McCall. *Polish Logic*. Oxford: Oxford University Press.

Maida, A. S. (1983). Knowing intensional individuals. *Proceedings of the IJCAI-83*. Los Altos, CA: Morgan Kaufmann.

Maida, A. S. (1986). Introspection and reasoning about the beliefs of other agents. *Proceedings of the 8th Annual Conference of the Cognitive Science Society*, pp. 187-195. Hillsdale, NJ: Lawrence Erlbaum Associates.

Maida, A. S. (1988). A syntactic approach to mental correspondence. *Proceedings of the Canadian Society for Computational Studies of Artificial Intelligence.* Edmonton, Canada.

Maida, A. S. and Shapiro, S. C. (1982). Intensional concepts in propositional semantic networks. *Cognitive Science*, 6, pp. 291-330.

Martins, H. (1988). *personal communication.*

Martins, H. and Shapiro, S. (1983). Reasoning in Multiple Belief Spaces. *Proceedings of the IJCAI-83*, pp. 370-373. Los Altos, CA: Morgan Kaufmann.

McCarthy, J. (1979). First order theories of individual concepts and propositions. Edited by B. Meltzer and D. Michie. *Machine Intelligence*, 9, pp. 120-147. Edinburgh: Edinburgh University Press.

McCarthy, J. and Hayes, P. (1969). Some Philosophical Problems from the Standpoint of Artificial Intellgience. Edited by B. Meltzer and D. Michie. *Machine Intelligence*, 4. Edinburgh: Edinburgh University Press.

McDermott, D. and Doyle, J. (1980). Non-Monotonic Logic I. *Artificial Intelligence*, 13, pp. 41-72.

McLoughlin, H. (1986). Personae: Models of Stereotypical Behaviour. In *Communication Failure in Dialogue*. Edited by R. Reilly. Amsterdam: North Holland.

Meehan, J. (1981). TALE-SPIN. In *Inside Computer Understanding: Five Programs plus Miniatures*. Edited by R. Schank and C. Riesbeck. pp. 197-226. Hillsdale, NJ: Lawrence Erlbaum Associates.

Minsky, M. (1968). Matter, Mind, and Models. In *Semantic Information Processing*. Edited by M. Minsky. pp. 425-432. Cambridge, MA: MIT Press.

Minsky, M. (1975). A Framework for Representing Knowledge. In *The Psychology of Computer Vision*. Edited by P.H. Winston. New York, NY: McGraw-Hill.

Montague, R. (1963). Syntactic Treatments of Modality. *Acta Philosophica Fennica*, 16, pp. 153-167.

Montague, R. (1974). *Formal Philosophy*. Edited by R. Thomason. New Haven, CT: Yale University Press.

Moore, R. (1977). Reasoning about knowledge and action. *Proceedings of the IJCAI-77*, pp. 223-227. Los Altos, CA: Morgan Kaufmann.

Moore, R. (1984). A Formal Theory of Knowledge and Action. In *Formal Theories of the Commonsense World*. Edited by J. R. Hobbs and R. C. Moore. Norwood, NJ: Ablex.

Moore, R. (1985). Semantic Considerations on Non-monotonic Logic. *Artificial Intelligence*, 25, pp. 75-94.

Moore, R. and Hendrix, G. (1979). Computational models of belief and the semantics of belief sentences. *SRI Technical Note No. 187*. Menlo Park, CA.

Moore, G. W. and Hutchins, G. M. (1981). A Hintikka possible worlds model for certainty levels in medical decision making. *Synthese*, 48, pp. 87-119.

Norman, D. and Bobrow, D.G. (1975). On Data-Limited and Resource-Limited Processes. *Cognitive Psychology*, 7, pp. 44-64.

Nutter, J. T. (1987). Default Reasoning. In *Encyclopedia of Artificial Intelligence*. Edited by S. C. Shapiro. pp. 840-848. New York, NY: John Wiley.

Pearl, J. (1985). Bayesian Networks: A Model of Self-Activated Memory for Evidential Reasoning. In *Proceedings of the Conference of the Cognitive Science Society*.

Pearl, J. (1987). Embracing Causality in Formal Reasoning. *Proceedings of AAAI-87*, pp. 369-373. Los Altos, CA: Morgan Kaufmann.

Perlis, D. (1986). Self-Reference, Knowledge, Belief and Modality. *Proceedings of AAAI-86*, pp. 416-420. Los Altos, CA: Morgan Kaufmann.

Perrault, R. and Allen, J. (1980). A plan-based analysis of indirect speech acts. *American Journal of Computational Linguistics*, 6, pp. 167-182.

Perry, J. (1977). Frege on Demonstratives. *Philosophical Review*, 86, 4.

Perry, J. (1979). The Problem of the Essential Indexical. *Nous*, 13.

Perry, J. (1983). Castaneda on He and I. In *Agent, Language and the Structure of the World*. Edited by J.E. Tomberlin. Indianapolis, IN: Hackett.

Petoefi, J. (1976). A frame for FRAMES: A few remarks on the methodology of semantically guided text processing. *Proceedings of the Second Annual Meeting of the Berkeley Linguistic Society*, pp. 319-29. Berkeley, CA: University of California Institute of Human Learning.

Pollack, M. (1986). A Model of Plan Inferences that Distinguishes between the Beliefs of Actors and Observers. *Proceedings of the Meeting of the Association for Computational Linguistics, 1986*, pp. 207-214.

Poole, D. (1988). A Logical Framework for Default Reasoning. *Artificial Intelligence*, 36, pp. 27-47.

Potts, T. (1975). Montague's Rhetoric: A Syllabus of Errors. In *Formal Semantics of Natural Language*. Edited by E. Keenan. Cambridge: Cambridge University Press.

Putnam, H. (1960). Minds and Machines. In *Dimensions of Mind*. Edited by S. Hook. pp. 138-164. New York, NY: New York University Press.

Quillian, M. R. (1968). Semantic Memory. In *Semantic Information Processing*. Edited by M. Minsky. pp. 216-270. Cambridge, MA: MIT Press.

Quine, W.V.O. (1943). Notes on Existence and Necessity. *Journal of Philosophy*, 40, pp. 113-127.

Quine, W.V.O. (1947). The Problem of Interpreting Modal Logic. *Journal of Symbolic Logic*, 12.

Quine, W.V.O. (1960). *Word and Object*. Cambridge, MA: MIT Press.

Ramsey, F. and Reddy, M. J. (1979). The conduit metaphor — a case of frame conflict in our language about language. In *Metaphor and Thought*. Edited by A. Ortony. Cambridge: Cambridge University Press.

Rao, A. and Foo, N. (1989). Minimal Change and Maximal Coherence: A Basis for Belief Revision and Reasoning about Actions. *Proceedings of the IJCAI-89*, pp. 966-971. Los Altos, CA: Morgan Kaufmann.

Rapaport, W. J. (1986). Logical Foundations for Belief Representation. *Cognitive Science*, 10, pp. 371-422. Norwood, NJ: Ablex.

Reichman, Rachel (1985). *Getting Computers to Talk like You and Me: Discourse Context, Focus and Semantics (An ATN Model)*. Cambridge, Ma.: MIT Press.

Reiter, R. (1978). On Reasoning by Default. *Proceedings of the 2nd Workshop on Theoretical Issues in Natural Language Processing*, pp. 210-218. University of Illinois at Urbana-Champaign.

Reiter, R. (1980). A Logic for Default Reasoning. *Artificial Intelligence*, 13, pp. 81-132.

Reeves, J. F. (1988). Ethical Understanding. *Proceedings of the National Conference on Artificial Intelligence,* pp. 227-232. Los Altos, CA: Morgan Kaufmann.

Reiter, R. and Kleer, J. de (1987). Foundations of Assumption-Based Truth Maintenance Systems. *Proceedings of AAAI-87,* pp. 183-188. Los Altos, CA: Morgan Kaufmann.

Rich, E. (1979). User Modeling via Stereotypes. *Cognitive Science,* 3, pp. 329-345.

Rich, E. (1983). *Artificial Intelligence.* New York, NY: McGraw-Hill.

Rich, E. (1988). Stereotypes and User Modeling. In *User Models in Dialog Systems.* Edited by W. Wahlster and A. Kobsa. Berlin: Springer Verlag.

Rieger, C. (1975). Conceptual Memory and Inference. In *Conceptual Information Processing.* Edited by R. Schank. Amsterdam: North Holland.

Rose, D. (1985). Towards a Unified Model of Deception. *Proceedings of the Annual Cognitive Science Conference,* pp. 346-350.

Rose, D. and Langley, P. (1987). Belief Revision and Induction. *Proceedings of the Annual Cognitive Science Conference,* pp. 748-52.

Ross, J. (1970). On Declarative Sentences. In *Readings in English Transformational Grammar.* Edited by R. Jacobs and S. Rosenbaum. Waltham, MA: Ginn.

Russell, B. (1919). Descriptions. In *Introduction to Mathematical Philosophy.* pp. 167-180. London: Allen and Unwin.

Schank, R. (1972). Conceptual Dependency. *Cognitive Psychology,* 3, pp. 552-631.

Schiffer, S. (1972). *Meaning.* Oxford: Oxford University Press.

Schiffer, S. (1978). The Basis of Reference. *Erkenntnis,* 13.

Searle, J. (1969). *Speech acts: an essay in the philosophy of language.* Cambridge: Cambridge University Press.

Searle, J. (1974). Chomsky's Revolution in Linguistics. In *Noam Chomsky: Critical Essays.* Edited by G. Harman. New York, NY: Anchor Books.

Searle, J. (1980). Minds, Brains and Programs. *Behavioral and Brain Sciences,* 3, pp. 417-424.

Shadbolt, N. (1983). Processing reference. *Journal of Semantics,* 2, pp. 63-98.

Shafer, G. (1976). *A mathematical theory of evidence*. Princeton, NJ: Princeton University Press.

Shapiro, S. C. and Rapaport, W. J. (1986). SNePS considered as a fully intensional propositional semantic network. *Proceedings of AAAI-86*, pp. 278-283. Los Altos, CA: Morgan Kaufmann.

Shoham, Y. and Moses, Y. (1989). Belief as Defeasible Knowledge. *Proceedings of the IJCAI-89*, pp. 1168-1173. Los Altos, CA: Morgan Kaufmann.

Sidner, C. L. and Israel, D. J. (1981). Recognizing Intended Meaning and Speakers' Plans. *International Joint Conference on Artificial Intelligence*, pp. 203-208. Los Altos, CA: Morgan Kaufmann.

Smith, N. (ed.) (1982). *Mutual Knowledge*. London: Academic.

Smith, P. (8 July, 1988). Review of Dennett, D., *The Intentional Stance*. In *The Times Higher Educational Supplement*. London.

Smolensky, P. (1988). On the Proper Treatment of Connectionism. *The Behavioral and Brain Sciences*, 11, pp. 1-23.

Sperber, D. and Wilson, D. (1982). Mutual Knowledge and Relevance in Theories of Comprehension. In *Mutual Knowledge*. Edited by N. Smith. London: Academic.

Sperber, D. and Wilson, D. (1986). *Relevance, communication and cognition*. Oxford: Basil Blackwell.

Stalnaker, R. (1981). Indexical Belief. *Synthese*, 49, pp. 129-151.

Steel, S. (1984). Simplifying Recursive Belief for Language Understanding. *Proceedings of the ECAI-84*, pp. 177-180.

Strawson, P. (1964). Intention and Convention in Speech Acts. *Philosophical Review*, 73.

Subramanian, D. and Genesereth, M. R. (1987). The relevance of irrelevance. *Proceedings of the IJCAI-87*, pp. 276-281. Los Altos, CA: Morgan Kaufmann.

Sullivan, M. and Cohen, P.R. (1985). An Endorsement-based Plan Recognition Program. *Proceedings of the IJCAI-85*, pp. 475-479. Los Altos, CA: Morgan Kaufmann.

Sycara, K. (1989). Argumentation: Planning Other Agents' Plans. *Proceedings of the IJCAI-89*, pp. 517-523. Los Altos, CA: Morgan Kaufmann.

Tarski, A. (1944). The Semantic Conception of Truth. *Philosophy and Phenomenological Research* , 4, pp. 341-375.

Taylor, G. B. and Whitehill, S. B. (1981). A Belief Representation for Understanding Deception. *Proceedings of the IJCAI-81*, pp. 388-393. Los Altos, CA: Morgan Kaufmann.

Thomason, R. (1980). A Note on Syntactical Treatments of Modality. *Synthese*, 44, pp. 391-395.

Touretzky, D., Horty, J., and Thomason, R. (1987). A Clash of Intuitions. *Proceedings of the IJCAI-87*, pp. 476-482. Los Altos, CA: Morgan Kaufmann.

Turing, A. (1950). Computing Machinery and Intelligence. *Mind*, LIX, pp. 433 - 460.

Turkle, S. (1987). *A New Romantic Reaction: The Computer as Precipitant of Anti-Mechanistic Definitions of the Human.* Paper given at conference on Humans, Animals, Machines: Boundaries and Projections, Stanford University.

Turner, R. (1984). *Logics for Artificial Intelligence.* Chichester, England: Ellis Horwood.

Vahinger, H. (1935). *The Philosophy of "as if "; a System of the Theoretical, Practical and Religious Fictions of Mankind.* London: Routledge and Kegan Paul.

Weyhrauch, R. (1980). Prologomena to a Theory of Formal Reasoning. *Artificial Intelligence*, 13, pp. 133-170.

Wiebe, J. and Rapaport, W. (1986). Representing *De Re* and *De Dicto* belief reports in Discourse and Narrative. *Proceedings of IEEE*, 74, pp. 1405-1413.

Wilkins, J. (1668). *An Essay Towards a Real Character and a Philosophical Language.* London.

Wilks, Y. (1971). Decidability and Natural Language. *Mind*, N.S. 80, pp. 497-516.

Wilks, Y. (1975). Preference Semantics. In *Formal Semantics of Natural Language.* Edited by E. Keenan. Cambridge: Cambridge University Press.

Wilks, Y. (1976). Parsing English. In *Computational Semantics.* Edited by E. Charniak and Y. Wilks. pp. 155-184. New York, NY: North Holland.

Wilks, Y. (1977). Making Preferences More Active. *Artificial Intelligence*, 8, pp. 75-97.

Wilks, Y. (1980). Frames, Semantics and Novelty. In *Frame Conceptions and Text Understanding*. Edited by D. Metzing. Berlin: de Gruyter.

Wilks, Y. (1982). Some Thoughts on Procedural Semantics. In *Strategies for Natural Language Processing*. Edited by W. Lehnert and M. Ringle. pp. 495-516. Hillsdale, NJ: Lawrence Erlbaum Associates.

Wilks, Y. (1984). Machines and Consciousness. In *Minds, Machines, and Evolution*. Edited by C. Hookaway. Cambridge: Cambridge University Press.

Wilks, Y., Huang, X., and Fass, D. (1985). Syntax, Preference, and Right Attachment. *Proceedings of the IJCAI-85*, 2, pp. 779-784. Los Angeles, CA.

Wilks, Y. (1986). Relevance and beliefs. In *Reasoning and Discourse Processes*. Edited by T. Myers, K. Brown, and B. McGonigle. London: Academic Press.

Wilks, Y. (1990). Some Comments on Smolensky and Fodor. In *The Foundations of Artificial Intelligence*. Edited by D. Partridge and Y. Wilks. Cambridge: Cambridge University Press.

Wilks, Y. and Ballim, A. (1987). Multiple Agents and the Heuristic Ascription of Belief. *Proceedings of the IJCAI-87*, pp. 118-124. Los Altos, CA: Morgan Kaufmann.

Wilks, Y. and Ballim, A. (1988). Shifting the belief engine into higher gear. In *Proceedings of the International Conference on AI Methodology and Systems Applications*. Edited by T. O'Shea and V. Sgurev. Amsterdam: Elsevier.

Wilks, Y. and Ballim, A. (1989). Ascribing Belief. In *Kuenstliche Intelligenz*. Edited by T. Christaller. New York, NY: Springer Verlag.

Wilks, Y. and Bien, J. (1979). Speech Acts and Multiple Environments. *Proceedings of the IJCAI-79*, pp. 968-970. Los Altos, CA: Morgan Kaufmann.

Wilks, Y. and Bien, J. (1983). Beliefs, Points of View and Multiple Environments. *Cognitive Science*, 8, pp. 120-146.

Wilks, Y., Fass, D., Guo, C-M., McDonald, J., Plate, T., and Slator, B. (1988). A Tractable Machine Dictionary as a Resource for Computational Semantics. In *Computational lexicography for natural language processing*. Edited by B. K. Boguraev and T. Briscoe. Harlow, England: Longman.

Wilks, Y., Fass, D., Guo, C-M., McDonald, J., Plate, T., and Slator, B. (1990). Providing machine tractable dictionary tools. *Machine Translation*, 5, pp. 99-

155.

Winograd, T. (1972). *Understanding Natural Language.* New York, NY: Academic Press.

Winograd, T. (1987). Cognition, Attunement and Modularity. *Mind and Language,* 2.

Winograd, T. and Flores, C. (1986). *Understanding Computers and Cognition: A New Foundation for Design.* Norwood, NJ: Ablex.

Wittgenstein, L. (1958). *Philosophical Investigations.* Oxford: Basil Blackwell.

Zadeh, L.A. (1978). Fuzzy sets as a basis for a theory of possibility. *Fuzzy Sets and Systems,* 1, pp. 3-28.

Subject & Author Index

Bold numbers indicate basic citations.